Dishonor Everywhere, But Who Cares??????

CURTIS E. DIXON

iUniverse, Inc.
New York   Bloomington

iUniverse books may be ordered through booksellers or by contacting:

iUniverse
1663 Liberty Drive
Bloomington, IN 47403
www.iuniverse.com
1-800-Authors (1-800-288-4677)

Because of the dynamic nature of the Internet, any Web addresses or links contained in this book may have changed since publication and may no longer be valid. The views expressed in this work are solely those of the author and do not necessarily reflect the views of the publisher, and the publisher hereby disclaims any responsibility for them.

ISBN: 978-1-4502-0660-0 (sc)
ISBN: 978-1-4502-0661-7 (ebook)
ISBN: 978-1-4502-0662-4 (dj)

Printed in the United States of America

iUniverse rev. date: 02/02/2010

CONTENTS

PREFACE

From the nineteenth century until the present time, dishonor seemed to be more prevalent and accepted in our society than discrimination of any kind, retaliation and harassment, drug and alcohol addiction and abuse, corruption in the work force, demoralization in families, sacrilege, or the many prefabricated legal strategies and movements that were afforded to that environment because dishonor was the master of all of the above. When people in authority should have used their powers and influences to promote honor, many of them advocated dishonor as the appropriate path to success.

Jesus walked this earth as a humble and most honorable man, but he was persecuted and crucified, because his goodness and helpfulness were considered too good to be true and a threat to those in authority. It was only after his death that people all over the world acknowledged and recognized his worth. One of the most honorable presidents of the United States was ridiculed, criticized, and humiliated by many people in high places during his administration, because he practiced what he preached. It was only after he left office that the leaders and citizens of this great nation recognized and appreciated his honor.

Do most people see HONOR as the enemy to mankind? If not, why does dishonor show its ugly face at all levels of our society? And why is it so easily accepted? This autobiography covers every important aspect of my life. The book clearly shows that dishonor has no boundaries. It was in my family, in my schools, in the military, in the work force, in my church, in my neighborhood, and throughout my experiences with the legal system. The more honorable I was, the more I was insulted, betrayed, and denied any semblance of the success that had been afforded to the dishonorable men and women I had to confront in an effort to rectify the many wrongs against me.

Where there is no honor, there is no righteousness, no faith, no integrity, no prosperity, no compassion, no gratitude, and no justice.

After you have read this book, answer three questions to the best of your ability. Why do you suppose I, Curtis E. Dixon, was chosen to be dishonorably treated by so many different people from different strata of our society? Why do you suppose that I was able to survive and continued to serve those in greatest need, the young and the elderly? What do you think you would have done if you had to walk in my shoes?

DEDICATION

First, I dedicate this book to God and my mother, Mrs. Georgia M. Dixon. God was my rock, my shield, and my fortress, who kept me strong, honorable, and grateful. My mother was the best mother that a child could wish for, because she loved me unconditionally, she corrected me when I was wrong, she praised me when I was successful, and she made sure that I put God first in everything that I did. She was also my best friend, because when supposed friends made excuses for not assisting me in times of need, my mother always stepped up to the plate without any reservations.

Second, I dedicate this book to my mother-in-law, Kimie Iwanami; teachers B.N. Cook, C.I. Sawyer, T. Sledge, Julie Weidl, Susan Nemeth, Mary Woody, Penny Underwood, Sharon Strachan, and Dorothy Jackson; Professor Harold, Major Rakestraw, Colonel Horne, Planner Marjorie L. Gregory, Compliance Manager Jerry L. Clark, Coordinator Mary Freas, Police Chief Surratt, Fire Chief Lester Ervin; secretaries Patricia Gentry, Geraldine Jones, and Mae Thompson; Professor Jim Svara, PhD; Principals Ben Henderson and Mike Shrader, EdD; Shirley Larson, RN; Marilyn Cooper, friend; Sheila McDaniel, my niece; Personnel Director Mike Lee; and CERTL Director Ann Lambros. Without these positive and honorable people in my life as I traveled many rough and dark roads, my educational journey would not have been as successful as it was; my military experiences would not have been as rewarding; my work experiences and accomplishments would not have continued as magnificently as so many people perceived them; and my teaching achievements would not have been accepted with the utmost appreciation by administrators, teachers, parents, and students. Each one of the above-mentioned people played a special and unique role in championing my existence, my contributions, and my will to persevere and live my life to the fullest.

Third, I dedicate this book to the hundreds of students that I taught and preached to about honesty and respect for at least one year of their lives. Each and every one of them gave me a real purpose in life that touched the depths of my soul and made me fully understand how God uses us to edify his many words of wisdom, righteousness, and strength.

Fourth, I dedicate this book to my daughter, Cheryl, my two granddaughters, Cynthia and Charlene, and my godson, Kenny. They have been my driving force to stay on the battlefield, to remain responsible, and to continue to provide valuable services to those that I love unconditionally.

INTRODUCTION

One peaceful spring day, as I was playing with my two beautiful granddaughters, I thought about the innocence and loveliness of the moment and how great it would be if it could last forever for them. They were so carefree and happy. Then the history of my entire life flashed before my eyes, and I knew I had to make sure that they would not experience any of the traumas that I had. Many thoughts went through my mind. Would they be prepared for this world if I wasn't there? What would they remember about their granddaddy? Who would bother to tell them the truth about their granddaddy and the contributions he made to society? At that moment, I knew what I had to do. I had to be the person to tell them. Therefore, my tribute to my granddaughters and generations to come is this book. It will let the world know that I was a man of honor, who never floundered under the worst circumstances, and that I accepted God as my savior and protector, knowing that he gave me wisdom and strength to be the master of my fate.

I, Curtis Eugene Dixon, was born on May 28, 1939, the fifth and youngest surviving son of Mr. and Mrs. Frank Dixon, in Winston-Salem, North Carolina. When I was very young, my mother told me that I was her seventh son, and to her, that meant I was special and different from all of her other sons. I had no idea what she meant, but my many experiences should speak for themselves, because I certainly was treated differently. In any event, no person, whether he or she is a child, teenager, or adult, should have to endure what I endured simply for being an honorable person.

My family had strict and family-oriented rules. We ate breakfast together every morning, and dinner together every Sunday. Church and school were sacred institutions in the Dixon household. Until we were eighteen years old, my brothers and I were not permitted to miss church or school, unless we were so sick that we had to spend most of the day in bed. I was completely different from my brothers, because I never made excuses to skip church or school. After my parents enrolled me in kindergarten with my brother Artemas, where I learned to read and write before entering public school, I loved going to church and school. In fact, I was only absent on two occasions: the first, when my arm was broken, and the second, when I let my brother and friends convince me to skip church and go to the park. Everyone in the Dixon home also had designated duties, and we performed them without complaining. My third brother William challenged our father's rules many times, and had to spend many cold nights on our front porch.

My parents and brothers were very special to me, and I loved them unconditionally. After my father had a heart attack and was unable to work, I noticed that he had very little patience with me and treated me differently from my brothers. My father was about forty-nine years old, and I was eight years old at the time. My father blamed me for everything that went wrong in the home without trying to find out what really happened. Even when my brothers tried to admit to doing something wrong, my father still insisted that I caused the problem. My mother, on the other hand, was always very consistent with me. She rewarded me when I deserved it and she punished me when I disobeyed her. There was no gray area with her. As a teenager, I learned to appreciate the structure and discipline that my mother had instilled in me. She had shown me that I was her special son, who was mentally, psychologically, and physically stronger than my brothers.

Consequently, I was a model student throughout my school years, with occasional disappointments from a few of my teachers and administrators. I was very active in church, even after some disappointments from my ministers. I was supportive and considerate to any adult or authority figure, even when they were not supportive of and honest with me. I was always supportive of my brothers, but they rarely supported me. I was well liked and respected by my peers and most of my teachers, but many of them showed their biases when I excelled over them. Athletically, I was always ranked among the best in tennis and football, but I gave up sports, when the coach who taught me how to play tennis told my opponent how to beat me during a tournament match. I truly loved being useful and productive, and I gave little consideration to my own personal wants if everyone around me was happy and appreciative. Everyone I knew and worked with understood that they could come to me in time of need, and I would assist them if I could. For as long as I could remember, I was told that I was too good and giving to others, too nice and accommodating, and people considered my kindness a weakness. I heard what they were saying, but all I knew how to do was to be myself. I never felt threatened by any forces that worked against me. For the strangest reason, I became more confident and determined to overcome any barriers with ease. After my fifth grade teacher at Kimberley Park Elementary School told me in front of her accelerated class that I had weak math skills, I excelled in mathematics over every student at my grade level during my next three years in elementary school.

After elementary school, my pursuit for happiness and success was severely tarnished by the dishonor of high school administrators, college professors, my brothers, my friends, entrepreneurs, my superiors in the military and the civilian work force, ministers, attorneys, and judges. The more honorable I was, the greater my punishments from powerful and influential individuals. Despite their many reprisals, I held steadfast to my honor. I never gave up on me, because I was never convinced that I deserved the cruel and inhuman treatments that so many supposedly decent and influential people inflicted on me.

My purpose in writing this book is threefold. First, I would like my daughter, godson, granddaughters, extended family members, and my friends and their offspring to remember me for who I really was, an honorable man caught in a web of dishonorable people with power and influence. Second, I would like the American society as a whole to know that dishonor is alive and thriving. It is in our homes, in our churches, in our schools, in the military, in the workplace, and throughout our judicial system. Too much dishonor has been traditionally hidden from public view, and could be the main cause for the many crimes and immoral acts of our present generation. Third, in 1988 I published a 583-page documentary entitled *Evil for Good in Winston-Salem*, which exposed many dishonorable leaders. Several small bookstore owners in Durham, North Carolina, who wanted several hundred copies of my book, told me that my publisher had informed them that he would not be printing any more copies of my book. Subsequently, I was unable to get in touch with my publisher. This occurred after at least four hundred copies of my book had been sold the first month that it was released. Was this my oppressors' way of trying to keep people who lived outside of Winston-Salem from knowing how dishonorable they were? Why do you think that a publisher would stop selling a book that had sold several hundred copies in a month? Why do you suppose my publisher stopped communicating with me?

Shortly after the above occurred, my immediate supervisor with the City of Winston-Salem (hereafter referred to as City) escalated his harassment tactics against me; a judge decided the disposition of my complaint while eating breakfast at the local Jolly House Restaurant the day before he heard my testimony; the city manager felt secure terminating me from my nineteen-year position with the City using false information; and two complaints were filed in federal court on my behalf, without my knowledge. They were immediately dismissed by the same federal judge who had dismissed my first complaint ten years earlier. The American public needs to know what lengths dishonorable leaders will go to maintain a corrupt sovereignty.

The following chapters of this book will clearly describe examples of how dishonor was cleverly and secretly discharged. Do not be dismayed by the gravity of the beginning chapters. The severity of the dishonor elevates as I move from the educational arena to the workforce. This book will also show that many leaders whom the average person would turn to for advice, direction, and resolution are among the most dishonorable. Who would ever think that ministers and judges would sanction the persecution of an innocent person, when it was within their powers to do the honorable thing? But they did. Who would think that City leaders would intentionally lie in a court of law to destroy an honorable man? But they did. Who would think that elected officials would sanction such reprehensible behavior of people under their auspices? But they did. Who would think that entrepreneurs would intentionally charge a customer for services not provided? But they did. Who would think that attorneys would not represent their client in his best interest? But they did. Who would think that judges would deviate from and distort the facts presented in a court of law? But they did. Who would think that the news media would refuse to publish any facts about an honorable man? But they did.

EARLY EDUCATIONAL EXPERIENCES

"Blessed is the child who honors the Lord, his mother, and father, and who knows that he is on the path of righteousness."

When I was about ten years old, two of my older brothers and I were looking out of the window of our home during a violent thunderstorm. All of a sudden, the storm blew the tin roof off our daddy's hunting dogs' house. Of course, we immediately told our daddy. His solution was that I should go out in the storm and fix the roof, as my two older brothers laughed. My mother pleaded with him not to send me out in to the storm, but to no avail. Being the dutiful and obedient son that I was, with tears flowing down my cheeks, I went out into the storm and fixed the roof. When I came back into the house, blood was all over my hands and clothing. In fixing the roof, I had almost cut one of my fingers off. My mother took care of everything while my daddy showed no remorse for sending me out into the storm to do a man's job. He complained that I should have been more careful working on a tin roof.

My elementary teachers really worried about my going to high school, because I was so quiet and soft-spoken in school.

I was never confrontational or disruptive in class. When I could read all of the books for first and second graders after only being in school two months, my first grade teacher accused me of memorizing the books. When my older brother Lorenza did the same thing, he was skipped to the second grade and placed in the accelerated class for gifted students. I was never considered for the highest academic class, even though I demonstrated the same academic skills and abilities as my brother. In fact, several of my teachers penalized me and ridiculed me in front of my classmates. After I learned to love mathematics and was the best in my class, my fourth grade teacher threatened to retain me if I did not recite the multiplication tables from one through twelve without error before the gifted fourth grade class. I completed this task with tears running down my cheeks. I never told my parents for fear of reprisals from my father, who never supported anything I said or did. I sought quietness and cooperation as a means of survival throughout my entire educational career.

In my community, however, I had a completely different personality. I was very outgoing, talkative, and confrontational, because my father never criticized any of my actions as long as they did not interfere with the church or school. Everyone in my neighborhood, including my minister, thought I would be a preacher when I grew up, because of the respect and appreciation that I had for education and religion, as well as the respect and honesty I demanded from my neighborhood buddies. I would give any of my friends the shirt off my back and the food off my mother's table if they needed it. On the other hand, if and when my buddies betrayed me after taking advantage of my goodness, I would show them my bad side. I once fought and beat three brothers, because they ate all of my mother's food, and then refused to live up to their promise to help me clean up around the house before my mother got home from work. They laughed at me as they left the house, and that triggered my bad side. When my good side reappeared, the three brothers were lying on the ground crying.

When I was a freshman at Atkins High School, Albert Poage, the varsity football coach, gave me a C in PE, and I was not even in his class. When I would not challenge the grade, my female academic teachers did and had it removed from my transcript.

Pete Odem, who was an assistant football coach, gave me my second C when I was a sophomore in his history class. His justification was that I had to be cheating because I rarely took notes, yet made the highest grade on all the quizzes and tests. I had simply bought the textbook that Mr. Odem was using and read it several times. (The class had only two textbooks, one for the students and one for Mr. Odem.) When I received the C, I did not challenge it.

I was a model student, participating in all school activities while maintaining a close relationship with my neighborhood friends, who were mediocre students. The majority of the students and teachers, both male and female, liked and admired me, because I was modest and multi-talented; and I was determined to be as good as or better than the superior, arrogant rich boys in my class. I went from being the smartest boy in my class to playing sports and a musical instrument, and to being a good dancer, and even to writing notes on the blackboard for several of my female teachers. I was also the only boy in my class group inducted into the National Honor Society. I won my school its first tennis trophy, and represented the school by being selected an outstanding cellist in the state-wide symphony orchestra contest. When I was elected president of the student body by ninety percent of the students, and was chosen captain of the tennis team and president of the athletic society, the administrators of the school turned on me, acting as if I were competing for their jobs. At first, I thought that the administrators were treating me so negatively because most of the boys in my class were sons of teachers, lawyers, ministers, doctors, and successful entrepreneurs. Then it dawned on me that the parents of the valedictorian and salutatorian of the class one year ahead of mine were not well educated. I became concerned as to what I might be doing wrong. Many of my female teachers and Mr. Sawyer, my ninth grade math teacher, assured me that I was not doing anything wrong, and they encouraged me to keep up the good work. Mr. Sawyer often told me that he wished his son was like me, talented and highly motivated to succeed in life.

My senior year in high school, my English teacher, Medora Hill, told me that it did not matter what the quality of my work was in her class. The principal, John Carter, had told her that I was to receive a B in her class all year.

Assistant Principal Togo West, whom I considered a great mathematics teacher, gave me my only two Bs in mathematics in high school, after labeling me his first and only genius student. I never failed to solve all of his problems, even the ones that students were not expected to solve.

As my brother Artemas and I were preparing for graduation, my brother bought a cheap navy blue suit to graduate in, and my mother and I purchased for me a very nice, expensive-looking navy blue suit. As we were getting ready for graduation, our father noticed the difference in the quality and appearance of the two suits. Immediately, he took my suit and gave it to my brother. For the first time that I could remember, my mother spoke up on my behalf, and I was able to wear the suit that I had purchased to graduation.

At my high school graduation in 1957, I excelled over every student in science, foreign language, and mathematics, but I was only given recognition for my achievement in mathematics at the end of graduation. All other students received recognition at the beginning of the ceremony. Assistant Principal West told the audience that they had inadvertently left my name off the program. My science and foreign language teachers told me after graduation that I had the highest average in their classes. That should have made me the valedictorian of my class, but Principal Carter blocked it. I was also told by one of my teachers that my test for a scholarship to college had been pulled by the principal before being sent for grading, ensuring that I would not receive any assistance toward college.

Instead of Principal Carter promoting my abilities and encouraging me, he made it his personal goal to destroy anything great that I stood for. The principal's attitude toward me made me more determined to excel and succeed. I graduated from high school without knowing why the principal disliked me so much. The year after I graduated, I learned that Principal Carter committed suicide after it was discovered that he had been embezzling school funds for years.

If I had not been a strong, God fearing individual, who believed in myself regardless of what others said and did to me, I definitely could have been a failure my first twelve years of school. Just think of the thousands of boys and girls who were not as strong and determined as I, and had very low self-esteem. Their dreams, hopes, and aspirations were possibly altered long before they even had a chance, by the dishonor of many people whom society has entrusted to help our children. This could still be happening today, tomorrow, and forever, with dishonor being so prevalent throughout our society.

I always remembered my mother's words: "You are my special son who is completely different from my other sons. God has blessed you with certain qualities that are completely different from most people, and they might bring out the worst in some people."

NOTHING IS IMPOSSIBLE
IF YOU WANT IT BADLY ENOUGH

"The things a man has to have are hope and confidence in himself against odds, and sometimes he needs somebody, his pal or his mother or his wife or God, to give him that confidence. He's got to have some inner standards worth fighting for or there won't be any way to bring him into conflict. And he must be ready to choose death before dishonor without making too much song and dance about it. That's all there is to it."

—Clark Gable

I only received a $10.00 award from my high school for all of my accomplishments, but I was still determined to go to college. My minister had told the congregation that he could get scholarships to Lane Methodist University in Memphis, Tennessee, for faithful church members. My brother Artemas and I were the most faithful young male members at our church, and our father was the treasurer of the Trustee Board and a member of the Deacon Board. After graduation, the minister announced to the church congregation that he had gotten his daughter Carrie a full scholarship to Lane Methodist University. He did not acknowledge me and five other students who had also graduated from high school that year. My mother had to remind him in front of the congregation.

My father was terminally ill with cancer at the time, and there was no money available for me to go to college. Still, I completed all of the necessary paperwork to be accepted into North Carolina Agricultural and Technical College, and I was accepted. Despite having no money to finalize my registration, I drove to the college with some friends and completed all of the necessary paperwork. When I got back home after all of my friends had finalized their registrations and I had not, my father said for the first time, "This boy really and truly wants to go to college and make something of himself, and I can't help him." With tears in her eyes, my mother said, "I can." The next day my mother and I took the bus into town, where my mother borrowed enough money, using all of her five sons' insurance policies as collateral, so that I could commute to college for one semester.

After I completed the registration process, I was able to take the English and mathematics placement tests with approximately fifteen hundred other freshmen. When the results came back, I had made the highest score on both tests. At that time, the college administrators became concerned as to why I had not received a scholarship to the college.

My father passed away my freshman year in college. That year I earned a 3.65 grade point average, and the university gave me a working scholarship and made me a dormitory counselor, which was to begin my sophomore year. This gift from God and the university eliminated all of my college financial problems. Further, this enabled me to save everything that I earned working in the factory in my hometown during the summers. I was also able to purchase all of my school clothes and supplies, as well as clothes and supplies for my nephew, because I did not want him to wear to school the used clothes that my brother Lorenza had bought him from Goodwill. I even made enough money during the school year to help my mother maintain her household. Our minister's solution to my mother's financial problems was for her to sign her house over to him, and he would let her stay in the house as long as she lived. I told the minister, "Thanks, but no thanks. My brothers and I will take care of all of our mother's needs."

During the three summers while I was a college student, I was fortunate enough to get employment with R. J. Reynolds Tobacco Company. However, the job that I was given was the hardest of hard labor, working from 7 AM to 4 PM Monday through Friday in the Turkish Tobacco Curing Department. When I reported to work my first day, all of the rough- and tough-looking men who worked in these warehouses made a bet that I would not last two days. I weighed only 135 pounds at the time, and I was expected to lift and turn bundles of tobacco that weighed at least forty pounds all day. Everyone else who worked in the warehouses weighed at least 170 pounds. At the end of the first week, I was still working and was creating an educational experience for all of the regular workers and my supervisor. The work was extremely difficult at first, but after my body adjusted to the routine and my mind took charge, the weight factor no longer existed. I taught the other employees to sing and tell jokes while they worked.

My supervisor, Mr. Hauser, only had a sixth grade education, and he loved exerting his authority. For some reason, he wanted to challenge me, perhaps because I was the only college student among the men. His first challenge was to have me get snack orders from the rest of the men and bring them to him before each break. He would then tell me the total cost of each order in an effort to show me that he was as smart, or smarter, than I, even without as much formal education. But every day he ended up spending five or more dollars of his own money, because he undercharged the crew for what they had ordered. I knew this and laughed each day, because Mr. Hauser had too much pride to admit that he could not add, even after I tried to tell him that he was undercharging everyone for the snacks. He would rather pay out of his own pocket than have me tell him what the correct cost should be.

After working at this site for two weeks and becoming proficient at the job, I went to Mr. Hauser and asked him if there was a required amount of bundles each worker had to complete in a day. Without knowing how to perform a quality analysis of production, he immediately told me that every employee under his supervision had to complete at most six rows of bundles per day. During our next break, I asked the supervisor to tell all of the workers what was required of them. The entire crew knew that they could do six rows of bundles in half a day with ease, and said nothing. With the extra time, we sang and told even more jokes.

Mr. Hauser felt very proud when he made his rounds and everyone had their hands on a bundle. When he caught me once without my hands on a bundle, he freaked out. He called me to his office and started to reprimand me, but I reminded him that I had met the daily requirement, even though I was taking a rest break when he saw me. Mr. Hauser just wanted all of the workers to fear him when he showed up. I accommodated him most of the time, but on occasion, I would make his day by teasing him. At the end of each summer, Mr. Hauser would tell me that he would not have me back the next summer. As the next summer was about to begin, Mr. Hauser would start asking my brothers when was I coming back to work. My last summer at this work site, Mr. Hauser told me that he would see me the next spring as a permanent employee. I just smiled and said, "Yes, in your dreams." I was told by my brothers, who stayed on under Mr. Hauser, that he was terminated from the company, because he could not pass an eighth grade reading and mathematics competency test, which all employees had to pass in order to keep their jobs (a new job guideline implemented by the company).

During this great and unique experience in college, it seemed to me that the more I excelled, the more the professors I admired the most worked against me. During my freshman year, my math professor considered me so gifted he let me teach his algebra class in his absence. And he told his students that I was only sixteen years old. Professor Harold bragged so much about my mathematical ability, the department chairman assigned himself as the only teacher for calculus III, so that he could determine if what Professor Harold was saying was true. The first day of class, this professor stated, "In my class, only the teacher receives an A." Of course, he and all of the students looked directly at me. I aced all of this professor's quizzes and tests, and I received a B for the semester. This department chairman even had the audacity to say, "Curtis, I know that you must be disappointed about making less than an A in my class, after being told by your prior professors and classmates that you are a mathematical genius. I warned you in the beginning that I did not give anyone an A, even if he or she earns one." Then the professor that I admired as being the most brilliant mathematician I had met scarred my record in a worse way by giving me a C in his complex functions class. He knew that I was the only student who met his requirements for an A by completing a problem that took twelve hand-written pages. That undeserved C in an elective class that I did not have to take was my graduation gift from my favorite professor, who knew that I had all As and one B in mathematics on my transcript.

MILITARY EXPOSURE AND ITS HONOR CODE

"We define character as the sum of those qualities of moral excellence that stimulates a person to do the right thing, which is manifested through right and proper actions despite internal or external pressures to the contrary."

United States Air Force Academy

I was commissioned a second lieutenant into the United States Air Force one month after graduating from college. The first thing I did when I went on active duty was to authorize a fifty dollar monthly allotment to my mother. My monthly pay was less than three hundred dollars. At my first training site, my civilian instructor told me that I was one in a million to ask him if I could lay my head on the desk, because I had not had any sleep the night before. However, after the instructor gave me permission to lay my head on my desk, he wrote me up for sleeping in class without his permission. He recommended to my major that I be dropped from the training program. When I talked with the major, he believed me and overturned the instructor's recommendation. Further, the major informed me that this type of activity was a common occurrence with

11

this instructor, and that I was the only junior officer who had challenged him. After my meeting with the major, I had no more problems with the instructor. Of course, I was the only black junior officer in the class.

The first week that I was at the military training site, I fell in love with a young lady named Katie. We were born on the same day four years apart. The six months that I was at the training site, we spent all of our free time together. Leaving her to go to Japan was the hardest decision I ever had to make. I truly loved Katie, but I also knew that I was not ready to get married. At that point in my life, I was not even able to get into any clubs without having to show my identification card. At twenty-two years of age, I still looked sixteen.

After I graduated from my training program, I was assigned to the Communications Squadron at Yokota Air Force Base, Japan, as a new first lieutenant.

During my tour in Japan, I sponsored two Air Force Academy cadets, and received national exposure when I was chosen as an outstanding junior officer on the rise in the Air Force. When my boss was reassigned to the United States, the commander of my squadron, Colonel Horne, appointed me Detachment Commander at Johnson Air Base. This was a tremendous honor, because although I was only a First Lieutenant, I was to perform the duties of a major. Under my leadership, the detachment was given an outstanding unit award by the Johnson Air Force Base Commander. I was the only black officer assigned to this squadron.

After two lovely years in Japan, I married a Japanese model and was transferred to Tucson, Arizona. I was promoted to captain within days after I arrived in Tucson. The Air Force Communications Headquarters Commander came to visit my unit, and he told me I would remain in Tucson for at least three years. Afterwards I would be eligible for another overseas assignment. After sixteen months in Tucson, I received orders assigning me to Tan Son Nut Air Base, Saigon, Vietnam. Immediately, my local commander called headquarters. The general's response was, "Something is seriously wrong and I will do my best to correct it." The general called back the same day to tell me that a civilian civil serviceman had taken his friend's name off the overseas list and put my name on. It was the policy of the general's command that all returning overseas service personnel remain in the United States for at least thirty-six months before they were reassigned overseas, with at least a two-month departure notice. Since my reporting date to Vietnam was less than three weeks, the general could not get my orders rescinded. I was sent to Vietnam, and my wife went back to Japan to live with her parents.

While in Vietnam, I had the unique experience of working for two supervisors. My first supervisor, a major, whom I sat beside every Sunday in church, rated my performance so poorly, even after telling me repeatedly that I was doing a great job, that his boss, a full colonel, destroyed the performance report. The colonel knew I had successfully removed many of my troops from lethal fire from the Vietcong in the Ca Mau area via helicopter; and had gone to Pleiku when it was under attack to provide supplies and materials to troops in that area. Further, it was known throughout my division that I had volunteered for both of the above assignments, because no one else in my unit was willing to go into the fighting zones. The administrative officer of the division presented me with a superior rated performance report, which was signed by the colonel.

My next supervisor was a lieutenant colonel. He told me he did not know how to evaluate me, because I never socialized with him at the officers' club, as the other officers in the division did. I did not drink any form of alcohol, and consequently, I did not frequent the officers' club as often as my boss and fellow officers, who got inebriated almost every night. Of course, I indulged my boss and met him at the club one night. We hung out together for several hours, just enough time for my boss to become completely wasted. I was riding a motorcycle, and he was riding a bicycle. I had no problem riding my motorcycle to my quarters, but my boss was so drunk, he kept falling off his bicycle and begging me not to leave him. After I got him safely to his quarters, he begged me not to tell anyone what had happened. Despite that, this lieutenant colonel still rated my performance average, and he recommended that I only receive a commendation medal for my outstanding job performance in the war zone. This lieutenant colonel's superior, the same full colonel as before, overrode his recommendation and changed the performance evaluation to outstanding, and awarded me the Bronze Star Medal. The lieutenant colonel consequently lost the respect of every military personnel under his supervision.

Just before the above incident, the lieutenant colonel walked into the office one morning and said, "Captain Dixon, I want you to fly to Da Nang and assess what is going on there. And that's *an order!*"

Everyone stopped what they were doing, and the warrant officer told the lieutenant colonel that the base was under an attack so severe, no one was entering or leaving the area. When I refused his order and everyone in the office supported me, the lieutenant colonel did not know what to do. His solution to his blunder was to take me outside and beg me to tell everyone in the office that everything was okay between us. For the next few months, the lieutenant colonel received no respect and cooperation from anyone in the office except me. But he still gave every one of the other officers a superior performance report and the Bronze Star medal. Prior to leaving Vietnam, I received a citation that stated that my division had been given the outstanding unit award. Of course, I was the only black officer in my unit.

I left Vietnam to accept another assignment in Japan, so that I could reunite with my wife. We bought a home on base and spent considerable time counseling the young troops in my unit about furthering their education. Only one of my troops enrolled in a degree program, but many of them enrolled in my adult education class at the base educational institute, where I was employed part-time as a teacher. After a year, my sergeant reported to me that my one and only college student was sexually assaulting several of the other troops when they were asleep at night. My commanding officer told me to conduct my own investigation before turning anything over to the base commander. I talked to the four young troops who had been victims, and they each said that the soldier who was in college, whom they still considered their friend, performed oral sex on them while they slept. They further stated that they would not do anything to cause him to be punished or dishonorably discharged from the military. They just wanted him to stop. When I talked to the perpetrator, who was making As in all of his classes, he gave no defense for his actions. The sergeant who initiated the investigation wanted the young soldier recommended for a dishonorable discharge. Since my commander had given me full authority to make the final decision, I decided to give the man a chance in life. I moved him into a private barracks away from other troops, pending his early dismissal from the military. This action was acceptable to the young soldier and my commander.

Ten years after my departure from the military, I received a letter from the young man whom I had saved from a court martial and a dishonorable discharge. The letter read: *"Dear Captain Dixon, I know that it has been many years since you saved my life and I should have written to you sooner. First, I want to sincerely thank you for giving me a second chance when I knew that no one else would have. Second, I want you to know that I have not disappointed you, because I immediately sought counseling for my problem, finished college and even got my doctoral degree, and I married my high school sweet heart. I am now a college professor. Again, thanks for giving me a second chance in life. I named my second son after you.*

To me, you were my guarding angel and I'll never forget you. May God bless and keep you safe always."

I valued my military experiences, because they taught me how to survive in any environment or situation. Further, I was exposed to many different cultures, which gave me a greater appreciation for the differences in people who were of the same ethnic group, as well as people from different ethnic groups. The one thing I saw as a military man was that children, the elderly, and dogs were the same all over the world. The children were innocent, though devious sometime. The elderly were humble and subservient most of the time. And dogs were loyal to their masters all of the time, regardless of how they were treated. I remembered and lived by the phrase, "When in Rome, do as the Romans do." Consequently, I learned to love the foods of the many countries that I visited, and I attempted to speak the language of three of those countries. I socialized with the local citizens, and was often welcomed into their homes and to their dinner tables. When I left the military, I left with the feeling that I was a whole man who could and would stand tall and honorable, anywhere and anytime.

GOOD GUYS FINISH LAST

*"It is better to deserve honors and not have them
than to have them and not deserve them."*

—*Mark Twain (Samuel Clemens)*

As a civilian, I arrived home with my Japanese wife and no employment. Within two weeks of my arrival, I was offered two jobs: one as a teacher with the Winston-Salem Forsyth County School System, and the other as director of operations, development, and training with a local federal manpower program called CEP. I accepted the job with the manpower program. My first day on the job, the director called a staff meeting so that he could introduce me. Over 98 percent of the staff was black. This was just the opposite of what I had been exposed to in the military. My first week on the job, everything that went wrong seemed to be a black on black issue, and they were totally unrelated to the mission of the program.

Director Henry Mack, the retired army major who had hired me, started displaying a love/ hate relationship with me. Mack shared everything with me, and I was most appreciative and dedicated to him. Mack gave a formal party for his top administrative staff immediately after I came on board. It was first class, and he introduced me as his right hand man on the job. When Mack told me that he wanted me to go to a party given by one of the local professors, I did. The next day Mack told me in the presence of other department directors that at the party I had denigrated him and the program. After he adjourned the meeting, he apologized to me, telling me that he had said those things to satisfy Lafayette Jones, his personal assistant.

When staff personnel came to me for professional advice at Mack's request, he would tell me in the presence of other directors that I was not in charge, and I should refer all staff complaints and concerns to him. Later, he would apologize when no one else was around, saying, "I was only joking. I want you to get to know Lafayette better. He is feeling threatened by you, since I no longer need him to live in my home and walk my dog." Then Mack's white secretary told me that Mack had told her *that I was going to build a new house and not have a job to pay for it.* She further said that Mack had a hit list of people he planned to fire, and I was at the top of the list. By this time, I had only been on the job less than a year, and I had experienced the worst work ethics and an unbelievable ghetto mentality.

Before Mack could implement his plan to fire people, he was brought up on sexual harassment charges by several black female employees. A meeting was held with all the employees and Louise Wilson, Mack's boss. It was a very sad day. Mack had no defense for the many accusations that the women cited. Without knowing the outcome, I came in to work the next day to find out that Mack had vacated the premises and left town, never to be heard of or seen again. Mack's personal assistant, Lafayette Jones, contributed greatly to Mack's downfall, because he kept most of the staff in an uproar all of the time. It was rumored that Lafayette did more than just walk Mack's dog, and that he hated the thought of sharing Mack with anyone. Lafayette once told Rev. Hunt, my friend and subordinate manager, that he hated me, because I thought I was smarter than everyone, and I was always so cool, even when falsely accused. When I called Lafayette and his cronies out in a public meeting, he came to me for the first time with an apology. He said that he truly admired my veracity, and that he had never dreamed my convictions were so profound and solid. Less than two years after Mack left the city, Lafayette, less than thirty-five years old, was diagnosed with prostate cancer. He died several months later.

CEO Louise Wilson appointed John P. Bond as the CEP director. Bond, a light-skinned black man with nappy hair, kept a short white man named George by his side at all times. In fact, George lived with Bond, even though both George's wife and Bond's wife disapproved. Bond, who had been a captain in the Army, befriended me. Thinking that Bond was an ally because we had similar backgrounds, I went out to lunch with him and George almost every day. We attended the same social functions, and we talked candidly on and off the job. I also invited Bond and his shadow George, along with their families, to my house-warming party. After the party, I heard that Bond had told George *that he could not stand rich and smart blacks like Curtis Dixon.* George would often tell me just to let Bond have his way with me, and the sky would be the limit. I could not be Bond's flunky as George was. Consequently, Bond eliminated my position as operations director with the manpower program, and I was without a job *six months after I moved into my new home.*

The year and a half when I worked with 98 percent black people was the experience of a lifetime for me. Most of the black employees concentrated most, if not all, of their efforts on sexual activities of any type on and off the job; drinking beer and liquor during office hours; backstabbing one another in order to be favored by the boss; and developing the worst work ethics humanly possible, by frequently being late for work and never completing assignments satisfactorily. I felt like a total misfit, but I maintained my high standards, even as my black brothers tried to put me down by saying that I wanted to be white, and I thought that I was smarter and better than they were. In reality, all I wanted was the best from and for everyone, black and white. My type of honor made me the enemy to my black brothers, and caused me problem after problem.

Before my position as operations director was eliminated, lies echoed through Winston-Salem that my new home was state of the art. People claimed that I had outdone prominent black lawyers and doctors throughout the city. It was rumored that automatic drapes covered the windows in every room, that each room was carpeted a different color and represented a different country, and that the pictures on the walls were originals from five different countries. The above were all lies, but still many black people disliked and envied me.

Shortly after the above rumors began, my wife accidentally burned down our new home. Instead of Bond and the manpower staff having any sympathy for me, *half of my black staff had a party to celebrate the burning of my home.* Ten months later, God blessed me and my wife with a healthy, beautiful baby girl. My insurance company paid me the full value for all of our clothing and furniture, in addition to restoring our home to its original state.

In haste, I took a job as head of a new business that I thought was going to become my business after six months. I was highly recommended for the job by John Bond. Jim Hansley, who was black, was the director for economic development. Everything he told me about the venture was not true, and the job turned into a nightmare. The initial goal of the business was to make bandoleers for the U.S. Army, something that I knew nothing about. But I felt that I could learn and do this job, as long as I did not have negative forces working against me. And I did make the business a success. I worked day and night seven days a week. To the amazement of the Army supply representative, Bond, and everyone with CEP, I met every shipment date for six months. Once the business became successful and newsworthy, Hansley informed me that the business belonged to him. It would not be turned over to me as promised. This ended the success of this business venture. Hansley, with the support of my floor supervisor, Betty Squires, who was a welfare recipient, set out to discredit and destroy me, so that they could take over the business. Squires sabotaged each weekly shipment after Hansley decided to keep the business for himself. She made sure that each shipment would be rejected by the Army. She did this while I was busy running in and out of the city, picking up materials and supplies for the business.

Hansley asked me to meet him for breakfast one morning before I was made aware of the bad shipments. I thought this was just one of our regular monthly meetings. Before we'd even received our food, Hansley said, "It has been reported to me by Dr. Brandon that you are never on the job. Therefore, you have completely neglected all of your duties as manager of the plant. As of now, you are fired."

I took the insults from this fellow and the lies told to him by Dr. Brandon—who served on Hansley's board—in stride, because by now I had learned that weak, insecure black men considered me to be their enemy. They would do anything to destroy the positive and stimulating vibrations that I always projected. Dr. Brandon, who was a black dentist, was one of my brother's neighbors. He and I had talked on several occasions when I visited my brother. Though he was on Hansley's board, he had never visited my plant.

Less than a week after this horrible fiasco, I was offered three jobs: two with R. J. Reynolds Tobacco Industry (the largest employer in the city), and the other with the City of Winston-Salem (the second largest employer in the city at the time). The administrators of each of these companies told me that they knew I had been given a raw deal, and they were impressed that I had succeeded with a venture that every businessman in the city had said was impossible. They further stated that they were not pleased with Hansley's track record.

Hansley became the manager of the business I had been running, and promoted Squires as his assistant manager of day-to-day operations. Less than a month after I was terminated, the business was shut down for lack of adequate production and inefficient management. Hansley told me he wanted to apologize to me for his actions, in the presence of my family and at a professional gathering. This dishonorable fellow literally got on his knees and begged for my forgiveness. I refused even to look at him and to acknowledge this demon's presence, because he was not sincere. He was apologizing only because the business had failed, and because the two largest employers in the city supported me. During the next year, Hansley failed at everything that he attempted, and eventually left Winston-Salem. Hansley was an "I" man who had failed himself. Once again, I had been a victim of the insecurities and jealousies of other black people—James Hansley, a well-educated black leader; Dr. Brandon, a prominent black dentist; and Betty Squires, an uneducated black welfare recipient.

I took the job with the City in October 1970, because it matched my prior training and experience, even though opportunities for advancement were much better with the tobacco company. My main reason for not going to work for the tobacco company was because of the black man I would have to work for. He had touched me inappropriately at a swimming pool gathering a year earlier. Further, John Bond was campaigning for me to take the job with his friend at the tobacco company. I was just not into that "guys' night out drinking" thing that seemed to be their game.

I loved my new job as director of evaluations with the Model City Department, because I was working directly with my lifelong black friend, Winfred, and I had lots of responsibilities and challenges. Without any warning, Winfred sabotaged everything that I was attempting to do on my new job. I learned from his previous supervisor, Florence Creque (black), that she had told Winfred that she wanted him to have the position I had been given. One day Winfred would tell me that he was acting the way he was because he was not happy at home, and I was the only person that he could take his anger out on. And then the next day Winfred would violate every office policy there was, as everyone looked on. These actions were completely out of character for him. During all of this nonsense, Winfred would visit my home every weekend, walk in the front door, and go out of the side door without saying two words to anyone in the house. After Florence told Winfred, in my presence, that she wished he had the talents and confidence that I displayed in performing my duties, he brought a pistol to work so that he could kill me. He called me over to his car to shoot me at point blank range. He told me later that he changed his mind after looking into my eyes and seeing that I was truly his friend. I cared about his welfare, and I had not done anything to jeopardize his job with the City. He even told me that Florence Creque had turned him against me with her many comments for and against both of us. After Winfred was transferred to the Planning Department and he had no contact with me, I was told by an alderman that Winfred had made negative comments about me to Bond.

Jim Wilson (black) resigned his position as director of the Model City Department, and a new black director named Robert McClain was hired. Also, the Deputy Director of Budgeting and Planning, Gus Ulrich (white), resigned his position and recommended that I be promoted into his position. Instead of promoting me, Jim Wilson suggested that it would be better to let me perform my duties as director of evaluation, as well as the duties of the deputy director of budgeting and planning, until the new director came on board. I agreed to this arrangement. I knew that Jim Wilson was resigning his directorship, because he had refused to terminate most of his black staff after the City was awarded a $5.3 million planned variations grant. McClain, the new director, gravitated to me immediately upon his arrival on the job, because I was more knowledgeable about the most important aspects of the department than anyone. McClain even invited me and my wife to his home for dinner to meet his family. I was shocked that no other employees were invited, not even Florence, his deputy director of programs and operations.

As usual, I worked long hours to make McClain look good to the City leaders. The more work I did, the more the City leaders said that the department's staff was not measuring up to the City's standards, at least, according to McClain. I took it upon myself to find out exactly what the City leaders were expecting from the staff. I caught McClain telling them that his staff was completely incompetent and could not complete any of the assignments that he gave them. When I walked through the door, McClain looked shocked. He said that he was not talking about me, and that he had all of my completed assignments in his back pocket. As he pulled out several folded papers, I left the room without saying anything. I felt completely betrayed again by this friend and boss. McClain ran behind me, trying to make his wrongs right. But I could not listen to anything he was saying, because I was so angry and disappointed. As I drove back to my office, I wondered, *What am I doing wrong to be betrayed by everyone that I support faithfully?*

Within two months, McClain lost all credibility with the City leaders. That paved the way for John Bond, who had been hired as an assistant to the mayor, to move into the assistant city manager's position that had been created for McClain. Prior to Bond being hired as assistant city manager, the members of the Community Development Commission, who were appointed by the Board of Aldermen, told Bond that his male companion had to move out of his home. Such an arrangement was unnatural, and it was causing too many problems in his marriage and with city residents and leaders.

Even though I was doing all of the duties of the deputy director of planning and budgeting very efficiently, McClain refused to promote me into that position. After he resigned, McClain told the City leaders that I would make an excellent administrative assistant doing the deputy director's duties. This would have been a significant downgrade in pay and job grade status for me. McClain left the city without any contact or communication with me. However, he sent word back that he had tried to destroy my career with the City, because I would not resign my position in support of him.

In the midst of all of this confusion and destruction, John Bond had successfully campaigned for and gotten the assistant city manager's position. Prior to his selection, Bond had asked me to join his team and provide derogatory information on McClain, who was also a contender for the assistant city manager's position, and most of the black staff in the department. I told Bond that I would prefer just to do my job and be judged on my merits. Bond said, "You are either with me or against me. And if you do not get me the information that I need to get these incompetent black people terminated, you are against me. I hope that you don't learn the hard way. The two things that you cannot beat in Winston-Salem are racism and perversion. You either join in, or you suffer the consequences. You just watch how a pro takes over your little clannish town. I already have two black aldermen eating out of my hand."

I listened in amazement and disbelief. The names that Bond gave me were men who had not been very supportive of me and the mission of the department, but I could not be a part of destroying the lives or the livelihood of other people, especially under these evil, selfish conditions. It never crossed my mind that Bond would spend the rest of my career and his life trying to destroy everything that I stood for, and that the entire bureaucratic system would buy into his game. To Bond, any member of his team had to be subservient to him. George, Bond's confidant for years, said to me just before he left the city at his family's request, "Curtis, get away from Bond. He is like a fat boy who has always had his way. He feels compelled to destroy any guy he cannot control. You can rest assured that if anyone is catering to Bond, Bond is having his way with that person. I am glad I'm finally getting free of this albatross. Money is not as important as my pride and my family." Before George left Winston-Salem, he told me he was returning to the New York City area so that he could reunite with his wife and children. They had hated the life he lived with Bond.

It seemed that the world was coming to an end for me. While I was having all of these problems on the job, I received a telephone call, informing me that my oldest brother had just been taken to the emergency room. When I arrived at the hospital, James was in the critical care unit. He was unconscious and could not be revived. James had been down on his luck ever since his wife had gotten him fired from the job he'd held for twenty years with the Hanes Hosiery Company. Every time my mother and I had gone to visit James, he had been drunk on wine and talking out of his head. My other brothers refused to check on him, because he was living in an impoverished area of the city. Where James lived was of no concern to my mother and me; we were concerned about James and his health. After a week went by, James finally came out of the coma. My mother and I had rarely left his side. When he was released from the hospital, he went to live at my mother's home, because he had no other place to go. His wife had made it known he could not live with her. I bought him bedroom furniture, and when he was able to get out of the house, I let him use one of my cars. I also gave him a weekly allowance so that he would have some spending money.

During James's better days, he had owned and managed a lucrative business. He told me that he wanted to start his business again, but he did not have any money. Before I could say anything, he asked me to be his partner. He stated further that if I put up the money to get the business started again, he would give me 25 percent of what he made for as long as the business lasted. I agreed with James's proposal, and gave him as much money as he needed to get the business up and running. In less than six months, he had about twenty of his old customers trading with him again. Many of his customers said to me that James had told them he had never dreamed I loved him so much, and I would do anything to make his life whole again. His customers wanted to know if I really gave James a weekly allowance and let him use the new car he was driving. When I told them I had done those things, because I loved my brother and was willing to do anything to help him get back on his feet, they asked me if I would be their brother. Several of James's customers told me that I was one in a million, because they had never known anyone who cared that much about someone else.

My brother showed his appreciation by never sharing any of the profits of our business with me. And I never asked him, because I felt that any initial profits were being used to get the business running smoothly. Then James gave me $1000 to deposit in my bank for him. His credit was so bad he could not have any money saved in his name. I did not question James's actions. In the meantime, he was still driving my car, and sleeping and eating at our mother's at my expense.

One year after James's illness, he met and married a young lady, and he told me that he did not need me as a partner in his business anymore. He handed me about $400, saying that he wanted to buy the car that I had been letting him drive. I never questioned any of James's actions, even though they showed no genuine love and appreciation for what I had done for him. He lied to my other three brothers, telling them that I had asked him to pay back the money I had invested in his business, because I did not want to be a part of it. Further, James completely dishonored our mother, who had taken him in and fed him for over a year.. In an angry and belligerent state of mind, he told our ninety-year-old mother that the only person who had ever done anything for him was his new wife. He further told her that she was going to die and go to hell if she did not honor and obey the wishes of his new wife. All of the above transpired after my mother told James that she was too old to be hauling her food to his home every Sunday, and his wife stopped speaking to her. Then this new wife convinced James that she was the one being persecuted by our mother. To satisfy his wife, James decided to insult his mother when no one was around. This brother, to whom our mother and I had shown undying love and devotion, betrayed me for the love of money, and he betrayed our mother for the love of a woman. My mother died unexpectedly two months after her ninetieth birthday. After her oldest son broke her heart, she complained every day to me that maybe she was living too long for two of her daughter-in-laws. As expected, they celebrated ridiculously at her funeral, so much so that James had to tell his wife to cool it.

Many years later, as James was getting too old to handle his business, he offered to train his son-in-law and transfer many of his customers over to him. When his son-in-law said he was not interested, I spoke up and said that I was interested in the business. My brother James said, "You have to be a special type of person to handle this kind of business." Then he quickly changed the subject. For some ungodly reason, he was not about to help the hands that had fed and clothed him when no one else would. In essence, James still lacked honor and gratitude for me, but he spent at least four days out of every week in church.

The week after Robert McClain left the city and Deputy Director Florence Creque became acting director, she informed me that John Bond had hired a man named Gary Brown, a small fellow similar in statute to George, to take over my primary duties as director of evaluation. Bond also promoted Nick Jamison to be the deputy director of budgeting and planning. In essence, two young, inexperienced white fellows were hired to replace me. And I was told to continue doing both jobs until I had sufficiently shown each of them what their duties entailed. Florence said to me, "Curtis, you should have provided Bond with whatever information he wanted from you. I was assured the directorship of this department after I gave him the necessary information to get Robert McClain fired."

Bond spent his time outside of work in a motel room with the three white men he had hired to protect and entertain him. Two of the men were short like George, and they appeared to be his favorites: my new boss Gary Brown, and Bond's private consultant Tom Riley, whom I had introduced to Bond. Initially, Bond didn't accept Tom Riley. I told Tom that if he really wanted to be the consultant for the City's Planned Variation Federal Program, he would have to be completely subservient to Bond. I never suspected that Tom would do anything to get a job, but he said or did something that made Bond welcome him as his personal consultant and after-hours companion. After he was hired, Tom never spoke to me again. The third person was a PhD candidate named Frank DeGiovanni, who had just married a beautiful six-foot tall woman, whom Bond loved just to look at as he stroked Gary's or Tom's heads in my presence. Frank was given the position of assistant director of planning, and he had no prior work experience at all. He voluntarily left the position after one year, stating to anyone who would listen that he could not continue in that position doing the extracurricular duties that Bond expected from him.

The planning experts with the University of North Carolina in Chapel Hill, where Frank was trying to finalize his PhD degree, were hired to evaluate the effectiveness of Bond's new management team and its strategies for using the planned variation grant. This team would be responsible for planning, implementing, and managing all present and future federal grants. The report from the professors at UNC-Chapel Hill concluded that the administrators of the federal grants were not productive, and that their actions were not in the best interest of the City, the community, and its residents. In essence, Bond was intentionally violating the grants' guidelines in order to satisfy his own personal desires. But it seemed that anything he did met with the approval of the Board of Aldermen and the city manager, because the university's report was disparaged, and Bond said in my presence that he would not be using their services anymore.

And then there was Alexander Beaty (black), who did what I would not do, and more. It seemed that his major role was to destroy any program that employed a large number of black employees.

Many seasoned City employees who knew that I played major roles in enabling the City to receive the $5.3 million planned variation grant and many other federal programs, approached me and told me that I would surely be promoted by the time I was as old as the individuals who had been promoted over me. When I told them that I was older than everyone promoted over me except Bond, they did not believe me. It seemed that most City employees thought I had just graduated from college, and that I had plenty time to advance on the job. Then several of them wanted to know what was going on. Some employees even remembered that Beaty had always objected to my being appointed to any committee, saying that I was not ready or would not be an asset, or that I was a troublemaker.

During a weekend in June 1974, Jim Wilson, the Model City director who had hired me; Louise Wilson, ESR director; Florence Creque; and several of the original Model City employees met at my home for a reunion. Jim Wilson finally told us why he left the City. He said that John Gold, the city manager, had said to him, "If you want a successful future with the City, you must terminate the majority of your black employees after they have completed all of the leg work to qualify us for the planned variation funds." Jim said that he told

Gold he could not do that, and that was the end of his career with the City.

"Curtis," Jim said to me, "Bond was hired to get rid of black employees, because I would not. You have gotten caught in the cross fire, because the city manager and the other managers were highly impressed with you." Louise Wilson added that whenever she recommended me for a management position in the monthly directors meetings, Bond always spoke against me and no one ever challenged him. Florence, she went on to say, was at those meeting and never said anything.

Florence defended herself. "Curtis, you know how Bond is. I know that you came to the City as an outstanding manager, but Bond would have my job if I did not support him. You know what happened to you when you did not do what he wanted you to do. He gave your position of evaluation director to Gary Brown." I did not know what to say.

Bond called a special meeting the first week that all of Bond's cronies were supposed to assume their new positions. Of course, he insisted that I attend, because I was the only person who knew what was going on in the federal program. I had been the sole keeper of the program's budget and program modifications. Florence, who now had been promoted to Model City director, had always taken me with her to all local, area, regional, state, and federal meetings, so that I could learn about any new information about the federal programs, and answer any questions or concerns that the federal representatives had about the City's federal programs. As I sat at Bond's meeting, he stated that I would work with everyone there until they felt proficient in their roles. After which, I would assume my new duties as an evaluator. Everyone in the meeting knew I was being demoted because I would not be subservient to Bond as they were. Still, Aldermen Larry Little pointed out to City Manager Orville Powell that I had more education and job-related experience than everyone being promoted, including Bond.

As assistant city manager, Bond was given unlimited access to City funds. He used them to buy a master's degree from the Babcock School of Management at Wake Forest University. I heard this directly from Bond, as he said in my presence that he was not capable of completing the assignments required for a master's degree at this prestigious university. In his capacity of assistant city manager over all federal grants, Bond made sure that Wake Forest University's School of Management received at least $100,000 in consultant fees. Bond got his masters degree in business administration. Bond bragged throughout the City offices that he did not attend classes often, and he did not complete most of the assignments. The City also paid Bond's tuition expenses of $25,000 per year for three years, even though the MBA program was a two-year program. I knew that because I had applied for the same MBA program at Wake Forest. My supervisor at the time refused to pay my $25,000 per year tuition, even though it had been approved by the City and federal representatives over the Model City program. Bond's name came up during my interview as a possible candidate. Instead, I completed my master's degree in mathematics and enrolled in the doctoral program at UNC-Greensboro.

Shortly after Bond received his MBA from WFU, Gary Brown enrolled in the same management program at earned his MBA. Then Beaty, Bond's number one crony, enrolled in an MBA program with Appalachian University at WSSU. In my opinion, he did not meet the minimum qualifications required to attend WFU. When he tried to use the same tactics that Bond had used, he was unsuccessful. As expected, he did not receive his master's degree. While all of the above individuals were getting qualified for their positions, I had a master's degree in mathematics, the number one prerequisite for the director of evaluation position.

For the next four years, Gary Brown kept Bond happy day and night as I ran the evaluation office. Gary did not even report to the office on a daily basis. When a city official or a professor or administrator from a university called Gary about anything pertaining to evaluation, he referred them to me. Even though I was doing everything to keep the evaluation office afloat, Bond's primary mission was still to destroy me. Therefore, when the first evaluation study was completed under Bond's administration, he called a special meeting, including his cronies and me, as well as other employees, to critique what he thought was my work. He tore apart every aspect of the evaluation, until a young woman he had hired, Brenda, started crying uncontrollably.

"I wrote this entire study," she managed to say, "the way that I was taught in college."

Bond tried to backtrack, saying the study really wasn't as bad as he had said it was.

Brenda went on. "Why do you all hate Curtis so much? He does all of the work around here while you guys all sit around criticizing him and playing with one another like a bunch of homos. What do you homos want from Curtis? He is more man than all of you put together. I have already told him that he needs to get the hell away from you jackasses."

Brenda felt free to speak honestly, because she was leaving this madhouse to go to medical school in California. In my mind, betrayal and demons were all around me, and would be anywhere I ran to. As I smiled in the meeting, Bond and his cronies hung their heads in shame. Bond adjourned the meeting, but he kept Brenda in his office to console her before she could get to her father, who was an executive at R. J. Reynolds Tobacco Company.

When Tom Riley arrived on the scene, Gary worried that he was losing his special relationship with Bond. So Gary called me into his office after I turned in an evaluation study to him. Gary attempted to criticize my evaluation study as Bond had done. When he finished going over the study with a red pen, I looked Gary in the eyes and said, "Are you sure those are the changes that must be made because they are grammatically incorrect?"

Gary said with confidence, "Yes, I will show you later how to write an evaluation."

I went to Gary's bookshelf, picked up one of his business administration textbooks, handed it to him, and told him to turn to page 125 and read for a while. Everything that Gary had redlined as being incorrect, I had copied verbatim from that textbook. Gary did not know what to say or do. He sat there just like the little boy he was, trying to degrade a man.

Finally he looked up at me and said, "Bond hates you and has all of us committed to destroying your life at any cost. I am tired of this game, the hugs and kisses from Bond in the presence of others."

Somehow, Bond got wind of Gary's confession to me. Gary was dropped from Bond's inner circle. In less than a week, Bond had relocated the evaluation office out of City Hall and into the NCNB building. Feeling rejected and lost, and without any appreciable skills to be successful, Gary set out to prove to Bond that he could destroy me for him. Gary asked me to complete a special study for a management professor at Wake Forest University. Of course, the study required academic and sophisticated strategies beyond the scope of my past experiences. Knowing what I was up against, I contacted some of my professor friends at UNC-Greensboro for their assistance. After I completed the study, I gave it to Gary. I received no response from him. After several weeks went by, I asked Gary about the outcome of the study. Gary said without any reservations, "The professors were very disappointed and said that it was completely unacceptable."

Two weeks later, while sitting in a meeting at WFU with Bond, Gary, and all of Bond's cronies, the same professor for whom I had completed the special study was in charge of the meeting. When he started reading excerpts from my study, I looked over at Gary. Gary hid his face in shame and refused to look in my direction. Then the professor went so far as to ask me to stand and said to the audience, "This is the author of this study. Without his expertise, this meeting would not have happened and we would not be able to continue with this project."

After the meeting, I never said anything to Gary, because I knew the deal. And Gary never critiqued another study that I completed.

To further insult me, the MISS Department adjacent to the Evaluation Office created an industrial engineering position salaried a pay grade above my position. The young man, Sandy, who was hired in that position, did not know what was expected of him. Neither did his boss, Sam Owen. According to Gary, who requested several of my evaluation studies so that Sam and Sandy could use them as a guide, Sandy completed one study that was not favorably received. After that, his position was upgraded to supervisory status, and two technician positions were created for him to supervise, so that he would not have to complete any studies. Several years later, he was promoted to a division head within the City.

The City was bombarded with huge grant opportunities all at the same time. Even though more than a half-dozen young white men had recently been promoted to management positions by Bond and Powell, no one seemed to know what to do in order to qualify for the millions of dollars. We black employees had been told that these young white managers were highly qualified, and were equipped with the latest planning and managerial skills and techniques to move the city into the next millennium. A young Harvard graduate named Joe Sauser was hired in the evaluation office to complete a housing study, so that the City could qualify for urban development money. The City's manpower department had failed miserably under the management of Alexander Beaty, Bond's number one crony, who had been caught spying on black employees and been threatened with bodily harm just before he was promoted into that position.

Immediately, Florence Creque was moved into the manpower director's position, in the hopes that she could plan and implement the million dollar federal grant program within six weeks. For destroying the manpower program, Bond moved Beaty to the personnel department as a personnel supervisor, pending the retirement of the personnel director. Bond hired Douglas Hearn as Florence's assistant director of planning. Tom Riley had told Bond that Hearn could put together a plan for the million dollar federal grant. After two weeks went by and no plan was developed, Florence asked her operations supervisor, Marjorie Gregory, who was also my best friend, to ask me to help write a plan. As always, I was eager to help, even though I had never been rewarded for my efforts. In my mind, cream had to rise to the top one day, and I was patiently waiting on my day. I thought that Orville Powell, who had been city manager for about two years, would be my "knight in shining armor." I agreed to help Florence on my terms. They were: I was to select two employees from her staff to work with me away from any City office; I was not to be disturbed by anyone during the two-week period left to develop the plan; and she was to give me complete authority over the project. Florence, Bond, and Powell accepted my terms, because all of the great young white managers that they had hired and promoted said unequivocally that they could not handle such a monumental task.

One day shy of two weeks, Marjorie, Lewis Jones, and I presented our proposal to the mayor, the members of the Board of Aldermen, Powell and Bond, the City's attorney, Rodey Ligon, and many other distinguished guests. When the presentation was finished and only one person, the City's attorney, had a question, the mayor stood and said that the presentation was by far the most impressive and well thought out plan he had ever heard. Florence never stopped grinning and shaking hands with the dignitaries, as they found their way to me to congratulate me for doing an outstanding job.

Now it was reward and promotion time, because the federal manpower office approved my plan without changing anything, and awarded the City one million dollars. When I met with Florence concerning her new organizational plan, she told me that the only position she could offer me was an evaluation position under the supervision of her new assistant director, Doug Hearn. This was the gratitude that Florence offered me for saving her job and professional standing. Without saying anything other than forget it, I left Florence's office, hurt and angry. A month went by, and Florence and Doug could not implement my plan. They tried to get Marjorie, whom Florence had promised to promote to operations director, to implement the plan, but Marjorie told Florence that she did not know how to implement it without my expertise. Of course, Florence went to Bond with her dilemma, and Bond went to Gary, my immediate supervisor. Justifiably, everyone was afraid to ask me to help them do their job after the way they had treated me, intentionally overlooking me for any upgrade or promotion, while others were upgraded or promoted for contributing nothing. Pretending to be my friend and supporter, Gary asked me to help get the manpower program off the ground. He said, though with an unconvincing look on his face, "Curtis, if you do this favor for us, we will promote you to a management position when the new community development department is formed." Though I doubted anything Bond or his subordinates said, I agreed to implement my plan for Florence.

When I went to Florence's office, everyone knew there was some tension between us. I asked Florence to convene her entire operational and planning staff for a meeting. She summoned everyone to the conference room and turned the meeting over to me.

As I was giving assignments to each of the staff personnel, including Doug Hearn, Florence said angrily, "Stop, this is not going to work. These people are not experienced enough to handle the assignments that you are giving them."

"Am I in charge of this project or not?" I asked. "Just let me know now, so that I can leave. And I will not be coming back down here to help in any form or fashion."

"Do it your way," Florence said, "but I'm telling you it will not work."

I gave everyone one week to complete their part in the project, and then they would report back to me and Florence. Of course, I met with each employee daily to make sure they were on target. When there was a problem with a particular agency, I met with the director of the agency and alleviated the problem. At the end of one week, the project was up and running and all of the funds were allocated throughout the entire city. Hundreds of jobs were created, ranging from secretaries to attorneys to directors of programs to managers of agencies. Florence called me to her office and asked, "How did you manage to pull this off? Where did you get all of this talent?"

I did not attempt to answer her questions. I thanked her for her comments and the opportunity to contribute to a worthy cause.

I already knew how Florence really felt about me, because Louise Wilson had told me that Florence and Bond always made negative comments about me every time she recommended me for a promotion. Florence hated me, because I could do things that she could not do, things she had not even thought of doing. When she first saw my new home, she had her home completely redecorated in a similar fashion. Many times she would catch herself when she was saying something complimentary to me, like, "You are really a talented and brilliant young man. Where did you learn so much?"

Florence invited me to her board meeting, where she presented my proposal and implementation schedule. At the end of her presentation, she came over to me and asked how she'd done. All smiles, I said, "You were great. You covered all bases." I thought to myself, *who am I that everyone wants to be like me, but they don't want me to succeed and prosper in life? How can they live with themselves?*

As a result of my expertise and willingness to assist, everyone received a promotion except me. Bond's position was upgraded to deputy city manager, Creque's position was upgraded to human services director, Beaty was promoted to personnel director, and Marjorie, who assisted me with the million dollar project, was promoted to operations director of the Human Services Department. Doug Hearn received an upgrade in position status, and Lewis Jones, the junior employee, was hired as the personnel director at the School of the Arts University in Winston-Salem.

Deputy City Manager Bond successfully destroyed my marriage by telling my wife that I had been unfaithful to her, and that he would testify on her behalf at our separation proceeding. He told my wife that she could get custody of our child and could keep our house. I was separated and divorced from my wife a year later because of the abasement my wife put me through, unjustifiably so. She did not really want a divorce, because six months before I divorced her she pleaded with me for a reconciliation. She was betrayed by Bond, who did not show up for court as her witness, even after he was subpoenaed.

The judge presiding over the case helped me terminate my marriage, when he gave custody of our child to my wife, even after stating that I was the better and more stable parent for the child and should continue in that role. The judge's final decision was that my wife should receive monthly child support payments from me. He further stated that I should continue rearing and caring for our daughter in my home until the child was grown. The child support decree was changed by another judge when our daughter was eleven years old, and my wife was ordered to pay me child support.

When the court summoned my ex-wife and me to court for not paying child support as ordered, the judge automatically assumed I was the defendant. He started criticizing me as a deadbeat dad. When my ex-wife spoke up and said that she was the defendant, the judge said, "Well, I'll be damned. This is a first in my courtroom." My ex-wife had all of the back payments with her. When she told me that the money came from her business, which was in serious danger of failing because customers were stealing her blind, I permitted her to keep the money for the business and to open up a saving account for our daughter. In complete shock, the judge said, "Where have you been all of my life? Nobody gives money back, but the decision is yours to make."

From that point on, my ex-wife respected me and treated me as though I was her best friend. When her mother and sister came to the United States from Japan for two weeks, they visited me every day, and had dinner at my home at least five times. When my ex-wife's job was in jeopardy, she came to me and I wrote a supportive letter on her behalf. She was able to remain on her job, until she retired with full benefits. I remained my ex-wife's friend, completely dismissing the many cruel and destructive things she had done to me. Just before my ex-wife went into a coma, she told me that I was her best and most loyal friend. She never regained consciousness, and died after being in a coma for over a year.

Having rewarded me with only betrayals and insults for my outstanding contributions, Gary Brown and Florence Creque had the audacity to ask me to monitor the Human Services Department's daily operations. In the meantime, the new evaluator, Joe Sauser, who was housed in the same office with me, was given the responsibility of completing a detailed evaluation of Winston-Salem's Housing Redevelopment Program. He had to make the appropriate recommendations, which would enable the City to get millions of dollars to form its own Community Development Department. After six months had passed, Joe had done absolutely nothing, and Gary was afraid even to address the problem. I was the mediator between the two young men. Joe would tell me that he did not plan to complete the study, and Gary would tell me that he did not know what to do.

I perceived this as a very simple problem with a very simple solution. Gary should exercise his authority as director of the office and order Joe to complete the study. Joe knew that Gary would not challenge him because of their after-work relationship. Whatever it was, it definitely superseded Gary's authority over Joe on the job. Instead of being a leader, Gary begged me to complete the study that everyone, from the federal level to the state level to the regional level to the area level, was waiting for. Gary promised me that if I completed the study, he would definitely promote me to one of the two assistant director positions that were in the proposal. I agreed to do Joe's work. I also continued with my regular evaluation duties with manpower and other City departments, while Joe did absolutely nothing every day on the job. It took me six months to complete the study, but I covered every aspect of the existing housing operations throughout the city. My study was received with the same enthusiasm as my manpower proposal. When the study was linked with the housing proposal that Gary had put together, the City was awarded millions of dollars to take over the housing and urban development activities for the entire city. Immediately, Gary was promoted to director of the newly formed Community Development Department, and Joe was promoted to assistant director of planning. I waited to be told that I would be promoted to assistant director of operations, as Gary had promised, but Gary avoided me for weeks. Joe told me every day that Gary had to give me the promotion, because without my input there would not be a new department.

In the midst of all of the above, Florence got sick, and her doctor ordered her not to work for an indefinite period of time. Bond assigned Beaty as the interim director of the Human Services Department. In less than a week, Beaty completely undermined the work that I had set in motion. The entire staff rebelled against Beaty's mismanagement practices. Of course, Bond convinced Powell that I was the cause of Beaty's problems with the Human Services Department's staff. At this time, I was in Denver working on a special assignment for Police Chief Surratt. When Florence's doctor told her she had to resign her position with the City if she wanted to live, she chose to take a leave of absence instead of resigning.

The Federal Manpower Representative for the City, a woman named Nancy, had befriended Marjorie and me. Still, she met secretly with City Manager Powell and Deputy City Manager Bond, and recommended her girlfriend Nellie for the directorship of the Human Services Department. Prior to that meeting, she had told Marjorie and me that she was going to recommend one of us for the directorship, because she considered both of us the most qualified for the job. My favorite high school science teacher, Mrs. O'Kelly was friends with Nancy, and she told me what Nancy had done and why. Marjorie and I never saw Nancy again, and her girlfriend Nellie was hired as the director of the Human Services Department. In less than one year, Nancy's position with the Federal Manpower Office in Atlanta was eliminated, and she had no job. She told Mrs. O'Kelly that she felt that she was being punished for betraying the two best friends and workers that she had ever known.

As a result of my working so closely with the housing personnel, I discovered that my mother's house was part of the relocation component of urban renewal. The Housing Relocation Director Thurmond Howell worked with my mother and me to get her the maximum amount of money for her house. I signed an agreement with Thurmond that I would bring the substandard home that my mother bought from my brother, Lorenza, up to standard within one month. With me as the administrator of my mother's funds, she authorized me to give each of her sons $1000, and to give Lorenza $2000 per his request, and to pay off the $3000 balance owed on his substandard house. My brother William and I refused the $1000 that our mother offered us. For the next twenty years, my mother had no expenses, because I took care of everything for her. When she wanted to buy all new kitchen appliances for her new home, I bought them. When she wanted a new carpet, air conditioning, and special screen doors, I bought them for her. When all of her funds were completely exhausted, I continued to buy my mother anything that she wanted.

A few weeks later, as I was still waiting to hear about my promotion to the assistant director of operation position under Gary, I received a call from Alderman Larry Little. He told me that Powell had called Florence Creque and asked her to take the assistant director of operations position, so that he would not have to promote me. Alderman Little stated further that Bond now owned Powell. They had gotten an apartment together so that they could do their thing secretly as often as they wanted to. I went by Florence's house to confirm what Alderman Little had told me. Florence lied to my face, saying, "I have not been offered any job with the City, and I have no plans of coming back to the City. My doctor told me that that environment would definitely kill me if I worked there again." Florence returned to work for the City as the assistant director of operations in the newly formed Community Development Department the following Monday. I knew that this situation would not work, because Florence had told me that she could not work with Gary Brown, and Gary never had anything nice to say about Florence. It became crystal clear to me that Florence would do anything to keep the world from seeing me perform administrative duties more proficiently than she. Florence lived a miserable life on and off the job for the next two years. When she was completely ostracized by Gary and most of the Community Development Department's staff, she tried unsuccessfully to resurrect a working relationship and friendship with me. She was never given any responsibility in Gary's administration. In fact, she was not even told when there was going to be a staff meeting. Suddenly, Florence's illness reappeared, and she had to take a leave of absence again. Florence sacrificed her health and life to assist Bond and Powell in destroying my career.

Joe Sauser felt really hurt that while I had done his work, he had been promoted and I had not. He tried to convince me that maybe Powell was going to give me Gary's position as evaluation director, after Gary was promoted to the new Community Development Department. Then, without any announcement, Powell's administrative assistant, Allen Joines, showed up and said that Powell had appointed him director of the Evaluation Office. The position had never been advertised. Joe had another month before he reported to his new position, and he told Joines that he was not going to do a damn thing for him. And he didn't. Joines just smiled and turned to me. He said that he knew I carried the office, and that I should continue running it as I had done under Gary's administration, because he did not know anything about evaluation. He was only there for the money and the promotion, not the responsibility.

Whenever anyone called or came to the office concerning evaluation, Joines escorted them to my office. Almost everyone ended his conversation with me by asking, "Why aren't you the director of this office? Everything seems to be directed to you." I never gave a direct answer to the question, as the disgust and hurt could clearly be seen on my face. Every evaluation request that came into the office was given to me. When Joines received two requests for studies to be completed as soon as possible for the police department and the fire department, he asked me if I would work on the studies in my spare time. Again, all of the work for the office was given to me. Without complaining, I completed both studies, which required extensive preparation, such as surveys, visiting other cities from the east coast to the west coast, and writing up the studies. Both studies were well received by Police Chief Tom Surratt and Fire Chief Lester Ervin. The police chief was most appreciative, and gave all the credit for the report to me when he presented it to his officers and the Board of Aldermen. The fire chief was also very appreciative, but Allen Joines and Tom Fredericks, the budget director, wanted to be present when I briefed the fire chief on my study, since it projected a million dollar savings for the City. Two nights later my telephone rang, and I was told to turn my television to channel 12. I saw and heard Joines presenting my study as if it was his work. The next weekend, Joines made a spectacle of himself by getting falling down drunk at Joe Sauser's wedding. When he reported to work on the following Monday, he told me that Powell had promoted him to public safety director. Then he thanked me for my outstanding work on the fire and police studies. He knew he would never have gotten the promotion without them. As Joines was packing up to leave that day, I said to him, "Who is going to become the director of evaluation?"

"I don't have anything to do with that," Joines said. "You should hear something in the next few days."

During the next week, I was the only person assigned to the Evaluation Office. Joe was packing up to move to his new position. The secretary, who only had a high school diploma, was promoted to an accountant position with the Human Services Department and left the office. When I called the city manager's office to find out what was going on, he was not available. So I made an appointment to meet with

Powell. Shortly after my telephone call to Powell's office, Tom Fredericks, the budget director, came to the Evaluation Office and told me that I had been assigned to his office. He stated that the evaluation duties were being transferred to the budget office so that he could be promoted to budget and evaluation director. I said very politely, "You should not be telling me this. I should have received an official reassignment notification in writing from the personnel department." It took another week before the official request was sent to me. In the meantime I sat in the office alone, wondering, *What have I done to be treated so cruelly and betrayed by everyone that I have helped? Why is everyone catering to John Bond? What has Bond done to Powell, my idol?*

In the City's newly formed Public Safety Office, two junior officers were hired, one from the fire department and one from the police department. Having been told about my expertise in planning, implementing, evaluating, and managing programs of any type, both men found their way to my lonely office to review my practices and studies. They wanted to use the benefit of my expertise to be successful in their jobs and move up the promotional ladder, as Joines had done. In record time, both of these white men were promoted to high administrative positions. George Sweat became the police chief, and Pete Harley became the deputy fire chief.

When I went to talk with City Manager Powell on the day of my appointment with him, his secretary told me that Powell had gone flying with Tom Riley. I had overheard Bond tell Riley to win Powell over to his way of thinking so that he could run the City his way and get rid of anyone he wanted. After flying with Riley about three times, Powell took flying lessons and rented an apartment with Bond and Riley. According to Bond's talkative cronies, Bond, Powell, and Riley met regularly after work and on the weekends at their apartment. Bond, however, never let the men stay around very long.

When I finally got to see Powell, he was a perfect gentleman and appeared to be very supportive of me. He said, "Curtis, in my eyes you are one of my best employees. I wish I had more dedicated and hardworking employees like you. But what can I do if Bond and Florence are always saying that you are not ready for a management position? Also, many of my managers and I feel that we don't know anything about your personal life and convictions. All we know is that you come to work every day; you are in graduate school several nights a week; and you take care of your young daughter and your mother full-time. Other than those things, we know nothing about you."

"What can I say?" I asked. "You met my family at the picnic. I live a very simple life, with my family and my church, and I try to be an asset on my job at all times. What else do you want to know about me? I don't drink or smoke. Is that a bad thing?" Powell was silent, as if he did not know what to say. I said, "What must I do in order to be promoted to a management position under your administration?"

Powell looked me straight in my eyes and said, "*If you had a master's degree in public administration, I will promote you into a management position without any reservations or comments from anyone.*"

I left Powell's office feeling that he was going to do the right and honorable thing by me.

When I finally moved back to City Hall in the Budget Office, the young female budget analysts (white) came running to my office to welcome me. They also wanted to convince me to make Tom Fredericks famous, as I had done for Allen Joines, by completing those unique and magnificent studies that everyone was raving about. Right away Fredericks, who received about a $7500 increase in pay because I was transferred to his department, accepted an invitation from the State Council of Governments to brief them on effective evaluations techniques for use by local governments. Of course, Fredericks did not know anything about evaluation techniques. My first assignment was to prepare a presentation for Fredericks to give at the meeting. As past directors had done, Fredericks requested that I accompany him to the meeting. During Fredericks's entire presentation, he kept looking at me for approval of what he was saying. On occasion, he asked me if certain comments he made were correct. Everyone at the meeting constantly looked at me as I sat quietly to the side. The moderator of the meeting did comment to Fredericks that I must be his expert on evaluation.

Having made Fredericks look good, I thought he would set aside his childish games, but he did not. When he learned I was in graduate school pursuing a master's degree in public administration, he did everything humanly possible to cause me to fail my classes. He refused to approve any leave requests that I submitted to him. He gave me assignments that he knew conflicted with my class schedule. After I made an appointment to talk with Powell concerning my problems with Fredericks, as Powell had told me to do, I was called in to meet with Personnel Director Beaty and Fredericks, who had already decided my outcome. They were shocked when I refused to address my problem with them until after I had met with the city manager, as he had requested I do. This comment ended the meeting with Beaty and Fredericks looking at each other like two buffoons.

It took Powell a couple of weeks before he could get up enough nerve to meet with me. In the meantime, it was business as usual with Fredericks. When the time came to give out budget assignments, he gave me all of the most difficult department directors to work with, and he made sure that he and the two young women got their favorite departments. The six-month budgeting process was designed in such a way that it should have been impossible for me to continue my graduate studies. Fredericks and the women spent at least three evening a week working on their budgets. Fredericks had anticipated that I would also have to spend at least three evening a week on my assignments. Having been the sole budget administrator for federal programs in the past, and having planned and implemented the Manpower Program, I did not complain about this task. I completed the budgets for all of my departments in less than three months.

All departments had shut down requesting evaluations after I was assigned to the budget office. Several managers told me that they were rebelling against Powell's method of promoting City employees without advertising the positions. During my extra time, I assisted the two women in the office with their budget assignments, and I was even able to work on my graduate studies.

When Powell finally got around to meeting with me and Fredericks, his first comment was, "I should have known that this arrangement was not going to work, a boy supervising a man." Powell's solution to the problem was: Fredericks was to leave me alone and enroll in a management program, so that he could learn how to be an effective manager.

The secretary assigned to the Budget Office once told me that she believed that if she came to the office without any clothes on, Tom Fredericks would not even notice. While at a Christmas party, Tom's wife said that she never planned to have any children with him. She further stated that if he wanted to have children, he could have some with the mutt that slept between them. All Tom did at the time was laugh. What were these ladies trying to tell me about one of Powell's favorite employees?

One year from the day that Powell told me I needed a master's degree in public administration to be promoted to a management position, I earned that master's degree from the University of North Carolina in Greensboro. During that year, I went to work every day from 7:30 AM until 5 PM. I would drop my daughter off at her school in the morning, and make sure she arrived safely at my mother's house after school. Whenever I wasn't working on the job, I was working on my degree. For my accomplishment, Powell hired a consultant firm to upgrade all City employees' positions except one. Out of the 1800 City employees, the consultant firm recommended that my job position be downgraded three pay grades, which would have reduced my annual salary by $2000. The Board of Aldermen's response to Powell's clear misuse of power was to void the study and ask for Powell's resignation. Six months prior, this same board had asked for the resignation of Deputy City Manager Bond, because he had misappropriated over $50,000 of the City's federal funds, by giving the funds to Tom Riley for personal and unsubstantiated services. According to Gary Brown, Bond paid Riley $21,000 for spending a weekend with him. Gary also told Joe Sauser and me that instead of firing both of these managers, the aldermen gave them credit cards with an unlimited dollar value so that they could seek employment elsewhere. Further, the aldermen gave Bond a written resolution, citing all of my accomplishments as Bond's accomplishments to make sure that he was marketable. Frankly speaking, the only thing I could remember Bond doing was feeling for something between his legs whenever we met in his office, and I don't think he ever found it. Both Bond and Powell landed comparable positions in other cities in another state. And according to the local media, they both resigned those positions because they were considered to be ineffective managers.

Under Powell's administration, every white employee with an MPA degree was promoted, and the two black employees— myself and a young woman—with MPA degrees were harassed, humiliated, and/or recommended for a downgrade in position status and pay. At no time did the members of the Board of Aldermen consider rectifying the many wrongs bestowed upon me or the young woman. Was it because we were not administrators or white, and our lives and the lives of our loved ones were not considered important enough? The mayor and five of the eight members of the Board of Aldermen had talked to me personally and assured me that I had done nothing wrong, and that I would be vindicated and promoted, as I should have been many years ago. But they betrayed me to favor dishonor.

Shortly after the above incidents, William Brandon told me that Gary Brown, the director of the Community Development Department, had completely mismanaged that department to the tune of about $200,000. His reprimand was to receive all the time he needed to seek employment elsewhere, with the highest recommendation from City management. And of course, he landed a better position as an assistant city manager in Colorado.

Lewis Cutright, a high school graduate with almost thirty years of service with the City, was appointed interim city manager by the mayor and the Board of Aldermen. This man exemplified more management savvy than both Powell and Bond put together. Immediately, he moved me from under the supervision of Fredericks, whom he considered to be one of Powell's personal cronies, and directly under his supervision. He spoke with me candidly on a daily basis, and told me that he was quite aware of how wrongly I had been treated, despite being a dedicated employee with the City. *He further said that he wanted to promote me to a management position because it was the right thing to do, but the members of the Board of Aldermen would not sanction his desires.* Once again, these board members, both black and white, had betrayed me.

In 1980, the board hired a new city manager, Bryce A. Stuart. According to the local newspaper article that was released to the public, he was the least qualified of six finalists for the city manager's position. He was the only candidate who did not have a master's degree. During a visit to the city of Charlotte on official business, I happened to meet former co-workers and employees of Stuart's. They told me that he had married a divorced woman with two or three children a few months before, or during, the interviewing process for his new position. He had also stopped being the happy hour king, and had gotten religion, because he'd heard the Board of Aldermen in Winston-Salem was looking for a family man with Christian values. At least two of the aldermen told me that the majority of the board members had completely overlooked any real qualifications for the position. They hired Bryce A. Stuart because he had blond hair and blue eyes, and because he agreed to cater to their desires. Based on the new city manager's immediate attacks on me, the members of the board evidently desired a city manager who would destroy Curtis Dixon's career and reputation for excellence at any cost.

Stuart, the poseur, hated me even before he met me. Interim City Manager Cutright told me that he had met with Stuart and did not consider him to be an honorable man. "He has never met you," Cutright said, "and he had nothing good to say about you any time that I mentioned your name. Stuart was most grateful when I gave him your organizational charts, which gave him important history on all of his managers and their staff, until I told him that you had prepared them. Then he started criticizing insignificant aspects of the charts, but he continued to refer to the charts when he was talking to me about any department. I will not work for this fellow. I will be retiring as soon as possible."

The wolf in sheep clothing finally arrived, and summoned me to his office his first day on the job. Stuart's initial comment was, "I know all about you, and I just want you to know that I don't have anything to do with your situation." From that point forward, I could do nothing right for Stuart.

When Stuart first arrived in Winston-Salem, he was invited to join the Piedmont Triad Chapter of the American Society for Public Administration (ASPA), and he joined without knowing that I was the president of the Triad Chapter. When he found out that I was the president, he refused to have anything to do with the organization. However, after he transferred me to the MISS Department and my reign as president was over, the City refused to pay for my membership in the Triad Chapter. Stuart told me that I was no longer eligible for this service, because my new duties were outside the scope of the policy. I was told that after Stuart had done the devil's deed of making me inactive with ASPA, he became active in the Piedmont Triad ASPA Chapter.

In Stuart's initial meetings with all of his assistant city managers, department heads, and me, he told each of us that he wanted a detailed written report of our activities. This report was to be handed in to him before his next staff meeting. When I was the only employee to complete the assignment for the next meeting, Stuart criticized my report in the presence of the higher ranking managers at the meeting. He told them that he did not need a five-page research paper from them. He held up my report and said, "This is too much. You all can just give me a handwritten note of your activities." Many of the managers laughed, because Stuart was looking directly at me the entire time that he was talking.

In the next manager's staff meeting, Stuart verbally reprimanded me for being unprepared. He thought he had asked me to have something ready for the meeting, but I politely told him that I had not been given any assignment.

"Are you challenging me?" Stuart asked angrily.

Silence filled the room, and I softly asked to be excused for a moment. When Stuart asked why, I said, "I would like to get my minutes on the last meeting and read them back to you, so that everyone here can be clear on what transpired."

Stuart was silent for a moment, and then he said, "Minutes. Oh, I should have known that you keep track of everything that is said and done around here. Just forget the entire matter."

After that meeting, whenever I completed any task for City Manager Stuart, he told me to give it to Allen Joines, so that Joines could present it to him and the staff. This was Stuart's way of showing all of his managers that he was more dishonorable than Powell and Bond when it came to dealing with me. Stuart acted as if he had met with Powell and Bond before coming to the City, because his every action mimicked Powell's and Bond's management style. He gravitated to every administrator who had been a favorite of Powell and Bond, especially Tom Fredericks and Alexander Beaty. It appeared to me that the aldermen had given Stuart the authority to continue Bond's and Powell's vendetta against me. Therefore, he felt secure in treating me as if I was immaterial, an expert going nowhere under his administration.

My office was adjacent to the city manager's office, with a door between them. Three months after Stuart's arrival, the major renovation plans that Powell had had for the city manager's wing began under the supervision of Beaty. Everyone involved in the renovation was told when and where to move before the renovation began except me. I was left in the middle of the renovation as everyone else was moved to safe locations. When the construction workers complained about an employee still being housed in their work area, I was moved into the City's old windowless vault for several months. When I got sick and rashes broke out all over my body, I was moved out of City Hall and into the basement of the NCNB building, where water from the sewage pipes leaked constantly. There the director of the auditing department complained that it was inhuman to treat anyone the way that I was being treated, and that he did not want to be seen as sanctioning management's actions, by permitting me to be housed in an area of his office that was not fit for human habitation. I was moved back to City Hall to the old Budget Office, and was assigned the duties of an engineer. Stuart's comment as he gave me the duties were, *"I have been told that you can perform any job proficiently and effectively around here, so I expect the same outstanding quality of work from you even though this job is outside your training and expertise. And furthermore, you will no longer report to me, but to Allen Joines."* At this point, I considered Stuart to be a reprobate and sadist.

Uncontested excerpts from my previous book: Joines' talents to Powell and now Stuart were well hidden from public view. On May 14, 1980, City Manager Stuart transferred me under the supervision of Allen Joines who at the time had the title of public safety coordinator. Around City Hall, Joines was referred to as the "Golden Boy" who got credit for other employees' work accomplishments. The day that Joines became my supervisor, he said, "First, I would like for you to complete the taxicab rate increase study by next Thursday, May 22 so that it can be presented to the Public Safety Committee on May 27, 1980. I thought to myself, *So this is why I am being transferred, to do Allen Joines' work as I once did in the past so that he can get the credit.* On Thursday, May 22nd, I completed the taxicab study and gave it to Allen. I left the office for a few minutes and when I returned, there was a note on my desk which read: "The study is Okay. Please complete the cover memorandum for the taxicab study for Bill Stuart, signed Allen."

Then the next day, I received a call from Mrs. Vivian Burke, the black alderperson who was chairperson for the Public Safety Committee. She said, "Curt, I know that you did the study because I asked Allen and he said that both of you worked on it. I want you at the meeting Tuesday night so that you can present your study." She said, "I know that Mr. Stuart plans to use Allen so that he can get credit, but you just be there and I'll handle the rest." When I arrived at the meeting, Mr. Stuart was surprised. He spoke to Allen, then to Mrs. Burke. He came over to me and said, "Curt, I would like for you to give a five minute briefing on the taxicab study. I know that this is a short notice. Do you think you will have any problems?" I said with confidence, "I can handle it." My presentation must have taken twenty-five to thirty minutes because there were many questions. Mrs. Burke thanked me for bringing to them (herself and Jon DeVries, a white alderman) the first complete, well organized and planned study since she had been elected to the board. Mr. DeVries even stated how satisfied he was with the report, my presentation and the timeliness in which I had completed it. He said, "The report was thorough and well thought out." He cited some examples from the report. I felt proud and grateful for the first time in almost ten years. I was being allowed to present my work and receive credit, all because of Mrs. Vivian Burke, a God fearing, decent and honest human being who had picked up on what the system was trying to do to me.

The committee delayed approving the rate increase until the staff could come up with some formulas that would justify the rate increase. Allen said to me, "Maybe you can get with the taxicab manager and come up with something." Then Allen said, "Curt, you did a beautiful job last night." Later Mr. Stuart told me that I had done a fine job at the Public Safety Committee meeting and that I handled myself real well during my presentation.

On Friday, May 30, 1980, Allen said, "Curt, how are you coming with the formulas?" I said, "I'm not." He said, "You know I've got to let Mrs. Burke know something today." I said to Allen, "I'll have something on your desk about 5 PM So tell Mrs. Burke that everything's for go." At 2:30 PM that same afternoon, I had not accomplished anything. Then it was almost as if God said, "I will show you the way and it will be done." I started writing, erasing, and writing. I didn't have the slightest idea what I was doing. At 4:45 PM, I had written five pages of formulas with examples. As I read them, I understood what I was trying to say fully, but feared that Allen would not. So I wrote him a note and told him, "Only with God's help will you understand what I have written." I finished the handwritten assignment at 5:30 PM on Friday.

On Monday, June 9, 1980, I received a typed copy of the formulas from Allen's secretary. He had made several changes. On Tuesday, June 10, 1980, I returned to the office and my draft handwritten copy of the formulas had been placed on my desk. In reviewing my handwritten formulas and the typed the formulas, I noticed that Allen had changed what I had given him. I hesitated about telling him but I did. He was grateful and told me to correct them. As usual, Mrs. Burke called me and told me that she had talked with Allen who had informed her that he and I had derived the formulas. She said, "Curt, did you do most of the work." I said, "Yes, I did." She said, "I want you at that meeting tonight."

At the 7:30 PM Public Safety Committee meeting, Allen passed out the changes that I made to the formulas. Mr. Stuart whispered something to Mrs. Burke and then to Allen. Before Mr. Stuart could sit down, Mrs. Burke said, "I see we have Mr. Dixon in the audience. Come up to the podium, Mr. Dixon." Mrs. Burke said, "Mr. Dixon, are these your formulas?" I looked at Mr. Stuart who nodded his approval for me to speak. I said, "Yes, they are." Mrs. Burke said, "Will you please explain your formulas to this committee?" I explained the formulas fully. Mrs. Burke thanked me. So did John DeVries and Larry Little, a black alderman, for an outstanding piece of work. At this point, Allen said, "Mr. Dixon worked extremely hard to come up with those formulas and deserves praise for doing such an outstanding job. I know because I watched him struggle each day until the task was complete."

The next morning Mrs. Burke called me and told me that she made those ending remarks, because just before the meeting started Mr. Stuart had whispered in her ear that he wanted Allen Joines to present his formulas. She said, "This infuriated me and made it crystal clear how young whites advance at the sacrifice of capable, qualified blacks." In the same conversation, Mrs. Burke said, "Curtis, beware of your own black folks because they will cause you more problems than anyone else. Be careful of whom you talk and about what you say. I was told by a black that you were helping the NAACP organize against the City on the Bert Weeks issue." I said, "But Mrs. Burke, I am not a member of the NAACP and never have been." Then she said, "I understand and I also told the person that she was lying because you were an honest, decent family man who did not get involved in that sort of thing. I told you the above to let you know how treacherous your own kind can be. I'm going to help you in any way I can because it is clear what predicament blacks have put you in."

Larry Little told me that the city manager was satisfied with my performance. And he was going to keep me on his team as an assistant to the city manager and use my talents doing special studies. At this point Larry said that he stated to Mr. Stuart, "Is it possible for Mr. Dixon to get into something permanent, something he can call his own instead of special and different types of assignments from one week to the next?" He said Stuart said, "I'm afraid not because he'll be working for Allen and there will be many different and changing duties." Larry said, "You didn't mean working for Allen Joines, did you? After all, Mr. Dixon has been with the City longer, has more experience, and is older. It is time that the system stop putting him under the supervision of young white men with less time and experience with the City than he has." Larry stated that Stuart then said, "Curt will be working for me and with Allen Joines on many assignments."

On July 3, 1980, Mr. Stuart told me that he had received a letter of commendation from the taxicab manager concerning my performance and that he concurred with it. He further stated that commendations should come from him and not the agency because it could be interpreted many ways.

Pete Mantius, a newspaper reporter for the Winston-Salem Journal said to me, "Curt, you are an amazing young man. You are not bitter. You still represent the City well and do not wallow in self-pity. I really admire you and feel fairly confident that everything's going to work out okay for you. I think that Bill Stuart will be fair with you because he knows what you stand for, especially since you demonstrated clearly to him that you are capable the way in which you handled the taxicab situation. By the way, I would like to congratulate you for doing such an outstanding job. You were simply fantastic. I know that you are suing the City, but I feel that Bill Stuart will not let that stand in the way of his being fair and objective about promoting you. The man has clearly demonstrated that he is a good, decent, Christian man and I feel that he, if anyone, will do right by you. I know that you probably applied for the ABC administrator's position. So don't be surprised if you get it. Just be sure and call me first thing. Curt, I am serious. The city manager is going to set everything straight."

I decided to complete a detailed Energy Conservation Plan for the City and present it to the city manager and Joines. I completed the fifteen page plan, typed it myself since I did not have clerical support and sent copies with a cover memorandum to the city manager and my supervisor, Joines on January 16, 1981. Without a word from the city manager and my supervisor, I received a memorandum on January 20, 1981 telling me to implement the plan. I was to be the engineer, accountant, manager and everything. I was to be the master of all trades.

A meeting was held with the public works director on February 18, 1981 at my insistence, after five attempts, to solicit technical support. During a prior interview, this public works director had said to me, "Curt, I must admit that you have one of the most impressive resumes that I have ever seen and you are well educated, but you do know that there are such people who are just educated fools and can not really perform satisfactorily on the job."

My comment to him at the time was, "My experiences and accomplishments which are also on my resume attest to the fact that I can perform more effectively and efficiently than most people in this system. Also, the projects that I worked on effectively for you in the past clearly showed you that I had proven myself theoretically and practically. So, for your information, I am not an educated fool, but a well educated, qualified manager and you know it."

Just as this meeting was about to begin, this public works director, Pat Swan, started with nonsense again. He said, "Curt, I'm going to get right to the point. Many of my people have told me that you said that you were not interested in energy and I personally feel that with this attitude, we will never get anything done."

Then I said, "Pat, I am not going to be the fall guy for you or any of your people. I don't want to hear about any gossip from you that anyone has said. I would appreciate it very much if you would just bring the liars in here and let them tell their lies in front of me. If you can't or won't do that, I don't want to hear anything else about such nonsense."

This public works director, who really considered himself to be someone special in the City, looked at me as if he could kill me, but he gracefully retreated. Then he said, "Curt, you need to work on your credibility." And Allen Joines spoke up and said, "I agree with Pat. Curt, if you worked on your credibility, staff support would come very easy for you." I looked at both of these white supervisors, smiled and said, "I can't believe that I just heard what you two managers said to me. It's a sad day when a manager does not know where credibility within any organization is originated. For your information, credibility within an organization starts at the top and works its way down through an organization, and not from the bottom up or the middle up and down." There was a long silence and stupid looks on two white faces for several minutes. Then I said, "Now that that is all taken care of, what about some technical support to help get this energy idea off the ground for the City."

Immediately, Pat Swan was a different man and supported everything that I said. When Building Management Superintendent Harold Bolick (white) arrived at the meeting, he resisted everything that his boss Pat Swan presented to him as I sat quietly listening to white superiors disagree with one another (for credibility). Then Pat said, "I want you to assign one of your engineers to work with Curt for a short while and show him what is required to complete an energy audit. After a couple of audits, Curt should be able to take on the full responsibility. If he can't, we should check with his university and see if he really graduated with all those honors." Pat smile and I said, "For your information, I am sure that I will not be prepared to be an engineer after a couple of detailed energy audits, not even after twenty." Then Harold Bolick said, "If you are prepared, please let me know so that I can write my Alma Mater Duke University and tell them to do away with their five year engineering program and get in touch with you." Quietness was everywhere. Then Pat Swan said, "Well, I agree that an engineer should be assigned to support this energy effort fulltime or for the time being." Bolick said, "If you are directing me to do this, I will." Then Pat Swan said, "I am directing you, but take care of your internal operations first." An engineer was not assigned to the energy effort until some two months after the above meeting.

The aldermen were very much aware of what was happening to me, and they avoided me as if I had the plague. One board member, Larry Little (black), did tell me that I was being used as a sacrificial lamb, with the majority of the board members' blessings. Then Alderman Little quickly got to why he was really visiting me so often. He wanted to make sure that he got accepted into the graduate program that I had just completed, and he wanted to use all of my materials. After Alderman Little retrieved my textbooks, notes, and research papers, and received his MPA degree, he betrayed me and did nothing to end the injustices being launched at me on a daily basis. In fact, Little was downright insulting to me when I asked him to be a character witness for me. Vivian Burke (black), a board member who lived across the street from one of my brothers, confirmed that the city manager was acting against me on orders from them when she told me that she told Stuart who to hire for the convention center director's position and he hired her person, William McGee. Burke boldly said to me, *"City Manager Stuart knows who he works for and he does exactly what we tell him to do."*

Uncontested excerpts from my book, *Evil for Good in Winston-Salem*, published in 1988: "Starting in 1983, each of the black aldermen which made up fifty percent of the full Board of Aldermen had me meet with them one by one in their homes or a place away from the office to tell me that they would never let my case go to trial because they knew without a doubt that I had been wronged.

Alderman Vivian Burke took the lead and talked and counseled with me often. Larry Little often told me that he stood firm with Mrs. Burke in my corner and that they had met many times with Mr. Stuart to correct the wrongs.

Larry Womble had me meet him at his home, where he assured me that my case would never go to trial and that justice would be given to me.

I met with Virginia Newell at her request in her home and at her office where she told me that she supported me wholeheartedly and that she would support a vote to correct the injustice that I had suffered for years, if the others stood firm.

In the final analysis, Mrs. Burke told me to give her a proposal of what I felt the City and my oppressors owed me for over ten years of inhuman treatment. Later, Larry Little told me that a decision had been reached to settle everything fairly and in my favor. He said that the Board of Aldermen was going to take care of the situation by giving me what he considered a fair settlement for my suffering. Then he said that he did not want me to question the members but just to take it and run because it would be a handsome settlement.

As my trial day came closer, the further away my black aldermen allies were. I could not see or hear from any of them. Then Larry Little and Vivian Burke on two separate occasions told me that Mr. Stuart had met with them and assured them that he had evidence to show that I was not deserving, and he needed their support since they had hired him to run the City. Later, Mrs. Burke could not remember having said anything to me about a conversation with Mr. Stuart. Larry Little only said to me that it was out of their hands and in the hands of the City Manager and City Attorneys.

Larry Womble said to me, "Curtis if we as Aldermen were truly in support of your truths and your type of integrity, we would have gone public long ago in your defense. I am telling you upfront that talk is cheap and we have been just blowing smoke up your behind. I would like to be the first to go public and tell this community what I feel about how the City has treated you for your outstanding performance and contributions to the City."

To my knowledge, Alderman Womble never made such a speech to the public. After the above, Larry Womble would not talk to me. After the above, several black aldermen suddenly became successful real estate owners and were awarded high paying contracts with the City."

It was clear to me that Stuart was a blue-eyed, blonde demon, even though he claimed that he was a born-again Christian. He hated everything good and pure that I stood for, and to me, Stuart enjoyed being evil. Without saying, "Discredit

Dixon," Stuart sent a clear message to his department heads that I had no clout or influence. Stuart aligned himself with the lowest of the low in ethical values. Allen Joines once told me that Stuart and Fredericks were the most destructive people he had ever known. He also said that he would never cross Stuart, for fear of the repercussions.

I was interviewed for the vacant Human Services Director's position by City Manager Stuart and Assistant City Manager Joe Berrier at 4:30 PM for all of ten minutes. The interview was very strange, because Berrier was quite emphatic with me. He said only this one thing to me during the interviewing process: *"Everyone in the City knows that you are the most qualified person for the human services director's position. But what I need to know is, is there anyone else employed with the City that you think can handle the job as successfully as you?"* All Stuart did was sit quietly and stare at me. The position was given to Walter Farabee, who had no knowledge or experience with manpower operations or practices. Aldermen Newell had told Stuart that she wanted Farabee to be promoted to this position, and he honored her desire. Walter Farabee was the nephew of Mrs. Newell's previous boss, the chancellor of Winston-Salem State University. Mrs. Newell told me the above as I sat at her kitchen table discussing my problems with the City. This was her way of telling me that my problems could easily go away if she or any other board members really and truly wanted them to go away.

Next, I was interviewed for the ABC administrator's position, and my interview went like this. *"Without a doubt, Dixon, you are the most qualified person for this position, but you are young and full of energy. Don't you think that you will become very bored with this position? Don't you think that this position is more for an older person who is thinking about retiring in the very need future?"* This was said by my fraternity brother Coach Gaines, who was one of three ABC board members interviewing me. The position was given to Lewis Cutright, who had told me he had been promised the position before the interviewing process began.

As planned by City Manager Stuart, I did not receive any promotions. I was granted interviews, in accordance with City policy, for the first time, after having been denied interviews my first ten years with the City. To me, Stuart enjoyed defying everything that he quoted, as a supposed Christian, in the local newspaper.

Even though Stuart had placed me under the supervision of Joines, he continuously gave me assignments that he felt that I was not qualified to complete. I completed top priority assignments that Allen Joines could not complete, and I even received a letter of commendation. Of course, this did not set well with Stuart. Then he gave me an assignment that required the support of the City's Purchasing Agent, Don Farmer, and several other department directors. Of course, I could not complete the report, because Farmer refused to provide me with any information. Knowing exactly what was going on, Stuart told me to use my imagination and get the report to him. Don Farmer said to me, "How do you feel knowing that you have all of that education and were a captain in the Air Force, and I have very little education and was only a sergeant in the Army, but you have to beg for my assistance?" I said proudly and boldly, "You are a poor excuse for a human being. I don't need a dam thing from you."

The next day I turned the report in to Joines with answers to everything that Stuart had requested. When Stuart asked me how was I able to get the information, I said, "I used my imagination, sir." After that confrontation, I distanced myself from the purchasing agent. Several years later I heard he developed many incurable illnesses that his doctors could not explain. He retired from the City as a very sick man.

After I planned, developed, and completed the City's first Comprehensive Energy Conservation Plan, I was told to implement the plan which required the expertise of an engineer. To further test my endurance, I was told to work directly with Harold Bolick, the building management division director, to find out exactly what was required of an energy coordinator. This little short man was known for not getting along with anyone black or white within the City. When I met with Bolick, he made it very clear to me and City Manager Stuart that it was impossible for me to do engineering duties without the proper training. Then Bolick assigned one of his engineers whose name was Dan Gilbert to work with me. After which time Bolick gathered up all of his clerical duties that had been overdue for the past three years and sent them to the vault where I was housed at the time. As everyone in the outer office looked on as the many boxes were hauled into the vault, I wrote 'return to the sender' and a note which read: "If you want a puppy to play with, buy one because I am not the one this day or any day forthcoming." Bolick never spoke to me again and transferred Gilbert out of his office to work with me permanently. After a couple of years, Bolick became critically ill and died of inoperable cancer. Many employees said that I had put a curse on him, because Bolick was unable to speak for several days after reading the note that I attached to his returned clerical papers.

The following comments are what Stuart reduced Allen Joines to: On January 8, 1981, Joines told me that he was impressed with both of my reports and that they covered everything and some more. On January 16, I completed the City's first Energy Conservation Plan and forwarded it to Joines and Stuart. A couple of weeks later, Joines said to me, "Damnit, Curt, I order you to complete those reports. I don't care if they are the Building Management Division's responsibility." On March 3, 1981, I received an unexpected memorandum from Joines which stated that my performance was inconsistent and inadequate for the period December 16, 1980 – February 16, 1981, because I took vacation during the Christmas/New

Year Holiday and I questioned why I had to complete another department's clerical duties.

As soon as the Energy Conservation Project became successful, City Manager Stuart called a staff meeting and introduced Allen Joines as the energy coordinator for the City. Then Stuart said as he and everyone in the meeting looked at me, "Allen will give us a complete report of his accomplishments to date." Allen proudly sat on the table in front of the department heads and told of his great accomplishments and how he had saved the City over $2200 in one month and $5500 the second month. Everyone in the meeting knew that I had done all of the work on energy conservation with resistance from Allen and Stuart.

Then Stuart told me that he wanted me to plan and implement a Drivers' Energy Conservation Program for the City. This really was the responsibility of the City's Employees' Safety Coordinator, Kemp Cummings, who was a genial and cooperative fellow. By now, I had learned not to question this city manager. I checked with the State Energy Office and discovered there was a Drivers' Conservation Training Program available for me to attend, and I did attend. After that, I planned and designed a special program for the City. Stuart told me to train the City's managerial and supervisory staff before turning the program over to Kemp. After I completed that task, Stuart told me the police department wanted me to train all of their police recruits. To do this effectively, it would take at least two people. Kemp volunteered to work with me, since he would be taking over this function. The first day of training, fifteen recruits showed up, but not Kemp. Therefore, I had to do the lecture part of the training, as well as the road part. The young recruits (all white) were very cooperative and worked with me. When I called Kemp to find out what had happened, he said that Stuart had given him another assignment for that day, but that he would be at the training site the next day. Knowing what Stuart was up to, I secured a backup person to come and help me for the rest of the week. As expected, Kemp did not show up the entire week, and he never called. The police chief and all of his officers considered the training an overwhelming success, but the city manager never commended me for a job well done. He just asked me, "How were you able to do two jobs at the same time?" I smiled and said, "I used my imagination, sir." After that, Stuart was no longer interested in a Drivers' Energy Conservation Program for the City, and it disappeared. Kemp Cummings, who had once had an excellent rapport with me, could not face or even talk to me.

Having been exposed to the most miserable working conditions possible under Stuart's administration, I became seriously ill without even being aware of it. As I was driving to work one morning, I lost my ability to talk, became dizzy, and started throwing up yellow mucous. I was barely able to drive, but I managed to make it to the hospital. Dr. Stewart in the family practice unit saw me immediately. She spent about one hour trying to calm me down, medicate me, and to get me to talk rationally. When I was able to talk, the doctor told me that I had to quit my job if I wanted to live. She further said that she had never had a patient who was being treated so inhumanely in her entire career. She made an appointment for me to see the hospital psychiatrist that same day.

For several months, I met with the psychiatrist at least twice a week. The psychiatrist prescribed Prozac for me, and told me that if my working conditions did not change, I would surely have a nervous breakdown. During this treatment, I went to work every day and did not let Stuart or anyone with the City know that my health was failing. All I could think about was the welfare of my daughter and mother, and the thought of wrong winning over right. I could not and would not accept that God wanted me to fail. I felt that City Manager Stuart, with the blessings of the mayor and the Board of Aldermen, was determined to make me fail at some task, even if it meant killing me. At this point and time in my career with the City, I was the only employee, out of over 1800 employees, who had been assigned duties that I had not expressed an interest in, and who had been denied access to any position that I was interested in and qualified for.

Allen Joines suddenly had the same role with Stuart that he had had with Powell, a special crony. Joines really wanted to do the honorable and right thing by everyone, so he came to me with a proposition. Stuart had given him the responsibility of completing the pre-application, application, and annual report for the Economic Development Project. This report had been Walter Farabee's responsibility, before Stuart promoted him to human services director. According to Farabee, it took him at least three months to complete the applications and report. Joines's first comments to me were, "We only have seven days to complete these documents and submit them for approval. You know that I don't know anything about this type of stuff, and I know that you don't either. I just want you to try to complete these tasks for me the way that you have always tackled the many impossible assignments given to you in the past. And I promise you that I will do whatever is in my power to right this serious wrong that has been launched against you. If you can complete this proposal, I will be promoted to economic development director for the City, and you can be my economic development coordinator."

Farabee refused to help me. "Curtis," he said, "I don't want you to take this personal, but helping you only makes Allen Joines shine. You know as well as I do that he will get all of the credit for your work, just as he has done in the past."

Three days before the due date, I wasn't able to come up with anything. With no information and lots of tears, I started writing and composing documents that only God was helping me put together. My greatest fear as I wrote the documents was that I'd give my betrayers and enemies the satisfaction of my failing. When Joines came to me on the day the assignments were due to be sent to the federal office, I handed him two completed documents, pre-application and the application, and said, "Don't ask me what I have written. There are documents and justifications for everything imaginable about economic development and a budget."

Joines said, *"Anything is better than nothing. Thanks, Curtis for all that you do and receive no appreciation or rewards. Further, Stuart will not even entertain the thought of your being promoted to the economic development coordinator's position. And I am afraid to speak out on your behalf for fear that he will turn on me and destroy my career. I hope that you understand. Between you and me, I think that Bryce Stuart and Tom Fredericks are alike. They like hurting people when the opportunity presents itself."*

Within two weeks, the city manager received a letter from the Federal Economic Development Office, stating that the proposal was one of the best they had received from any of their agencies, and by far the best that they had ever received from the City of Winston-Salem. The sophistication and quality of the proposal qualified the City for additional discretionary funds.

Instantly, Joines was promoted to the economic development director's position with a substantial pay increase. An outsider, Valerie Broadie, who had no economic development experience, was hired as economic development coordinator. *Joines told her to get with me to learn what was necessary for her to be successful in her job.* And once again, I got nothing for my contribution, except that I was transferred from under Joines's supervision, out of City Hall and back to the NCNB building.

Stuart reassigned me to the MISS Department under the supervision of Sam Owen. This fellow had offered me a computer supervisory position several years prior. I had no computer knowledge and skills, other than the information that I read before interviewing with Owen. Of course, I turned the job down. This also told me that Sam Owen had limited knowledge about computers himself. It was rumored throughout the City that Owen had gotten his promotion because he was related to Orville Powell. I was told by Joines that Stuart had assigned me to the MISS Department, because I ate breakfast every morning with one of the computer team leaders, Bobby Die, and therefore should be happier in that environment. This nonsense was never discussed with me, because only an idiot would determine another person's career based on whom he ate breakfast with. Further, such a move on Stuart's part confirmed that he was incapable of making his own decisions. Before City Manager Powell resigned, he had casually asked me if I would be happier working in and around people I socialized with, and he named the MISS Department. Of course, I told Powell that as a means for job advancement, the idea was ludicrous. Powell said he knew it was very unprofessional, and was not a basis for assigning a person to a department. City Manager Stuart just transferred me without any discussion, as only an evil, dishonorable coward would do.

By this time, Stuart had placed an engineer, Dan Gilbert, in the unofficial Energy Office with me, so that the engineering duties could be justified. I kept my old title, senior program evaluation analyst, as if it was part of my birth name. Dan and I worked side by side for several months without any conversations between us. After I took him to visit people all over the state with high administrative positions, Dan was most grateful and told many other City employees "how great and smart" he thought I was. Then he told me top management had said many repulsive things about me before he started to work with me. He said, "*They told me that you were a trouble maker and for me not to talk around you at all. Someone really hates you and wants to see you destroyed to do the things that they are attempting to do to you. I truly admire you because you are the only person that I know and have worked with who can work effectively and cooperatively with people you know hate you. I couldn't do it."* Dan then told me that his first wife had committed suicide because he refused to communicate effectively with her.

Dan was a strange person. The first three months we worked together, he wore the same clothes every day for weeks at a time. It was not until he started a secret boss/employee relationship with Sam Owen that he started wearing different outfits to work and changed his opinion of me. After Dan had been married less than a year, his wife called me one night in a panic. "I have got to talk to somebody," she said, "and you are the most decent and honest person that I know. Dan admitted to me that he spent the afternoon and evening at Lake Norman with Sam Owen. When I asked him if they had sex together, he refused to answer me. What should I do?"

I told Linda to calm down, and not to do anything she might regret later. "Continue to talk to Dan," I said. "Work things out. Don't let people like Sam destroy your marriage. Have you been happy with Dan?"

"Yes, I have," she answered, "but lately Sam has taken control of Dan's body and mind. He doesn't listen to anything I say."

Then I said, "Hang in there and work with him. Dan loves you, but he is caught in a web that he does not know how to handle. You are the only person who can save and help him at this point in his life."

Linda said, "I feel better after talking with you, and I am going to take your advice."

Before Dan spent that evening with Sam at Sam's Lake Norman home, he was known for making the following comments to me: *"Please don't used Tom Frederick's secretary as a witness in your case against the City. She told me that she* was going trick you and say what the City defendants wanted her to say, because she had been promised a promotion." However after Dan's rendezvous with Sam, he worshiped him and agreed with any and everything that Sam said and did to me.

The following weekend, two City employees whom I had just started working with stopped by my home. One of them said, "Curt, you must have stepped on someone's toes real hard because just before you came to work with us, top management called the entire staff in and told us all kinds of negative things about you. Man, after knowing you and working very closely with you the past two months, I know that they are all lies. Usually some of the things that you are told about a person are true, but everything that they said about you was a lie. Man, they hate you an awful lot."

About a month or so later, when Dan and I were at a conference, Dan said to me, "I guess you will want to have sex with me next." I pretended that I did not hear him and he did not repeat himself. Was Dan trying to tell me that Sam Owen had had sex with him? To me, Sam Owen was a strange bird. He popped his knees and switched when he walked. On one occasion, I thought that two ladies were laughing, smacking lips, and saying endearments to each other behind Sam's closed office door, until only Sam Owen and William Hill came out of his office.

Sam questioned my performance on an accounting assignment that he gave me, because neither of us had any knowledge of the subject. He was most insulting toward me in the presence of Dan and the telecommunications coordinator, Martha Weber. When I did not respond to Sam's ignorance, he left my office. After he left my office, both Dan and Martha remarked that Sam's action toward me had been very bias and unprofessional. Why was he treating me like that, especially in front of other people? I didn't respond to their concerns, because I did not know who to trust.

Whenever Sam had to submit any reports to the city manager or any other management personnel, he would have me critique them first. Stuart even responded in writing to Sam that the reports he received from Sam's department were always written in an outstanding and professional manner. Sam Owen gave me copies of the memoranda, and thanked me for my cooperation and expertise.

When it came time for performance evaluations of all of the employees assigned to the MISS Department, every employee received an above average to superior performance review, except me. My performance review had below standard ratings in most areas. I challenged the report, but Stuart refused to have anything to do with the situation. I was referred to Assistant City Manager Joe Berrier. When I met with Berrier, he invited Alderman Patrick Hairston (black) to sit in during the meeting. Alderman Hairston slept, or at least kept his eyes closed, the entire time that Berrier and I discussed my rebuttal of my performance evaluation. Just as Berrier was about to agree with me that my performance report was in error and should be rated much higher, based on the duties that I had been assigned outside my area of expertise, Alderman Hairston raised his head.

"I think the report is fair as written," he said. "Dixon's performance has been below standard, from what I have heard."

Assistant City Manager Berrier said, "Well Dixon, what can I say? Your alderman has decided for us. The report stands as written."

I just shook my head as I left Berrier's office, because Berrier knew that Hairston was not my alderman. Within months after the above, Patrick Hairston was awarded a cleaning contract for more than $200,000 at the One Triad Building, where the City's law firm resided. Also, the City was involved in the construction of the building. During the next election, Alderman Patrick Hairston lost his seat on the board. *The comment that came back to me from Hairston was that he showed me what smartness and sophistication got me. And he bet the next time that he offered me a drink of liquor at his house regardless of the time of day I will drink it or continue to suffer the consequences. The truly sad part was this man was a former NAACP president in Winston-Salem. This was black racism against a black.*

When I requested a transfer from the MISS Department, Stuart denied my request. Of course, things got worse for me under Sam Owen's supervision. When I told my attorneys about my job situation, they told me that there was nothing they could do. I had no one on my side except God.

Thinking that he was special after his rendezvous with Sam Owen, Dan was very disrespectful to Owen's secretary. Owen reprimanded Dan in the presence of other employees, and Dan resigned his position with the City. The telecommunication coordinator had resigned her position less than three months earlier. This left me in this created energy/telecommunication section as the only person to handle everything. I was required to do my clerical duties, Dan's engineering duties, and Martha's telecommunications duties. When Martha resigned, Owen did not hire a replacement for her. Two weeks after I took over all of these duties, the City's traffic engineer wrote a memorandum to Sam Owen, with a copy to the city manager, that stated that I was derelict in my duties of completing a monthly report regarding the energy conservation savings on the City's new traffic lighting system. Immediately, I made a copy of the report that I had sent to the engineer, and a copy of Dan's last report. My report showed a savings ten times more than Dan's report. In addition, I had justifications for everything written in my report. Dan's report only gave numbers with no justification. All Owen could say was, "Just forget the whole thing, Curtis. In the future, you will not have to do this report anymore. It's really the Traffic Engineering Department's responsibility."

My doctor took me out of work, because I was becoming agitated, and my blood pressure had gotten dangerously high. While I was out of work, I received a letter from the City's personnel director, informing me that my doctor had to provide his office with written notification before I could return to work. This personnel director further stated in his letter that he would make sure my supervisor. Sam Owen, was apprised of my status at all times. My doctor sent me a copy of the letter that he had sent to the personnel director on a Wednesday, advising City personnel that I would be returning to work the following Monday. When I went to work that Monday, Owen summoned me to his office. In the presence of his assistant director, he said, *"Curtis, I have not received any notification from your doctor that you should be here. Therefore, I want you to get the hell out of my department and out of this building."* When I tried to show Owen my copy of my doctor's letter, he refused to look at it. Then I politely asked him to call the personnel director, who had the same letter. Owen said, *"I am not calling any dam body. I want you out of my department right now or I am going to have security remove you from the building."*

At this point, everyone in the office could hear Owen yelling at me. Also, everyone in the office, including Owen, knew that my daughter dropped me off at work at 7:00, and that morning a violent thunderstorm was going on outside. Feeling protected by others, Owen walked me to the entrance of his department and put me out in the storm. I walked fifteen miles to my home in the storm. I never cried. I just prayed and thanked God for keeping me calm, because I knew I could have killed Owen before his assistant director could have known what was happening. As I entered my home, my telephone was ringing. When I answered it, William Hill, the personnel director, tried to apologize for what had just happened. I knew that the entire scene had been planned, because Owen and Hill talked several times every day. They were regular lip-smacking, hand-twirling, knee-popping partners. This was the same personnel director who had told Owen to document me and fire me. And as fate would have it, William K. Hill (black), who had been hired by Beaty, died before he was three score and ten years old.

Several of my City customers often commented about my superior performance in telecommunications, and said that I should be recognized somehow for doing such an outstanding job. I mentioned what was happening to me to my best friend Bobby Die, and he told me that whenever one of his customers said something like that to him, he would tell them to put it in writing. On several occasions after that, supervisors within the police and recreation departments commented to me that I needed recognition for the efficient and speedy services that I provided their departments. Remembering what Bobby had said, I told the supervisors to put their comments in writing to my supervisor, Sam Owen.

Less than a month after the above, and without any discussions of any kind with Owen, City Manager Stuart, acting like the timorous person he was, had Hill hand-deliver a letter of termination to my home. At this time, my doctor had ordered me to take a month off work. Stuart cited the following reasons for terminating my employment with the City: (1) Dixon falsified letters of recognition about his performance, (2) Dixon could not work cooperatively and effectively with his supervisors, and (3) Dixon violated City policy by publishing information about other employees. The local unemployment agency went along with Stuart's scheme to further betray and insult me. Nobody wanted to hear the truth. To them, it was much easier to go along with the crowd and have a promising career. Dishonor against Curtis Dixon was making its rounds in Winston-Salem.

Bryce Stuart and Sam Owen sold their souls to the devil by lying about every honorable quality that I possessed and lived by daily. *To them, who cared if I was performing the duties of three positions outside my area of expertise in an outstanding manner? Who cared if the letters of recognition were substantiated by the signatures of the two supervisors who wrote them? Who cared that Owen only gave me a below to standard performance evaluation after he considered me to be the only employee within the MISS Department talented enough to proof read and rewrite all outgoing correspondence? Who cared that I was well respected throughout the City by all of my co-workers who readily shared their performance ratings with me. They were confident that I was receiving outstanding performance ratings for the magnitude and quality of work that I performed daily?* To Stuart, my violation was sharing the outstanding performance reviews that all of my co-workers received. I was the only employee who had received an average to below standard performance review, even when one of the "outstanding" employees wrongfully completed a program that charged a citizen one million dollars for a two-month water bill.

The more Stuart tried to insult me and set out to destroy me professionally, physically, and emotionally, using dishonorable tactics, the more it seemed that the mayor and members of the Board of Aldermen echoed his superiority. It was as if Stuart was their god from hell. It appeared that most of the elected officials feared him and worshiped him, while several of them complained about his many inadequacies behind his back. Despite their many complaints about Stuart, the members of the board always gave him high annual increases in his salary. It was clear that God played no role in the management of the City under the auspices of Stuart and these elected officials, because it seemed that every manager or supervisor, who blatantly violated City policies, mismanaged City funds, or violated the rights of other employees, were rewarded handsomely. I was told that one assistant city manager had a book on his desk entitled *How To Succeed By Mismanaging,* and he bragged about practicing the principles of this book. He was considered one of the City's greatest administrators. For many years, this assistant city manager, and many of his subordinate managers, proved his philosophy was true by accomplishing absolutely nothing noteworthy throughout their careers; by becoming alcoholics and totally dysfunctional on the job; and by misallocating thousands of dollars of City funds.

I was the enemy to these City leaders, because I was too honest, too productive, too accommodating, and too efficient. Therefore, the many inefficient and unproductive managers felt that I had to be eliminated at all costs. According to the above assistant manager's administrative assistant, at least two City division heads were unable to function in their positions, because they had serious drinking problems. They were allowed to remain at their jobs for several years, until they had enough time in to retire. A third division head was permitted to lose a $3000 lawn mower, or some very expensive piece of lawn equipment, every summer, and to build a swimming pool in his backyard using City materials and equipment, without so much as a verbal reprimand for several years. The assistant director of the MISS Department only worked two or three days a week during the years that I was assigned to that department because of what appeared to be a drinking problem, without any repercussions from Owen or Stuart. And of course, all of the above employees were white. The only black administrators who were allowed to blatantly mismanage programs and funds without any repercussions were John Bond and Alexander Beaty. They were special, because they only mismanaged programs and funds that involved predominantly black employees or black citizens. But Owen and Stuart felt comfortable terminating me from my position with the City citing false allegations. Will hell be hot enough to hold these perverts and the elected officials who supported and condoned such repulsive management practices?

An anonymous caller told me that at least twelve attorneys were hired to read the book that I had published about the city managers and their management staff. The attorneys were trying to find any information that could be used to discredit, or even destroy me in court, but they could only find one possible gray area, information that I had written about the performance evaluations of my co-workers. The city managers, department heads, and many others mentioned in the 583 page book were not willing to challenge the information published about them, because they knew that every sentence echoed the truth. On the one gray area, I was told that the supervisor of the City employees involved did everything within his power to get those individuals to file charges against me. None of them would come forward, because they knew that we had talked freely throughout our offices about our performance ratings, and that I had not violated any of their rights.

The elected officials had shown their bias when they had completely overlooked City policies and supported City Manager Powell and Deputy City Manager Bond, helping them find comparable positions in other cities after they intentionally mismanaged thousands of tax dollars. The officials did nothing to protect my career, even knowing that I had saved the City hundreds of thousands of dollars, and had written proposals and plans that made it possible for the City to receive millions of dollars in grants. Could these elected leaders have shown any greater dishonor to God, mankind, and themselves? Do these elected leaders think that Stuart will be in a position to save them when their day of reckoning comes?

I had more education and outstanding contributions to the City than every person promoted over me, and I was denied any credit for any of my accomplishments under City Manager Stuart *after he told me personally that he knew that I could perform most City management positions very efficiently and effectively. Then he had me housed in construction areas, vaults, leaking basements and finally in an engineering position located in a computer operation, knowing that I did not have any expertise in this environment and he made sure that my performance under his administration was rated mediocre at best.* Stuart, who proclaimed to the entire community that he was a Christian, thought he had successfully destroyed my career and standing in my hometown. He then set out to make his wrongs against me right by promoting many black City employees who had not been promoted or upgraded in the past, as a means of showing all City employees and the community that he was not a biased and inhuman leader, as the facts had so elegantly and truthfully depicted him when I was under his administration. *What Bible was he reading that told him to take this road to repenting for his sins and crimes?* Promotions were made in the following management positions just before or shortly after Stuart terminated my employment with the City: assistant city manager (black woman), assistant finance director (black man), city revenue director (black woman), assistant planning director (black woman), fire chief (black man), police chief (black woman), assistant city attorney (black man), manpower director (black woman), and on and on. Sad to say, many of the persons promoted to these positions did not remain there very long. Further, several non-managerial employees who had once supported my efforts, were suddenly promoted or upgraded in pay status, and they began proclaiming throughout the City that I was a troublemaker, and I had got what I deserved. They suddenly considered their honor worthless after being given a few pieces of silver. *I strongly believe that none of the above would have ever happened without the fortitude and honor of Curtis Dixon. I made all of the above possible when I planned and implemented the million dollar federal program for the City which created many of the above positions and I filed charges against the City for refusing to promote me. I felt that God used me to show dishonorable leaders how they could be maneuvered to help many deserving individuals whom they would have never given a chance.*

What did the mayor and members of the Board of Aldermen, the city managers, and everyone involved in the demise of Curtis Dixon gain by trying to destroy something that God had ordained, and by spending what appeared to be millions of dollars to cover up the blatant dishonor that they bestowed upon one of God's children? *Why do you suppose the city manager and the City's elected officials were willing to spend millions of tax payers' dollars to destroy my honor?* As dishonorable people, all they could comprehend was discrediting the honor that I projected so vividly on the job, in the community, and in the courtroom.

After the mass promotions of many City employees who had worked indirectly or directly with me, most of them could not walk on the same side of the street with me, and many of them were known to exit restaurants or stores when I entered.

As I was going to a parking lot one afternoon to get into my car, I noticed that Sam Owen's car was parked beside mine. As I got closer to my car, I saw Owen get out of his car. But as soon as he spotted me, he got back in his car, locked his doors, and rolled up his car windows. I just got in my car and drove away, laughing and shaking my head. I was shopping at the farmer's market one Saturday morning, and I saw this same person working behind one of the stands. When he saw me, he hung his head in shame and ran from the market, never to be seen at the market again by me.

As I was leaving a department store, I noticed Alexander Beaty peeping around a car at me. Each time I looked in his direction, Beaty hid behind the car. As I stood there and watched him peep and hide about ten times, I got in my car and drove off. I thought to myself, *the City of Winston-Salem and the black citizens of this city are really in bad shape, if what I just witnessed represents its leadership.*

As I was shopping at the mall, I saw Bryce Stuart and his wife approaching me. When they saw me, they changed aisles. Then they came into the same shoe store where I was shopping. When they saw me, they spent at least fifteen minutes peeking at me as they looked at the same shoe. I purposefully stayed in the store, looking at every shoe, to see how intelligent the city's top leader really was. Of course, I had to leave the store first, because Stuart was not about to walk past me. I thought as I was leaving the store, *Where is there any honor in a coward who will throw a rock and hide?*

My family and I were eating out one evening, and I noticed that one of the aldermen and his wife were eating at the same restaurant. By coincidence, we were seated beside this alderman. Within minutes after we sat down, this fellow and his wife left most of their food uneaten and departed the restaurant.

Mayor J. Allen Joines was the guest speaker for the inauguration of the pastor at my church, Friendship Baptist. As he was speaking, he must have seen me looking directly at him, because his entire composure changed. When he finished speaking, he sat down and stared into space. While people were getting their food, Mayor Joines left the gathering without doing his regular hand shaking routine.

If dishonor causes such fear, discomfort and shame, why do so many people live that life? Did these men fear and hate the honor that God displayed through me?

WHY MANY ENTREPRENEURS FAIL

"I think the purpose of life is to be useful, to be responsible. It is, after all, to matter: to count, to stand for something, to have made some difference that you lived at all."

—*Leo C. Rosten*

In the midst of the many storms in my life, my brother Artemas came to me with a business proposition, which could possibly eliminate some of our job problems. The three of us, Artemas, Nathaniel, and me, agreed to purchase a tractor trailer rig. Nathaniel was a friend of my brother Artemas. They had worked together for several years in the truck driving industry. Before I embarked upon this venture that I knew nothing about, I consulted with the post office and several tobacco companies that used such rigs to haul their merchandise. I was told by all of them that such a business could be very profitable with the right driver. Nathaniel, who was going to be the driver, assured me that he was very dependable, and that he needed this opportunity to provide a living for himself and help take care of his elderly mother. We bought a two-year-old rig under my signature, with the written understanding that each of us would pay one third of the $550 monthly payment until the truck was paid off. My brother and I put up the $3000 down payment.

The business failed in less than one year, because Nathaniel could not stay away from the sex shops. When he should have been hauling merchandise, he would be at any peep shop in town, looking at naked women or looking at men and women having sex. Despite Nathaniel's irresponsibility, I paid him at least $50 per week and made the monthly payments on the rig from my regular job's salary, because Nathaniel was not making enough runs to meet our monthly obligations. After I thought he had gotten his sex problem under control, Nathaniel tried to steal all of the money from every run that he made, by requesting early withdrawals before completing a job. *When he could not make early withdrawals and get all of the money made on any run, he told all of his and my brother's friends that I was trying to take his truck away from him. Of course without inquiring, everyone assumed the worse about me and wanted to do me bodily harm. When my brother told the fellows the truth, they all wanted to apologize to me. Most of them said that they should have known better, because they never knew me to be dishonest with anyone. Before I could even talk to Nathaniel about his lies, he destroyed the engine in the truck and left it on the side of the road in another state. His wife called me and told me what Nathaniel had done. She further told me that Nathaniel had left town so that he would not have to face me and my brother.*

Still hoping to get the most out of our investment and make this venture work, I had the rig hauled to my home and spent $3000 to replace the engine. I advertised for a driver with at least ten years of experience, and received calls from three applicants the first week. I hired a friendly young black man, who was married, mechanical, and very business minded. For three months, the business made more money than it had the entire year when Nathaniel drove the rig. Then I received a call from one of the companies that we had contracted with. I had spoken with this woman many times, and we had established a bond. She did not hesitate at telling me that my driver Matt had told everyone in her office that my brother and I did not know anything about trucking, and that he would be the sole owner of the truck within a month. When I asked Matt about that conversation, he stated everything I had been told was true, and that he had planned to steal the truck by saying that someone had stolen it while he was on a run. His termination was very pleasant. When I asked him to bring the truck to my home, he did, and he apologized for his dishonesty. He said, "My wife told me that it would never work, because you were wise beyond man's comprehension, even though you are too trusting of others."

By now, I had paid for the rig with my own money at $550 per month. I desperately wanted to make this venture work, especially since I could not find a buyer for the rig. In haste, I hired a black man who lived in Cleveland Projects. Again, this third driver, Sam, started off doing a great job. During the first month, he made enough runs to earn $5000 for himself and $4000 for the business. Halfway through the second month, he called and asked me to come by his home so that he could discuss some truck-related business with me. *When I got inside his apartment, he cornered me and put a 12 inch butcher knife to my neck. He then told me if I said one word he would cut my head off. I did not say anything as this driver, who was completely drunk, rambled on and on about needing more money and that I was rich and should gladly pay him more money. All of a sudden, Sam stopped talking and removed the knife from my neck and said, "Get out of here before I kill you." I ran from the apartment like a frightened puppy. As I drove home, I could not stop crying and thanking God for protecting me.*

When I finally arrived home, my telephone was ringing. I was in no shape to talk to anyone. After an hour or so went by and the telephone was still ringing, I answered it. Sam said, "I am sorry, Mr. Dixon. I was just playing with you. I would never do anything to hurt you. You have been nicer to me than anyone in my entire life. I hope that you know that I was just playing with you." All I could say was, "I can't talk to you right now. I just can't do this anymore." I hung up the telephone. It continued to ring, but I did not answer it. The next day, I called Sam and calmly said, "I am out of the trucking business. I will pay you whatever you think that I owe you, but my truck will not leave my yard on another run by you or anyone."

Immediately, I put the rig up for sale. A black minister who lived about four miles from my home wanted to buy it, but he was unable to pay the full amount, and his credit record would not permit him to borrow the money. Again, I was a glutton for punishment. I typed a contract that required that the minister pay me $500 up front, and $100 per month for thirty-six months, $5000 less than what the truck was worth. I just wanted to get rid of it and get some of my money back. The minister made his payments on time for a year, and then disappeared off the face of the earth with the truck. I did not pursue the matter. My betrayers on and off the job were slowly killing me, and I had turned all of this over to God. Two years went by, and I did not hear anything from the minister. One rainy day my telephone rang and it was the minister. He asked me to go over to his house. When I arrived at the minister's home, his wife let me in and escorted me to her husband's bedside. The minister said as he cried, "God has told me to make things right with you. Here is $1000 for all of the trouble I may have caused you, and here are the keys to your truck. I hope and pray that you can forgive me."

I did not know what to say as I took the money and the keys to the truck. As I was leaving the minister's house, his wife said, "Did my husband tell you that he has terminal cancer and only has two weeks to live? He has been calling your name all day and night every since he was told he had cancer. Please tell him that you forgive him, so that he can die in peace." I went back into the bedroom and told the minister that I truly forgave him for what he had done. The minister hugged me and cried again. Then we prayed together for the next hour. Two weeks later, the minister's wife called me and told me that her husband had died in his sleep. She thanked me for making his last few days on earth peaceful.

Once again, I parked the rig in my yard to let it die. Then my oldest brother James told me that one of the men on his job wanted to buy it. I told James that I was selling the rig cash and carry only. When the man showed up at my home, he had only one third of my asking price. My brother told me he would vouch for the man, because he was a Christian man whom he had worked with and respected for many years. Knowing that this would not work, I let James's friend have the rig, on my brother's word that he would make it good if his friend did not pay. After the man made two payments on the truck, he disappeared. He changed all of his telephone numbers, and he was never home when I went to his house. When I approached my brother about my dilemma, he said, "The man still works with me, but I don't have anything to do with your arrangement." I did not say anything else. I just walked away and never saw my rig again. A year later, James told him that his friend who had stolen my truck had been fired from his job and arrested for selling drugs.

In 2004, when I was trying to get the transmission rebuilt on my 1984 Nissan 300ZX, I met a young black man who had just bought his own transmission shop under the name AAMCO Transmission. Duncan presented himself to me as a very responsible and honest gentleman, who even told me that he wanted to give one of the local high schools several thousand dollars to help tutor black students. I signed all of the appropriate paperwork for Duncan to rebuild the transmission in my car. When Duncan told me the transmission had been rebuilt and installed properly, I paid him over $3300, which included a three-year warranty. For the next three years, I continually had to return my car to this shop, because my transmission was operating worse than before the shop rebuilt it. For three years, this shop kept my vehicle for at least five days each of the five times I took it in for repair. I was told each time that the mechanic was going to rebuild the transmission properly, but no repairs were ever made. When I took my car to two Nissan dealers, I was told the transmission had never been rebuilt, and that I needed a new transmission or a replacement. When I informed Duncan, he admitted that his shop had not rebuilt the transmission, and that he would personally make sure the transmission was rebuilt to my satisfaction. When I took the vehicle in the last time, I was told that Duncan had sold the business and that the new owner refused to rebuild the transmission. In an effort to be fair with this new owner, I requested a meeting with him. He refused to meet with me to discuss the matter. When I contacted the Better Business Bureau, the BBB completely ignored the three-year warranty contract that guaranteed me free service from the shop, regardless of the owner. The bureau ruled in favor of the new owner.

I filed a complaint in Small Claims Court, citing my problem in complete detail. The magistrate who handled the case was definitely a man of honor, because he made sure that justice prevailed. When I first appeared before the magistrate, he told me that I had not completed the paperwork properly, and that I was filing my complaint against the wrong person. Instead of dismissing my complaint, he told me what I needed to do so that the complaint would be correct. Then he said that he would not have me pay another filing fee. I was just to resubmit my paperwork per his request and bring the updated complaint back to him. Before I left his office, he said, "Some of us are about justice and honor. Everyone desires a fair and honest hearing. Good luck." I did everything that I was instructed to do, and the magistrate ruled in my favor. The new transmission shop owner had to return the money that I spent to have the transmission rebuilt, plus interest and court cost. A week or so later, I saw Duncan at Sam's. He was in a wheelchair. When I spoke to him, he said, "I told the new manager of the shop to rebuild your transmission. I left him enough money to redo the job. I even told him that he could not win in court, because the transmission had not been rebuilt and two Nissan dealers had confirmed that." Before I could ask him why was he in a wheelchair, he said, "You know, strange things happen to you when you don't live right. I was playing soccer and made a wrong turn and broke both of my knees. The doctor told me that I was lucky, because I could have damaged them in such a way that I would have never been able to walk again. I took this as a warning, and I was prepared and willing to testify on your behalf concerning the transmission." I just smiled as I thought: *God is definitely in charge of this universe, and people just refuse to accept his grace and his power.*

I needed to hire a carpenter to do some odds and ends around my home. My sister-in-law Peaches recommended her carpenter and I hired the young black man named Button after I saw the quality of his work. Button worked for me for over a year, performing magnificent woodwork in my sunroom and throughout my home. Further, he was a jack of all trades. After he installed a new half bath in my game room, I became so comfortable and trusting of this individual, I gave him a key to my home so that he could come and go as he wanted to. When the Christmas holiday came around, Button told me that he and his family would not be able to have any kind of a Christmas, because he did not have any money. He had always borrowed his Christmas money from my brother William, and paid it back in cash or services, but William had passed away. Then he asked me if I would lend him $1200, so that he and his family could have a Christmas holiday. He promised me he would pay me back within three months, or he would work for me free until the amount had been repaid. I agreed reluctantly, because every black person that I had trusted in the past had disappointed me. Well, I never saw Button after I lent him the

$1200. He never returned to my home to finish the work that he had started, and he never answered any of my telephone calls. Two years later, my sister-in-law called me and told me that Button was in the hospital, critically ill. Every part of his body had begun to shut down, and the doctors could not determine the causes. Button did not die from his many illnesses, but he was never able to work again or take care of himself.

MORE HONOR AMONG THIEVES

"Dignity consists not in possessing honors, but in the consciousness that we deserve them."

—*Aristotle*

In most families, the youngest child is normally spoiled. This was not the case in my family. When I was a very young child, my responsibilities at home were equal to or greater than my older brothers. It seemed that I was always blamed for everything that went wrong around our home, and I was given a whipping by my mother almost every week, many times for something my brothers did. I had to run most of the errands and cut the grass, while my older brothers worked inside most of the time. If I questioned anything, my father would tell me to shut my mouth and do what I was told. I had to constantly fight throughout my neighborhood in order to prove myself and get the respect of my peers. My two favorite things were going to church and school. I remember missing Sunday school only one time, and I missed just ten days of school, because I broke my arm. The lessons that I learned in Sunday school really taught me how to understand and cope with life. And school was God's gift to me. I loved learning, and would not let anyone alter what education meant to me.

Even though my neighborhood was full of boys whom I played with daily, my best friend was my brother Artemas. I was always there for Artemas, but he was not always there for me. As children, if anyone challenged Artemas about anything, I backed him up. Whenever Artemas needed financial support as an adult, I would find a way to help him, even if I had to borrow the money. On the other hand, if I wanted to borrow something as simple as Artemas's tools to work on something around my home, I had to endure a sermon from him before he would finally let me use the tools.

My friendship with other boys was disastrous. One of my friends tried to make out with my girlfriend and got busted, because my girlfriend told on him. Another close neighborhood friend wanted to hump me during an overnight stay in my backyard tree house, but I raised an alarm. My parents made me come into the house and spend the night inside. I never tried the overnight, or even a night out, with the boys again. My high school buddy refused to get out of the car when I gave him a ride home from a dance. He pretended that he was asleep when I arrived at his house, and he would not wake up. My girlfriend, this friend, and I rode around for hours. I had to take my girlfriend home first, and then this friend was wide awake. After the above, I became a lady's man. This meant that I played sports with the fellows, but I spent my free time with the ladies, one on one.

While in college, I maintained a very close friendship with the fellows from my hometown, until I had three unpleasant experiences. While taking a physics test my sophomore year in college, a hometown friend took my test from my desk to copy all of my answers. When the professor noticed the strange, desperate look on my face, he started to come to the back of the room where I was sitting, but then he stopped. At the end of the class period, the professor asked me to move to the front of the classroom, telling me that I should always sit up front in all of my classes. The second incident occurred when I was a junior in college. One of my homeboys had the only car among our group, and he charged each homeboy fifty cents to ride home with him. This did not bother me. I simply saved fifty cents of the dollar that I had for the week, so that I could get a ride home each Friday. However, one Friday, this boy decided to make me get out of his car downtown, even though I lived two blocks from his home. When I asked him why I couldn't ride to his house as I had always done in the past, he said that he was not going home. I had to walk ten miles to get home. As I passed my homeboy's house, his car was parked in his driveway. I never said anything to him, but thereafter I walked downtown to the bus station and caught the Greyhound home.

My senior year in college, I bought a car. During the short time that the car was running, I hauled my homeboys and fraternity brothers anywhere they wanted to go. However, three months before I graduated, the car broke down and I was not able to have it fixed. All of a sudden, I did not have any friends. I could not get a ride anywhere. My homeboys who had cars always had some excuse as to why they could not give me a ride. I never complained or said anything to anyone. When my mom noticed what was happening, she asked me, "How are you dealing with this situation?" My comment was, "Every dog has his day and my day will come. I am concentrating all of my energies and efforts on graduating from college." Of the twenty homeboys who started college with me, I was one of three to graduate on time.

While serving more than six years in the military, I made many friends that I labeled associates. I did not want to endure any lasting hardships, as I had in the past. During my first assignment in Biloxi, Mississippi, I fell deeply in love, and I spent every day of the six-month assignment with my soul mate. I left that assignment as I had arrived there. I was told several years later that I had fathered a daughter, and that my soul mate had married her old boyfriend so that her child could have a father. When I was in Japan, the white female teachers, one black female teacher, and one black female lieutenant fed me and kept me happy during most of my tour. Then I met and fell in love with a Japanese model. To my own surprise, I married her four days before I departed Japan. This romance was a disaster after ten years, because my foreign wife listened to and followed the wrong people.

My lifelong goal was to build my own home, the one that most of my black college friends said I could never have. Having saved several thousand dollars before I was discharged from the Air Force, I was able to build my dream home. Just when I was about to give up on finding a contractor, I saw the perfect advertisement in the newspaper. I met with two young white brothers who were starting their own contracting business. I immediately hired them, because they offered me everything that I wanted in my dream home. Just as the workers were putting the final touches on the house, one of the brothers said he thought that I had too much house for what his company was charging me. I said, "My contract with your company reads that I will get a turn key job, which means that everything will be completed, including the garage ceiling, a deck, and a paved driveway." When I asked him why he was trying to renege on our signed contract, he said, "I had no idea that this house was this big and would look this beautiful. I just can't finish it unless you agree to pay me an extra $3000." Of course, I did not pay him any additional money. In fact, I withheld $3000, because the contractor refused to finish the garage ceiling and pave the driveway. After trying three or four times to get the $3000 from my lending institution, the contractor gave up.

I was the first person to move into my neighborhood, and I provided assistance to the first four black families that moved in after I did. Tom and Kaye Trollinger with their two children were the second family to move into the neighborhood. I was right there at least one day a week, helping them to move in and get their new home in order. I even strained myself helping Tom move his formal dining room furniture into the house, and I had to receive medical treatment. After the Trollingers were settled in their new home, they had a party in the new addition that Tom had built himself. Several of the guests asked me later why I was not at the party. When I told them I had not been invited, they were shocked. One of my close associates said, "But Tom stops by your home several days a week, and you are always at his house helping out or eating dinner with them."

A few years later, the owner of the lots in this new development held an auction for the remaining twenty or more lots that he had not sold. During the auction, I went to Tom and asked him if the two of us could be partners in purchasing several lots. Tom told me that he had partners already. Tom and his partners purchased several lots at very reasonable prices. I did not purchase any lots, because they were all sold before I returned to the auction with a fraternity brother as my partner. During my next visit to Tom's home, Kaye said, "Tom is having problems with the fellows he partnered with. I don't know why he partnered with strangers with you right out there during the auction." Before I could say anything, Tom arrived home and insisted that I stay for dinner. Feeling hurt and insulted, I stayed and ate dinner with Tom and his family for the last time. As the years went by, Tom continued to stop by on his way home for small talk. He even joined my fraternity, Omega Psi Phi. He always joked with me by saying, "One day I am going to be as successful and rich as you was." And I would respond, "If I had your money, I would not have to work another day in my life. How many checks did you pick up today from your post office?"

When Tom decided to become an entrepreneur and open up his own business, he asked everyone that we knew to partner with him, but he never asked me. Not one of the people that he asked would go into business with him, and still he refused to ask me. Determined not to have me, his loyal and devoted neighbor and friend, be a part of his venture, Tom told me that he had used his home, his cars, and everything he owned to start his business alone, because no one wanted to work with him. When he asked me to be his first customer, I let him replace my kitchen carpet, which really did not need to be replaced, and to carpet the bedroom in my guest house. Tom told me that I was the only person in our neighborhood who agreed to help him get started in his business. Two years or so later, Tom was written up in *Black Enterprise* magazine as an up and rising entrepreneur, who was worth at least four million dollars. It seemed that Tom's success was the beginning of my failure, all because of blacks. When he built his mansion, I only received an invitation to see the inside of the home after his house warming. For years, I really thought that Tom never involved me in anything he did because he thought I had more than I did, and he was not about to increase my wealth. That seemed to be the mind-set of too many black people that I came in contact with. I have prayed that Tom will one day remember how he treated me, and be as honorable with me has I have been to him. God has given him a second chance.

Reverend James Hunt (black) visited my new house, and fell in love with my home and the development. Immediately, I took Reverend Hunt to talk with A. E. White, the owner of the development, who also lived in the neighborhood. Reverend Hunt signed a contract to purchase the largest lot in the development, right across the street from me. For the next year, the reverend and I became close friends. Every weekend, our families ate dinner together. Our wives shopped and cooked special dinners together. After one and a half years, White told me that he was going to cancel his contract with Reverend Hunt, because the reverend had not made his $50 per month payments in over a year. White asked me to talk to Reverend Hunt, because he considered us to be close friends. When I talked to Reverend Hunt about this situation, I said to him, "If you are not going to pay for the lot, sign it over to me. I will pay White the balance due on the lot and return you your $500." Three months later, White told me that he had to cancel the reverend's contract. He did not give him any of the $500 back, because he had violated their agreement by not making any payments. I never asked the reverend why he would rather lose $500 instead of selling the lot to me. Our friendship was never the same after that incident. Within five years, Reverend Hunt developed heart disease and died before the age of fifty.

My brother's best friend Fred, who had bought a lot on the right side of mine, wanted to sell it because he could not afford to build a home in the neighborhood. When he came to me for assistance, I told him I would buy the lot. Fred's wife spoke up and said, "The lot is for sale to anyone but you, Curtis." I did not question her, because I knew she was the boss in that family. I simply backed away from my offer, even as Fred insisted that I find them someone to purchase the lot. They did not want to lose the land through foreclosure. Being the good guy that I always was, I got my fraternity brother Clarence to buy the lot. But God does not like ugly, and rewards it in his way and in his own time. Fred and his wife built a smaller home in another neighborhood, using a contractor that had a bad reputation for building shabby houses. Fred's wife told my brother not to tell me, but one night as they were sleeping, the floor to their bedroom gave way, and they ended up in the garage below. She further said to my brother, "Curtis was right about his assessment of the contractor that we used to build our house. I guess that I was too consumed with thinking that Curtis was acting superior and holier than thou."

I stayed away from any serious relationships with the many women that I dated after my divorce. I could not quite figure out what I had done wrong in my marriage, so I didn't know what to do differently. In any event, my divorce devastated me, and taught me that I should devote all of my energies and efforts to those persons who needed me the most, not necessarily those women who loved me sexually. Therefore, I continued to work under the most inhuman conditions, because of the love and devotion that I had for my daughter, mother, and godmother. Whenever I acted as a representative for the City of

Winston-Salem in Raleigh, North Carolina, Nashville, Atlanta, San Diego, and Denver, I was offered better job positions and working conditions. But I could not bring myself to abandon my family.

Even though I did not receive custody of my daughter until she was eleven years old, I was always the pivotal parent in her life. With my mother's assistance, I provided my daughter with all of her clothing, and covered her school expenses, her medical and dental expenses, and her after-school care. I attended all of her school functions, went on field trips with her, met with her teachers regularly, and took her on vacations to fun but educational sites in at least forty states and Canada. With all of these sacrifices and more, my daughter disappointed me by not putting forth any positive efforts in college. She dropped out of college her junior year. She could not see the value of a college education, after witnessing the heartaches and hardships that my education and outstanding accomplishments had caused me.

When I was going through so much turmoil with the City that my health had begun to deteriorate, Reverend Gilliam approached me. He said he wanted to help me in any way possible, to correct or reduce the many evils that were being levied upon me daily on my job. I was really impressed that someone cared about me and was willing to take a stand. This minister invited me to the local Black Baptist Ministers' Alliance monthly meeting, so that I could tell them how I was being treated every day as a City employee. My mother and my dear friend Shirley, who was a nurse, went with me to the meeting. When I arrived at the meeting, I discovered that the ministers had only one item on their agenda: Curtis Dixon and his problems with the City. I told these ministers about the many promotions that I had been denied the right even to apply for; about how my office had been in construction areas, vaults, and damp basements, until my blood pressure was 160/120, hives broke out all over my body, and my equilibrium was so distorted,

I could not walk or see properly. Every minister in the room listened intensely, and then asked questions about the many hideous incidents I was relating to them. The more I presented factual documents to support everything I was saying, the more the ministers believed me. Finally, every minister except one said they had heard enough. They were committed to ending this type of callous treatment from an organization that was supported by taxpayers' funds. Before they could ask me what could they do to help, Reverend Drayton stood up and said forcibly, "I am this ministry's representative on the State Advisory Committee, and I do not think that we should get involved in governmental matters."

Reverend Eversley, Reverend Mendez, and several other ministers disagreed with Reverend Drayton, but he eventually wore them down. At the end of the meeting, several of the ministers came up to me and said that they did not agree with Drayton, but they had to respect his voice because he was the senior minister in the group. The nurse who accompanied me to the meeting told me that Reverend Drayton had spent all of his time at the meeting trying to put his hands under her dress. My mother even said that she saw the nurse fighting the minister off. After this meeting, these ministers did not do or say anything to support me. Many of them avoided me whenever they saw me coming.

Reverend Gilliam talked to me quite often after the meeting, expressing his disappointment in his fellow ministers and even himself. He strongly felt that as disciples for God, they were supposed to intervene and make things right. To him, ministers could be the most powerful leaders in a community, because they had the fellowship of most of the people in the community, as well as God on their side. Reverend Gilliam constantly worried about not doing the right thing for me and not demonstrating that he truly put God and God's work first. I received a call from one of his church members, who said that Reverend Gilliam had been found dead in his recliner. She further said that he had worried himself to death, wondering if he had done all that he could have done for other people like me. Several years later, Reverend Drayton had both of his legs amputated.

Even though my brothers and I made sure that our mother had her own home with all of the necessities, I went the extra mile by escorting her to church every Sunday, by taking her on all of my summer vacations with my family, by buying her groceries, and by making sure that she had the best medical care on a regular basis. When my mother wanted to move into my home with my daughter and me, I welcomed her with open arms. At the young age of eighty-five, my mother thought that she had to be ill, because all of her sisters were ill. My brother Lorenza immediately arrived on the scene and had our mother sign her home over to him and his wife. My mother told me later that all of her Eastern Star Sisters and her closest friends told her that she should have left her house and everything to me, because I was her sole caretaker and provider, physically, emotionally, and socially. When my mother asked me if she had done something wrong, I simply said, "You did what you thought was the best thing at the time, and I accept your decision, because I love you for you, not because of what you have." Until my mother passed away, she would often say, "Your brother Lorenza will surely share with you, because he knows what you have done for me, his children, and even for him."

When she was ninety, my mother was admitted to the emergency room for the first time in her life. While I was tutoring a student, I received a call from my daughter Cheryl. She said in a panic, "Grandma was found unconscious lying across her bed and we cannot wake her up." I told Cheryl to call 911. When I arrived at the house, the medical emergency staff and my entire family were there. As I walked in, I was told that they could not move my mother onto the medical stretcher, because she was too heavy. Immediately, I said, "Bull. Where there's the will of God, there is a way." I lifted my mother up and put her on the stretcher. As the EMS personnel transported my mother from the house to the ambulance, the dark clouds of a tornado suddenly covered the city. My daughter rode in the ambulance with my mother, and I drove my car. I came within inches of having a serious head-on collision with another car, but suddenly the sky lighted, alerting the other driver that I was approaching. It was as if the world stopped for a moment to protect me from any harm.

Thinking that this storm was the worse part of this terrible night, I discovered that the doctor on duty at the emergency room was an intern who had no idea what she was supposed to do. The primary emergency room doctor refused to assist the intern for at least four of the five hours that my mother lay in the emergency room, passing in and out of consciousness. My daughter had admitted my mother at approximately 6:45 PM, and I arrived at the emergency room at 7:00 PM. When I asked the intern to contact my mother's physician, she disappeared for about an hour, only to return even more confused. The nurses on duty quietly said to me, "It's a shame that your mother has to just lie there and receive no medical care." I told the intern to get a real doctor in there to attend to my mother. The doctor disappeared for another hour, and when she returned she said, "Every test that has been run shows that your mother has no medical problem." Again, I said, "Get another doctor in here who can give us some answers."

After four hours went by, the head doctor on duty finally showed herself. The extent of her medical diagnosis of my mother was to ask my mother to identify me. My mother called my name and turned her face away from the doctor in disgust. I asked the doctor, "Where do we go from here? My mother has been lying here in this cold room for over four hours without any reasonable medical treatment." The doctor just walked away and left me with my mother, who looked up at me and said, "I love you, son." She held my hand very tightly and started gasping for air. Immediately, I screamed for help. The entire emergency room staff ran into the room and asked me to leave the area. Within minutes, the head doctor came into the waiting room to talk to my entire family. First, she said that our mother had been sent to the intensive care unit. Second, she said, "Your mother is ninety years old and has had a good life. You all have got to be prepared to lose her."

I said to the doctor, "I thought that your job was to save lives, not to give the family a minister's last rights speech. Why did it take the emergency room over five hours before our mother was sent to the Intensive Care Unit?" Without answering my question, the doctor gave us directions to ICU. When we arrived, the doctor on duty asked to speak with me. He said, "I could have saved your mother's life if she had been brought to ICU at least one hour sooner. Your mother just gave up from exhaustion." Then he asked how long my mother had been in the emergency room. When I told him over five hours, he just shook his head and said, "I am truly sorry for your loss. Just let me know if I can assist you in the future." God had called my mother home, because she really did not want to live with the hurt and shame that her oldest son, James, had caused her. When my daughter called James and told him that his mother had died, he still did not want to come to the hospital.

The medical report written up by the emergency room doctor after my mother passed away did not reflect anything that took place in that emergency room. The "cover your behind" report, which was the most dishonorable act a person could do to a defenseless, God-fearing ninety-year-old lady, stated the following: *The patient was a very pleasant 90-year old white female who had no significant past medical history and was presented to the emergency department with a 12 hour history of fever. The family stated that the patient had been in her usual state of good health until approximately 2:00 o'clock in the afternoon until arriving at the emergency room at approximately 6:30 PM…..Because the patient had previously been associated with the hospital, Family Practice was consulted for possible* *admission. During the evaluation by Family Practice resident and attendant the patient suddenly became unresponsive and apneic requiring endotracheal intubation and mechanical ventilation. At this point the **Medical Intensive** Care Unit service was contacted for admission to the unit. GENERAL: Patient was a well-developed slightly obese black female who was unconscious on the hospital stretcher being mechanically ventilated.* The hospital information is contradictory as to the race of the patient and how long the patient was sick, and gave no medical specifics for the five plus hours my mother lay unattended in the emergency room. Because there was no honor and dedication to the cause, my best friend and mother died.

I had a very special relationship with my third brother William. Our philosophies about family ties closely resembled our mother's. When William became terminally ill, he was given only a few months to live. The last month that he was in the hospital, he was uncooperative with his wife, his sister-in-law, and the nurses. He told them, "When my brother Curtis comes over here, he will take me home." When I finally arrived at the hospital, the nurses saw the gleam of hope in William's eyes and said to me, "You must be the brother that he has been asking for all day and night." As I hugged William, he whispered in my ear, "I want to go home. I promise you I will be good and cause no one any problems." I said to William, "We will take you home if your doctors say that it is okay." I went directly to William's wife and told her, "If there is nothing else that they can do for William here at the hospital, let's take him home. I promised him that we would take him home. I'll move in with you all if necessary to take care of him." Without any hesitation, William's wife Peaches said, "William cannot go home, because he has tests scheduled every day for the next three weeks."

I visited William every day after work for the next three weeks, and I watched him deteriorate from starvation. His wife continued to tell me that he was still being given tests and treatments. Finally, I said to Peaches, "Why is William in the Palliative Care Unit of the hospital if he is still receiving treatment for a possible cure and everyone around him is dying?" Again, without any reservation, Peaches said, "William is only in this unit because there were no other rooms available in the hospital. He is not like those patients who are dying." I did not want to overstep any boundaries, but I did insist that I be permitted to talk to the doctors with Peaches. I had promised my brother that I would make his last days on earth as comfortable as possible at his home. Somehow, Peaches kept William's doctors away from me. I did not pursue the matter, because I did not want to cause any family problems, especially with my brother so critically ill. My heart ached every day that I visited my brother, because the cancer was not killing him. He was literally starving to death, because he refused to eat. Finally, I said to Peaches, "Let's take William home." And she agreed.

The Wednesday morning that William was supposed to be taken home I left school and went to his house to discover that he had been sent to a hospice. Even then, Peaches said, "William will be fed intravenously, and we can stay with him for as long as we want to." Being totally ignorant of what a hospice was, I did not believe Peaches. Something told me to go visit William on that snowy day. When I first arrived at the hospice, I received the shock of my life. The facility's chaplain told me that this hospice was the last resting place for terminally ill patients, and that William had, at most, only a couple of days to live. I spent most of that day with my brother, because there was no one visiting him, not even his wife. Whenever I did leave, something drew me back to my brother's side. Somehow, William lived long enough for everyone to arrive at his bedside. When he passed away, Peaches tried to climb in the bed with him as she cried uncontrollably. Then she confessed by saying, *"Please forgive me for not taking you home from the emergency room when they told me that there was nothing else that could be done to save your life. Please forgive me for denying you the right to visit Las Vegas for the first time with your oldest brother before you died. Please forgive me for not taking you home after you said that Curtis would take you home when he arrived at the hospital."* Everyone was spellbound. Then I realized why William would stop talking to me or anyone when his wife entered his hospital room. He was very unhappy with her lying about his health and denying him his dying wish to go home and die peacefully. I loved William so much that I have worn his clothes every day in memory of him. Also, I have often thought of the joyous last moments William and I could have had if his last days had been at his home. To me, dishonor is a terrible and sinful trait that deprives too many people of small bits of happiness. *May God have mercy on the souls of such insensitive people who possess and use dishonor to cause anyone undue harm!*

After William's death, Peaches distanced herself from the Dixon family. When members of my family would attempt to visit her, she would not let them into her home. However, she did welcome me whenever I visited her. Shortly after William's death, Peaches cried on my shoulders that she missed my brother so much. Then she said that she did not have enough money to buy her medicines, because she had spent all of her money (more than $200,000) on her children and grandchildren. And of course, when she asked me to lend her money, I obliged her, even though I had not gotten over how cruel she had been to my brother and how she had lied to me. After Peaches borrowed a little less than $2000 from me and never paid me back, I discovered that she had done the same thing to another friend of hers. As fate would have it, Peaches, her children, and one of her grandchildren fell on hard times. The worst types of trauma seemed to plague her and her immediate family. It was rumored throughout the community that drug abuse, alcohol abuse, HIV, and many other unsavory diseases might have beset her family.

When my brother Lorenza decided to sell our mother's home, my oldest brother James found him a buyer. James told me that surely Lorenza would give me at least $6000 for all that I had done for our mother. After the sale of the house, James told me what the house sold for. When Lorenza finally got around to visiting me just before he returned to Indianapolis, Indiana, I asked him if he planned to give me any small token from the sale of our mother's home. He did not answer me and just left my home. After the above, I wrote Lorenza the following letter: *"I am writing this letter, because our mother told me to let you know how things really were if you sold her house and made no effort to share the profits with me. This is very hard for me, because I have always shared any and everything I had with my brothers while none of my brothers other than William have shared anything with me. Example: When I was going through my legal problems with the City, William was the only brother who said that my brothers should share in my expenses because I had always been there for all of you and he offered to give me $1000. However, you proudly informed me that you sent Bill McGee $100 toward his defense against the City (this was the same man who caused you to be removed from a principal's position and to leave the City in shame), but you never offered me anything toward my defense. This really hurt me and our mother and she wondered until she died why you were always so indifferent towards me. When I called you several years ago about borrowing some money and you turned me down before I could tell you how much or why, it was our mother's ideal that I call you to see if you really cared about my welfare. She cried after I hung up talking with you. Before she died, she always told me to love and be close to all of my brothers and hold no animosity toward any of them. And I have loved all of my brothers unconditionally, because first you are my brothers and second because my mother was my best friend and the wisest person that I have ever known and loved without any reservations… With the money being given for our old home place, immediately our mother wanted to give each of her sons $1000. However, you wanted $2000, which I sent to you. Consequently, I did not get a $1000 for myself as everyone else did. Then there was the pay off of your house that was* *another $3000......Our mother cried many tears after you had her sign the house over to you after I had spent thousands of dollars bringing it up to a very high standard, wondering if she had done the right thing by me...... Her comment to me was: "Your brother knows what you have done and he will do right by you." ......It seems that all of the brothers knew that you sold the house and what you sold it for from you except me. Was there a reason for not telling me?..... You must do what is in your heart. Regardless of what you do, I will continue to love you and be there for you."*

After receiving my letter, Lorenza immediately called James and Artemas, who said that they had not received any money from our mother when she sold her house. Without addressing anything that I had written in my letter, Lorenza sent me an official formatted memorandum with copies to our brothers, James and Artemas that read: *"I set out for you the following: You never had any ownership in the house; your assertion that you spent $10000 on the house is ludicrous; If any money was spent, it was mother's money, not yours; I did not discuss the sale of the house with you because it was really none of your business....... I hope that this clarifies this issue for you. If it doesn't, I am truly sorry because I will discuss it no further."*

When I called James and Artemas in regards to their lying to support Lorenza, they apologized by saying that they had forgotten about receiving the money from our mother. Further, when Lorenza visited our mother and brothers in Winston-Salem, he always stayed with me. He never spent one night with our other two brothers. Still, he told them about selling our mother's house, and he did not tell me because he did not consider it any of my business. This comment alone told me that Lorenza truly did not have any brotherly love in his heart for me, the only brother who visited him in Columbus, Ohio, and Indianapolis every year, helped raise his children, sent him money when he was in graduate school, and opened up my home to him and his family whenever they visited Winston-Salem. A week after

I received Lorenza's memo, his wife Nettie called and told me that Lorenza had less than six months to live, because cancer had spread throughout his body. As in the past, everyone looked to me to take care of our brother. And I did, because I loved my brother despite his feelings for me. During this time, it was very difficult for Lorenza to look at me and talk to me. When he did, he said things like, "Curt, you have always been healthy and caring." I never mentioned his memo or anything unpleasant. At Lorenza's funeral, his wife insisted that I speak for my brothers, and I did in a manner that our mother would have loved and approved of. In fact, I knew no other way.

My godmother Darsey Ryan never had any children of her own, and she met me after I was discharged from the Air Force. There was this instant mother-son attraction between us. My godmother was only four years younger than my mother, and her health was failing. I took her to the doctor whenever she needed to go, to the grocery store whenever she needed food, and to the emergency room, which was very often. I would stay with her day and night whenever she was not able to be alone, visited her every day of the week, and even cooked for her when the need arose. My godmother had over a dozen nieces and nephews who lived nearby, but none of them found time to do anything for her except beg her for money. It was routine for any of them to call me whenever there was an emergency concerning my godmother, because they refused to go out of their way to accommodate her. I took care of my godmother on a daily basis for more than twenty years. When she passed away, she left behind an estate that was valued at about $500,000, under the administration of her niece Vera Williams. Vera had never visited her aunt, or been in her aunt's home before she became terminally ill. Further, Vera refused to spend one night in her aunt's home after it became necessary for someone to spend evenings and nights with her. Before a full-time sitter was hired, I stayed with my godmother every night. The week before my godmother died, she said to me, "Curtis, I think that I made a mistake trusting my niece Vera. Now I am too sick to make any changes. I can only hope and pray that Vera is an honest girl. Other than her, you are the only person who knows what is in my will. Make sure that Lucy Ann gets to keep the furniture in the house. I told Vera, but I just don't know what to expect from her."

My godmother had given me a $30,000 Certificate of Deposit in my name five years before she got sick, but she asked me to give it back to her after she became seriously ill. She wanted to will me twice that amount, because, as she put it, "Curtis, you have been better to me than any of my relatives and a true godson." Two weeks before my godmother passed away, Vera was seen dragging her aunt from the courthouse. After my godmother died, everyone named in her will was not permitted to see the will or meet with her attorney, so that the will could be read in everyone's presence. I received a check for less than $5000 in the mail from Vera's lawyer. Darsey Ryan's favorite nephew, who had deposited $50,000 of his own money in his aunt's account so that she could live off the interest until she died, took exception to the $10,000 he received. He called Vera and told her that his attorney would be in touch with her concerning his money. This nephew received his $50,000 via overnight delivery before he even talked to his attorney. This confirmed to Darsey Ryan's family and me that Vera had falsified her aunt's will. If not, why had she been seen dragging her sick aunt into the courthouse? Why was everyone named in the will denied their legal right to see the will and have it read in their presence? Why and how did the rumor circulate that Vera's sister and son were witnesses to my godmother's will only a couple of weeks before she passed away? Why would Vera refuse to be in the same room with anyone named in Darsey Ryan's will before, during, and after the funeral?

All of my godmother's immediate family members wanted me to contest the will, because they thought their aunt had to have left most of her savings to me. She had told all of them that she was leaving most of her money to the person who had taken care of her the last ten years of her life. Everyone knew she trusted me more than she did anyone else, because she made it known whenever she needed any part of her business or personal life handled, she called on me. Still, I did not contest the will. Vera, who received the bulk of her aunt's estate, could not look me in the eyes. For years, she would turn and run in the opposite direction whenever she saw me coming, because she knew her aunt had told me everything about her affairs. Vera's reward for her unforgivable and dishonorable behavior came when her husband started hanging out with a group of young fellows who appeared to be homosexuals. What joy and happiness have her new home, the actions of her husband, and her dishonesty brought her? Is it possible to escape the wrath of God for sinful deeds?

When I attended graduate school to earn my master's degree in public administration, I was told by several of my black classmates who were a semester ahead of me that it did not matter how hard I worked in my classes. I would never receive a grade above a B. They said that all black students only received Bs and below at this university. I proved them to be wrong, because I made all As and one B. Further, my professors considered me to be very intelligent and charismatic. Consequently, I became friends with several of my professors. On several occasions my family and I would get together with Dr. Jim and his family, and Dr. Mike, who recommended me for the presidency of the Triad Chapter for the American Society of Public Administration (ASPA). Our social gatherings were both academic and affable, because of the wealth of practical knowledge that I brought to the table, which either supported or refuted the professors' theoretical and academic knowledge. Also, as president of the Triad ASPA Chapter, I was fortunate enough to interact regularly with Dr. Olson, the chairman of the Political Science Department, and his wife Mary; and with the city managers and county manager of Greensboro, High Point, Burlington, and Guilford County (all white). This experience was by far the most rewarding and enjoyable of all of my adult experiences.

After I completed my master's degree in public administration, Alderman Larry Little used me as a character reference so that he could be accepted into the MPA program at my alma mater. After the director of the program talked with me, Little was accepted. Then Little asked to borrow my textbooks, notes, previous assignments, and tests to use as study guides. I was told by one of his classmates that he used the materials unethically and was reported to the department's chairman. When the director of the program refused to let Little graduate, Little badgered me at work until I called and talked with the professors who had given him incomplete grades in their classes. Those grades were changed to passing grades, and he was permitted to graduate, because the professors did not want him to cause me any further problems on my job. Even after the above, Alderman Little refused to return my materials to me, and he ceased supporting me in my struggle against the City. As a matter of fact, Little was downright insulting when I asked him to be a favorable witness in my complaint against the City. As a result of my assistance, Larry Little was able to get a job at Winston-Salem State University as a political science instructor.

Velma Watts, who worked with me during the Model City days, showed up at my home to borrow the research papers I had written when I was pursuing a doctoral degree in administration at the University of North Carolina in Greensboro. She had been accepted in the doctoral program at Duke University. Her comments to me were, "I was told that you were the person to come to in order to get the best quality research papers, and I promise to bring all of them back to you. Curtis, you are going to discover that no one is going to support you in your struggle with the City, especially the black aldermen and the black leaders in Winston-Salem. Most of them know that you deserve better." Velma paused, and then said, "This is my first time seeing inside your home. It is as beautiful as they said it was. You must know that all of your problems have come from your building this house, marrying a foreigner, and having the audacity to be smart. Black people in Winston-Salem were not ready for you." I gave Velma all of my research papers, but I said nothing during her visit. Velma called me after she received her PhD, and she told me that it had taken her only two years to complete her doctoral program. She told me several times that she was going to return my research papers, but she never did. Further, she knew that I had given her my only copies. After the above, Dr. Watts was hired as the Associate Dean of Minority Affairs at Wake Forest University/ Medical Center.

It seemed that everyone's life that I touched with my knowledge and expertise was enriched, and they received promotions and rewards commensurate with their education or experience. In the meantime, the leaders of our entire bureaucratic system quietly and privately said that I was not deserving of anything. What was I doing wrong?

After the hospital psychiatrist (white) advised me to file legal action against my oppressors and I did, this psychiatrist told me that he could no longer be my doctor and that he would not be a favorable witness for me. When my doctor (white) in the hospital's Family Practice Unit found out about his decision, she volunteered to be a witness for me. She said, "The managers of the City were wrong for treating you so cruelly. And I am ashamed to be associated with fellow practitioners who support unhealthy practices in the workplace. I will be relocating to another city, where honesty is the policy and practice of my co-workers." Evidently, that one influential call on behalf of the City or the powers to be, that was always made to anyone who was in a position to expose the dishonesty of the City, did not work with her as it did with the psychiatrist and many others.

The state equal employment representative (black) who met and talked extensively with me about how I was being treated on my job, told me that the City was wrong on every count and that there was no way any court should rule in its favor. However, after one visit to the City's attorney's office, this representative refused even to meet with me again and tell me what had been discussed. He did call me to say that the people I had suggested he talk to had said they did not know me well enough to tell him anything to support my claims against the City. Therefore, he would not be able to pursue my allegations against the City any further. Having gone to school with the director of this agency, I called the director to find out what had really transpired. When the director finally returned my call, all he would say was, "My office sanctions you pursuing your claims in State Superior Court, and for some unknown reason, your representative from our office resigned his position the day before you called me." What message had the representative received from the City's attorney that had caused the above? The City's attorney was also black.

My neighbor Walter Marshall (black), who was a County Commissioner at the time, called me before my trial date in 1989 and voluntarily told me that Assistant City Manager Alexander Beaty told him that the City administrators were not worried about my prevailing in court over them, because they had made sure that my creditability and professional reputation throughout this community and in any court room had been destroyed with lies. He went on to say that Beaty told him that my complaint against the City would be dismissed by the presiding judge, and that City Manager Stuart was going to fire me right after the judge dismissed my complaint. This neighbor, who presented himself to students and the public as a loyal, law abiding citizen, refused to do the honorable thing and repeat in court what he had been told. The entire time he was testifying, he looked at City Manager Stuart and praised him and his staff. The City's attorney and the city manager smiled the entire time that Marshall was testifying.

Less than a month after I was terminated from my job with the City, I hastily married my daughter's piano teacher, who could sing and play the piano so heavenly. I was really a basket case. I had dizzy spells, threw up yellow mucous, and had rashes all over my body from the constant harassment imposed on me under Stuart's administration. My new wife's love and her ability to sing God's music as she played the piano brought joy and hope back into my life. Knowing that I was not completely mentally stable when I said I wanted to add my daughter's name to the title of my home, my new wife told me that she would assist me. She hired her lawyer to take care of everything, and I trusted her to do right by me. She told me that her lawyer said he could not put my daughter's name on the title, because she was too young. He could, however, put my wife's name on the title, with the written understanding that my daughter's name would replace her name when she became of age. I agreed to that arrangement. Trusting my new bride, I signed the completed title change without reading it.

My marriage was great for about five years. After that time, my wife misappropriated thousands of dollars from my checking and savings accounts, and ran up debts on my credit cards. When I discovered what was going on, I still tried to save our marriage by paying off all of her debts on my credit cards. Shortly thereafter, my wife lost her job, and she refused to do any housekeeping. The straw that broke the camel's back, as the old saying goes, was when I asked her to at least pick up after herself. Her response was, "I am no maid."

"You are right," I said, "but you are out of this house. I am through with you, your selfishness, and your attitude." With tears in her eyes, she said that she had no place to go. I told her that she could take all the time she needed, but she had to go. Within a month, she had moved out. Trying to be civilized and fair, I told my wife to write up our separation papers. When she presented the papers, which gave her half of everything that I had owned prior to our marriage, I put my foot down. I told her that she could have the house and all of her bills, and I would leave with all of the cars that I had paid for and were titled in my name. Immediately, my wife changed her stance about expecting half of the equity in the house, because she loved the new car I had bought her. She also knew she had been dishonest when she had had her attorney put in the deed that I awarded her half of my home as a wedding gift. We were finally able to make an amicable settlement. Losing this wife was like inhaling a fresh breath of air for the first time. Friends and family members started to visit my home again, and even the flowers started to grow abundantly in my yard.

Then I met the young lady whom I knew was "the one" for me. We were inseparable and loved doing everything together. As years went by, this woman maintained a secret romance with another man in another state. Still, she demanded to know every move that I made both day and night, even when she left town to be with her secret lover. She became so domineering I slowly lost all sexual attraction for her, even though I felt I still loved her. When I could no longer love her to her satisfaction, she retaliated against me in the cruelest manner possible. She told her family and my family that I was having relations with my godson, my godson's mother, my godson's grandmother, my godson's girlfriend's mother, and with any female teacher who talked to me or even walked anywhere with me on my job. She became so vindictive while still hoping to have a relationship with me, that she started canvassing my immediate family with insulting and damaging remarks. The only way I could stop her was to send her the following correspondence: *"With all of your intelligence, I am sure that you must know that 'Evil is as evil does'. And you certainly have been busy doing the devil's work. While on the other hand, I have been enjoying life to the fullest in your absence. It has been over five years since I have experienced this type of peace and tranquility, no stalking, no fortune-tellers, no suspicions and criticisms, no being controlled and harassed about decisions that I make............ Your actions with my immediate family members are the straws that broke the camel's back. Be very careful about what you are doing and saying. You are attempting to assassinate my character and defame me with slanderous comments. There are laws that prohibit such........... I thank God for making me strong enough to endure any evilness that is launched at me or about me and wise enough to know who my enemies are. You, not only went outside my family in an effort to destroy my character, you were bold enough to go inside to my immediate family with this garbage. I will never stop loving you, but I also know that I will never trust you or welcome you into my home again. I will forever cherish and hold dear those great times that we shared together. Have a good life.....You will always be in my prayers and may God have mercy on you and remove that destructive spirit you display when things do not go your way.*

I did not see or hear from this girlfriend for five years. But my oldest brother told me that he had talked to her, and her only comment was, "Your brother Curtis is a very good person and a fine gentleman." When I finally saw this ex-girlfriend in late 2008, it was like love all over again for both of us. We laughed and enjoyed each other's company. When we parted, she asked me to call her so that we could have lunch together soon. As she was walking away, she said, "I know that you won't call me, but I hope that you will." I said, "I might just take you up on your offer." And that was the end of that.

Everyone who came into contact with me felt comfortable requesting my assistance, anytime, anywhere and on their terms only. And I was always very accommodating. However, the vast majority of the black people I assisted never reciprocated. In fact, many of them worked against me, or plotted to make my life as uncomfortable as possible. It was as if they were punishing me for being there for them. They had to know that no one else would have given them the time of day.

During many of my quiet moments, I would ask God, *"Who am I? Why do I always provide good and perfect gifts to my neighbors and fellowmen, only to be rewarded the malfeasance of so many supposedly honorable people?*

ABUSE OF POWER

"Let not the wise man glory in his wisdom, let not the mighty man glory in his might, let not the rich man glory in his riches, but let he who glories glory in this, that he understands and knows me, that I am the Lord who practice steadfast love, justice, and righteousness in the earth; for in these things I delight"

—*Jeremiah9:23*

Exactly two years after I built a new home and bought a new car for my first wife, Akie, she burned down the house, wrecked the car, and charged me with assault. When we went to court, I went directly from work to the courtroom. My wife was not there. When my name was called, I stood before this southern white judge from hell, who angrily said to me, "Where is your wife?" Before I could answer, the judge said, "I think that I have a smart one here." The bailiff, who knew me, came up and put his hand on my shoulder, whispering to me, "Don't say anything." I did not say anything. When my wife and her attorney arrived a minute later, my wife said, "It's all a mistake." The judge asked her if I had told her to say that. My wife said, "No, your honor. He has not talked to me since the sheriff gave him the subpoena." The judge did everything within his power to provoke me, but I did not open my mouth. The judge was still talking to my wife's attorney as I was leaving the courtroom. All charges were dropped against me, but the humiliation lingered on.

Two years later, my wife and I filed for a separation, and we had to appear in court to decide who would get custody of our daughter. The judge awarded full custody to my wife and stated, "Without a doubt, Mr. Dixon, you are the better parent, but it is my belief and policy that mothers should have custody of their children. I want you to continue providing the love and stability to your daughter." As the judge was finalizing his decision, my wife handed our daughter to me and said, "I have an early flight to New York. I'll see you all when I return." In shock, the judge said, "Does this happen all of the time?" I smiled and said, "I have adjusted to this by now, your honor. This has been the story of my life." Then the judge said, "Keep me posted on what goes on, and if your wife continues this type of irresponsibility, I will reverse my decision."

One year later, my ex-wife's neighbors called me every day of the week, complaining that Akie was leaving our daughter Cheryl alone in their apartment. They begged me to get Cheryl away from her before something serious happened to her. Finally, I agreed to file for custody of my daughter, but only if the neighbors would testify in my favor. The neighbors, a husband and wife, agreed. But when they went to court, they changed their testimony, and Akie retained custody of our daughter. After the hearing was over, Akie's neighbors ran up to me to apologize. They said, "Your ex-wife's lawyer called us every day and convinced us that your daughter would be better off with her mother." Of course, Akie handed Cheryl to me as she and her lawyer left the courthouse, laughing. All the neighbors could say was, "We are so sorry, Curtis. What can we do to make up for this wrong?" I said, "Leave me alone, now and forever." They continued to call me for about a month, but finally stopped after I refused to talk to them. Their message on my answering machine was always, "We are truly sorry for being so dishonest with you. Your ex-wife is even more irresponsible with your daughter. Cheryl is wearing shoes that are two sizes too small for her."

Less than a month later, I went to Florence Creque's home to help her with a special project. When I rang the doorbell, the black woman who had acted as Akie's attorney at our separation hearing answered the door dressed in Florence's nightclothes. She even had on Florence's bedroom slippers. Florence informed me that this attorney friend had had an investigator following me for over a month, but had found no irregularities in my lifestyle. I said, "Why are you telling me this now? This is something that you should have told me when I was being investigated. Everyone makes mistakes." Florence said with a phony smile on her face, "But we all know that you don't make mistakes. I won the bet because the only skeleton in your closet was your taking an extra fifteen minutes for lunch every now and then." I told Florence that I could not help her with her project, and I left her. In my mind, Florence wanted me to fail, and she really did not care about my welfare at all. One and one half years later, the thirty-five-year-old attorney suddenly became critically ill and died within a month.

Two years later, my ex-wife filed for an increase in child support, even though I kept our daughter at least four days a week (Friday through Tuesday), bought her clothes, and picked her up every day from a private day care that I paid for. I hired a lawyer, and he assured me that my child support payments would not increase based on the services I was already providing my daughter. In court, however, this white lawyer refused to present any of the information that I had given him. Consequently, my monthly child support payment was doubled. When I looked disappointed, this lawyer had the audacity to tell me that I was ungrateful, because the payment could have tripled. I stopped him in the middle of traffic and said angrily, "How in the hell would you feel if you had your daughter every day and had to pay someone else who did absolutely nothing for the child? The money only benefits my daughter's mother. I take care of all of my daughter's needs." Looking like a fool, this lawyer said, "I really didn't get a chance to study your case. I am sorry. Maybe I can talk to the judge in his chambers." I left the lawyer standing in the street, as I said, "Forget it. All of you lawyers are full of shit."

When Cheryl was six years old, my ex-wife moved to another county to live with a man she knew absolutely nothing about, I refused to let my daughter move with her, even though she had full custody. When my daughter said that the man was obsessed with touching and hugging her the one weekend that she visited her mother, I did not let my daughter visit his home again. When the man realized that my daughter would not be moving into his house with her mother, he put my ex-wife out. She had no place to live. My daughter was living with me, and my ex-wife slept in her car in my mother's driveway. Without asking, my ex-wife moved into the guest quarters in the back of my home. When I filed for custody of our daughter *without a lawyer,* I was awarded full custody. My daughter was in the sixth grade at the time. I let my ex-wife live in my guest quarters until she got on her feet and bought a home.

After every management position that I played a major role in creating within the City had been filled with non-contributors, Gary Brown and many other employees started telling me that I was never going to be treated fairly unless I made the City accountable for its wrong actions against me. Every day for a month, I was told that I needed to file legal action against the City and its administrators.

In 1978, I decided to file a discrimination charge against the City and City Manager Powell for repeatedly violating City policies against me. Even in this system, I was betrayed and insulted. After a year, I had not heard anything from the Equal Employment Opportunity Commission in Greensboro, North Carolina. When I inquired, I was told that my file had been lost. Then I was told by a black EEOC representative that it had been sent to the Charlotte EEOC office. I had to go to Charlotte and look for my own file. A new white EEOC representative and I found it in the dead files. This EEOC representative spoke candidly and said, "A file with this much information was intentionally misplaced. The City has violated every federal policy possible against you. Someone with this EEOC agency has to be working with the City in order for a case with this type evidence to be misplaced." My file was finally returned to the Greensboro EEOC office in 1979, but my discrimination complaints were *never reviewed* by any EEOC office. After I filed a second EEOC retaliation charge against the City and City Manager Stuart in 1980, the Greensboro EEOC office only reviewed this complaint in 1981.

On May 27, 1981, the city manager, the City's attorney, the City's EEOC officer, and I had a meeting at the EEOC Office in Greensboro, North Carolina concerning my retaliation charge. At this meeting, I was treated with no respect by the black EEOC representative who was supposed to mediate the meeting. First, he had me wait outside the meeting room for thirty minutes while he conversed with the City's representatives. When I was finally permitted to enter the room, he let the city manager take charge of the meeting and discuss whatever issues he wanted to. I stood my ground, knowing that I was dealing with a black man in a responsible position who was intimidated by white people. Virtually nothing constructive came out of the meeting. The city manager and his band of renegades felt they had won, because they had preempted the EEOC system. The next day, I called the EEOC representative and told him that I wanted my February 1981 retaliation charge updated to cover the initial complaints that I had given his office. He had neglected to address them at my hearing. The EEOC representative said nervously, "Mr. Dixon, I don't think that is necessary, since you and your attorney plan to file for a right-to-sue letter." I told him I wanted it done, and that I would be in his office on June 1, 1981, to sign the amended complaint. The EEOC representative tried to make excuses about the workload in his office. I had smelled a rat at the hearing, after the hearing, and now while I was talking to this EEOC representative, who was buying time for the City. I said, "Sir, I have informed my attorney of your nebulous actions at the hearing, and he is very displeased and plans to talk to your superiors." The EEOC representative said, "Your amended complaint will be ready for your signature on June 1 at 2 PM."

When I arrived at the EEOC Office at 2 PM, the EEOC representative met me at the door and said, "Everything is ready just as you asked, Mr. Dixon, and I am very sorry for the inconvenience. I hope that you aren't too disappointed in my performance. *I only did what I was told to do.*" The scenario was a black working against a black, because a dishonorable white or racist black had requested it. I thought to myself as I was driving back to Winston-Salem, *Why would my black attorney meet with this EEOC Agency in my absence, instead of attending my hearing with me? Was he working with and for the City at my expense? Why does it always look as if blacks are working against blacks? Why are white complaints that are handled by black EEOC representatives more often than not resolved to the satisfaction of the white client? Will we as blacks ever learn that we are our own worst enemy?*

Before City Manager Powell left the City in 1979, he told the City's attorneys to hold off settling with me for five years. This alone was a clear indication that he knew he had intentionally discriminated against me, and that the City had full control of the situation. The City attorney's secretary told me about the above conversation. My complaint was kept out of the court system for five years, just as Powell had requested.

When I had to hire a lawyer, the professionals I respected the least based on my experiences with them, I thought I would fare better if I hired my fraternity brother and supposed friend, Walter Johnson (black), to represent me. Before Walter got heavily involved with my case, Henry Frye, another fraternity brother and a State Supreme Court judge, met with us for breakfast at a local restaurant. Judge Frye's comment to me was, "Curtis, if you and Walter are still friends when he finishes representing you, you will be the first in his career as an attorney. Walter is too busy doing everything but adequately presenting his clients." Walter smiled and said, "I have got to do right by Curtis or my wife will divorce me." Hiring Walter was a big mistake. He billed me $10,000 before he had done anything significant with my case. When I questioned his actions, he said, "I am confident that I can prevail over the City and get you awarded no less than $100,000. Then I will also get a judgment that will require the City to reimburse you for the $25,000 legal fees that I will be charging you." *After Attorney Johnson had charged me over $15,000 and received the money, I read in the local newspaper that he had been hired as director of the State Correction Division under Governor Hunt in Raleigh, North Carolina and that he would report to work within a week.*

When I finally caught up with Walter, he had shipped all of my documents to Julius Chambers in Charlotte, North Carolina, and had started his new job. Walter had never said anything to me about taking another job, or transferring my case to another attorney. I was very angry and afraid, because it seemed that no matter where I turned, nobody supported me. Dishonor was suffocating me, and I did not know what to do. When I met with Walter and Julius Chambers in late 1979, Walter's first comment to Julius was, "Don't try to pull the same mind games on Curtis that you use with your regular clients. Curtis was known as the mathematical genius in our class all through college. You will not be able to fool him with nonsense." I reluctantly accepted Julius as my attorney, because I felt I had no one else to turn to.

Attorney Julius Chambers (black) was worse than Walter. First, Julius said to me, "Even though you have information to show that the city manager and many of his managers have willfully and intentionally violated City policies against you, I will not be able to prevail in court without witnesses." When I asked him what he needed, he said, "If you get me at least four sworn affidavits from possible witnesses, I will win your case for you." When I provided Julius with twenty signed affidavits, he became very angry at me and turned my case over to one of his junior attorneys.

Uncontested excerpt from my first book: *"Only weeks before my trial, Julius Chambers fought with me about presenting the real facts against City administrators. When I disagreed with him and showed him about twenty signed affidavits to substantiate all of my allegations against the City, Chambers wrote me a letter threatening to withdraw from my case if he could not lose it the way that he knew best and with the letter he attached a $3,500 legal bill with a complete repeat of a previous bill that he had already sent me. Only this bill had changed several dates and things so that I would not associate it with any of the many bills that I had received in the past. Within days after I received Mr. Chambers unprofessional and fraudulent correspondence, I read in the local newspaper that Julius Chambers had accepted the position of NAACP legal defense director and that he was to begin work before my trial. This man had not said one word to me."*

Further, I had told Walter and Julius that I wanted a trial by jury. When Julius met with the judge, he told the judge the case would be tried without a jury, intentionally denying me my legal and constitutional rights. When I asked Julius to tell the judge that I wanted a trial by jury, Julius told me that Judge Ward would not permit him to make after the fact changes.

When I went to Julius's office to retrieve my documents so that I could turn them over to the junior attorney, all of my documents that incriminated Assistant City Manager Bond were missing. I wondered if this was intentional, because Julius and Bond were members of the same fraternity.

Uncontested excerpt from my first book: *"The Junior Attorney John Nockleby (white) was very weak and inexperienced at presenting any case before a judge. His primary concern was money and that Judge Ward might still rule against me, even though I had over two hundred exhibits and many witnesses.*

The discovery and pretrial period, the trial and the judgment were the worst miscarriages of justices that any court in America could force on any citizen. Any and everything evil took precedence over my excellence in the United States Middle District Court in the Winston-Salem proceedings, and even in the court's findings and conclusions of law under the auspices of Judge Hiram Ward.

The discovery and pretrial periods were rife with misrepresentation and falsification on the part of my white attorney John Nockleby (white), the City's EEOC/Affirmative Action Officer Beckie Goforth (white), the City's Attorney Tony Brett (black), and the magistrate (white) under Judge Ward's jurisdiction. For example: John Nockleby called all of my white witnesses and told them that he was not going to use them in court because he did not want to do anything to hurt their careers. Further, when the witnesses were honorable and insisted on being favorable witnesses for me, John told Joe Sauser (white) that he could possibly lose his job with the City if he testified and gave the real facts about my employment with the City. Of course, my witnesses apprised me of the junior attorney's actions and I told the associate attorney who was given the lead in representing me in court. This Associate Attorney John Gresham was very ethical and honorable in dealing with me and he immediately reprimanded the junior attorney in my presence.

Beckie Goforth willingly and intentionally wrote in a sworn affidavit that I had never supervised any employees since being employed by the City. This lady knew that I had supervised several employees, because she had attended all meetings concerning my case and had heard the truth. She knew without a doubt that I supervised at least four City employees when I was the director of evaluation and acting deputy director of budgeting and planning for the Model City Department in 1971 and 1972. Magistrate Stuart, who once worked for the City, denied my attorney access to certain personnel records in the pretrial preparation of my case. According to Attorney Gresham, this had never happened to him in the twenty years that he had been an attorney. Even the City's Attorneys Roddey Ligon and Tony Brett knowingly put false information throughout the pretrial document.

In the meantime, a young white female employee with the City of Winston-Salem filed an EEOC Reverse race discrimination complaint against the City of Winston-Salem in 1983, and the complaint was resolved by EEOC to her satisfaction within one year. Why do you suppose the City of Winston-Salem and the EEOC Office could come to an agreement on the above complaint so quickly when it took the same EEOC Office about a year to acknowledge receipt of my complaint that was found hidden in the dead files at a different EEOC Office from where I had originally filed it?

On October 3, 1984, I received a call from Mrs. Florence Creque, who was the only witness listed for me and the City of Winston-Salem. Her conversation went something like this: *"Curtis, I have had Brandon out looking for you all afternoon to tell you that the City does not plan to be honorable and fair with you tomorrow at your trial. I met with City Manager Stuart, Assistant City Manager Beaty, and the City Attorneys this morning and they were coaching me to lie about everything that you stand for. Everyone who testifies for the City tomorrow at your trial is going to lie about your performance, except me. I told them that they can take my job and even fire me, but that I was not going to lie about you because you are too fine a young man and because you have contributed too much to this City, to be treated in such a fashion. Curtis, Brandon knows the complete story because I told him to get this information to you. I wasn't going to call, but since he was unable to get in touch with you, I couldn't let you go into that court room thinking that you are about to get a fair trial. I am truly sorry Curtis, but you can rest assured that I will tell the truth about you for whatever good it will do. I'm sure that you can see that this whole thing is just a big conspiracy because, if you will remember, I told you that your trial would not be heard before Judge Ward until the Fall of 1984, even after you told me that the judge himself had told you that he was going to try your case in the Fall of 1983, for sure. Just think: How could Attorney Brett who told me when the case was going to be tried would know the exact date unless he or the Womble, Carlyle Law Firm had some inroads to the judge's office?"*

The Trial of Dixon vs the City of Winston-Salem began on October 4, 1984 at 9 AM in the U.S. Middle District Courtroom on the second floor of the Federal Building in Winston-Salem, with Judge Hiram Ward presiding. It lasted three days, even though it was scheduled for ten days. My attorneys and I entered the courtroom with over five boxes of exhibits and the City attorneys walked into the courtroom with no exhibits. The trial proceedings were three days of open and blatant slander, perjury, and conspiracy against me, a black man in a white man's arena. Judge Ward spent his time staring vehemently at me because I was able to trap each defendant and the defendant's witnesses with documented evidence. My attorneys, who were both white, tried to assure me that the Judge's stares were in my favor. To them, I was the most impressive plaintiff that they had ever seen and heard testify in a court of law. My mother and I thought differently about the judge's stares. We saw them as resentment of and despise for me, a black man who would dare display such intelligence, confidence, and courage in his courtroom against white men."

When Brandon met with me, he told me about the unethical and cruel tactics the City's leaders planned to use to discredit me in court. When I asked Brandon if he would testify to what Florence had told him, he agreed. The City's attorney requested that Brandon be deposed at his law firm's office. I told my attorneys that they needed to talk with this witness before he reported to the City's attorney's office, but they did not. When my attorneys and I arrived at the City's attorney's office, Brandon was already there. When he was deposed, the City's attorney asked Brandon if Mrs. Creque's comments to him were her opinion. Brandon said that he thought so. This incident never would have happened if my attorneys had listened to me. Brandon was permitted to testify, but Judge Ward refused to admit his testimony as evidence against the City, because Brandon had agreed that what he was told was "Mrs. Creque's opinion." Two other black department directors met with Stuart, Beaty, and the City's attorneys, and were coached to lie. They were Walter Farabee and Lester Ervin. I was told that they were not about to be a part of the City's vendetta, and would not perjure themselves in court. They disappeared before my trial date, so that they would not have to commit perjury against me in court. One went on a business trip to California and did not return until after the trial. The other checked himself into the hospital for surgery and was not able to be a part of the trial. On the other hand, my cousin, Alexander Beaty, willingly perjured himself about my performance and ability to work with my supervisors. My attorneys proved that he had never been my supervisor. Beaty's only ability on the job was being subservient to anyone in authority, especially white people and John Bond. He once told me that he would prostitute his own mother if his boss wanted him to.

Quotes from Evil for Good: *I had a white witness whose testimony would have been better than Brandon's. This witness, Mary Freas, was going to testify that City Manager Powell and Deputy City Manager Bond had called her in and tried to get her to implicate me in her department's problems with Beaty. They further had asked her to provide false testimony about me, such as my being a trouble maker and causing* unnecessary problems among City personnel. My attorneys and I both considered this young lady to be my strongest witness. After all of the City's witnesses and defendants made so many blunders, my attorneys decided that they did not need Mary's testimony. Feeling confident that they had prevailed on every aspect of my complaint, my attorneys concluded their case without informing me that they were not going to use Mrs. Freas. Of course, I panicked. Then Attorney Gresham calmed me down by telling me that they did not need her testimony, because they had already won my case according to all the rules of the law, previous cases, and statutes on the books. I was still petrified by the fact that my own attorneys would go against their promise to me by not using Mary to solidify my case. Then I remembered Julius Chambers' written comment to me which read: "I will not be a part of anything that will malign any City defendants." And my question was, "How can you win a lawsuit without presenting all of the key facts?"

My attorneys presented my case in such a way that no defendant's career would be maligned in any way. My mother who attended every court session said to me on day number 2, "Son, you are not going to win in this judge's courtroom. This judge has not taken his eyes off of you since your trial began. He is looking at you, even when other people are testifying. He will not be fair. Something tells me that he has already made up his mind. I want you to watch him throughout the rest of your trial." My mother's suspicions became evident when any of my witnesses spoke favorable of me. The Judge would interrupt them as he looked at me and say, "Those comments are irrelevant. We are not here to determine how well Mr. Dixon is respected or how smart Mr. Dixon is or what great accomplishments he has made since being employed with the City." The Judge took exception to the testimonies of most of my witnesses. My witnesses included aldermen, a university professor, a minister, the police chief, a psychiatrist, a physician, and many co-workers. Gary Brown, who was one of my supervisors, was so nervous on the stand that he perjured *himself every time that he opened his mouth to testify against me. When he said that I had not completed certain assignments accurately and timely, his own handwritten evaluation reports on me stated otherwise. This witness became so ridiculous that Judge Ward called for a recess in order to help the City save face. The City's attorney did not have to object to anything or request anything during the trial, because the judge did everything for him. When the City's witnesses could not defend their many wrongful actions against me properly and started perjuring themselves, Judge Ward would tell them in open court that they needed to go back to the drawing board and prepare a better defense. The judge did agree that he would disregard Brown's testimony if John Bond did not testify as a witness for the City and confirm Brown's testimony. As expected, Bond did not testify as a witness for the City and he did not appear in court. The City's leaders knew that Bond's history with the City would have been much more damaging than the perjury of Gary Brown. Bond created this entire drama against me, because he made it known throughout the city that he could not stand rich and smart blacks like me. This all began after I invited Bond to a house warming party at my new home and after he discovered that I was completing my master's degree in mathematics.*

It was as if my witnesses and I were just going through the motion, because the judge had already decided in favor of the City, with no regard for right or wrong. City Manager Powell admitted that he had not complied with City policies when promoting others employees over me. The testimonies of City management personnel seemed to be of no concern to Judge Ward, other than when he had to stop them from making buffoons of themselves in open court. In a real court of law, wouldn't the above practices be considered obstruction of justice?

Orville Powell, city manager from 1972-79, testified that based on his dealings with me, I would not be suited at all to dealing with and supervising people; that he suggested I apply for the assistant county manager's position that required that I interact and supervise people; that he recommended me to become the president of the Piedmont Triad Chapter of the American Society for Public Administration (ASPA), a professional organization that comprised of city managers, department heads, professional municipal employees and professors – dealing with people; that he did not advertise any of the positions that I qualified for; that he never supervised me and in fact did not even know who had been my supervisors (after appointing Allen Joines and Tom Fredericks as my supervisors within a twelve month time frame). This city manager whom I had once chosen as my idol sat in meetings and observed me perform John Bond's, Alexander Beaty's, Allen Joines's, Tom Frederick's, and Gary Brown's administrative responsibilities in an outstanding manner. Also, Powell only complimented me for my outstanding contributions when we were alone in his office because he was afraid that John Bond would get upset with him. Powell's testimony was contradictory in regards to my dealing and supervising people and he lied about not knowing who my supervisors were.

Bryce Stuart, city manager from 1980 until I departed the City, testified that he gave me a clean slate when he was hired. Then he verbally assigned me energy duties, knowing that I did not have any training or experience in engineering. He conveniently did not mention that he gave me three criteria for selecting an employee for an administrative position: recent supervisory experience which he denied me, performance which he had Joines and Owen rate me below standard to standard, and education that he told me that he did not consider in my situation at all. After I asked Mr. Stuart in writing where I fell short as far as being given an administrative position, he stated that he did not think that it was one of my rights to be told where I needed to improve in order to be promoted and that he had never had to give a written performance evaluation on anyone in his seventeen years in this type work. When I told him that as a commissioned officer in the military, I gave my troops yearly evaluations, Stuart said that the military was the worse managed organization in the country along with IBM. After which time, he ordered Allen Joines to give me low performance evaluation ratings; he relocated me to at least five different offices in less than a year; he made sure that my office telephone number changed at least a half-dozen times in an effort to make me an inefficient ASPA President; he made sure that my ten year superior performance rating with the City change to standard after he was only employed with the City six months, and he committed perjury in court by saying that I did not complete any energy assignments until the spring of 1981 even after he was shown at least four completed energy assignments dated before the spring of 1981. This was the same man who was quoted on March 21, 1980 in a newspaper article entitled, "Stuart Governs City with Bible at Side": "I think the thing Christians can do to help government is found in I Peter-Let your good lives be an example. The challenge is to maintain very scrupulously your standards of peace, of seeking understanding, of seeking truth, to be honest and forthright. Have these standards for yourself and seek to set an example for others so that they can learn from that and see that this is the appropriate way to be. I don't think God expects us to obey orders that require us to sin, to lie, or to cheat, but, at the same time, he gave us a will and I think that he expects us to use that to seek correctness and to do the proper thing." Did Stuart really give me a clean slate? Why would he get involved in Orville Powell's dishonorable practices and treat me worse than Powell after the above comments? Why would this man insult me, the city and its residents, and play with God publicly? Why did the city's elected officials and subordinate managers accept Stuart's dishonesty, his lies, and his complete disregard for the standards of peace? Was it because the elected officials, Stuart, and even Judge Ward knew that dishonor was acceptable everywhere and nobody cared?

James Allen Joines, development director at the time, testified emphatically that I did not work on the UDAG project, but Mr. Stuart testified that I did work on the project; that he did not sell beer illegally at the 1977 downtown street scene, but Tom Fredericks testified that Joines was with him when they sold beer illegally at the street scene and they were counseled by Powell who promoted both of them shortly after the incident. To support Stuart, Joines perjured himself by testifying that I had not completed any energy assignments from May 1980 until May 1981. However, Joines did not contradict the memorandum and other completed energy documents that were shown to him in court quoting his high praise of my accomplishments on energy assignments before May 1981. Joines harassed me so severely when my doctor took me out of work for two weeks that my doctor wrote him a letter stating that he had never known any employee to be treated as I was being treated. Why would Joines lie so ridiculously in court?

Roddey Ligon and Toney Brett, attorneys for the City, wrote in the Final Pretrial order that Mr. Harold Bolick would be one of their witnesses as my supervisor, but at trial they stated that Bolick was my witness after Dan Gilbert testified that Bolick was his supervisor and that Bolick was not cooperative with him or me toward the completion of energy assignments. The attorneys also wrote in their brief that I was a "Glory Grabber" because Louis Jones designed the floor space for the manpower program. But Mrs. Florence Creque, the human services director in charge of the manpower program, testified that she did not request a space layout from me, but hearing her talk about a need, I completed a space layout plan for twenty-five to thirty people and put it on her desk. The attorneys further wrote that Gary Brown had nothing to gain or loss from his (false) testimony because he was not an employee of the City when he testified, but they were in the court room when Brown testified that he was the community development director for the City. Even worse, Brown was maintained on the City's payroll until November 20, 1984 for pay purpose only, because he reported to his new position in Lakewood, Colorado on November 15, 1984. What happened to the honor code for these attorneys? Why were they so carefree in writing erroneous information in their brief?

Gary Brown, community development director in 1984, testified that as my supervisor from 1972-77 he was not satisfied with my performance and he cited three studies that I had completed as his primary reasons for his dissatisfaction with me, but Brown gave me a very good to superior performance evaluation report citing the same three studies as his reasons for the high ratings. Further, Joe Sauser, who worked in the office with Brown and me testified without any contradiction from Brown that Brown said in his and my presence that I was more qualified to be the evaluation director in 1977 than he and Joines. Brown testified further that I did not apply for any positions within the Community Development Department in 1978 and that he definitely did not consider me for any position within the department. Brown even testified that he had reviewed all of my exhibits before he testified and among them were several documents that clearly showed that I had applied for four positions within the Community Development Department in 1978 and that Brown had in fact interviewed me for several positions but had chosen someone else for three of the positions. Brown continued to perjure himself by testifying that I did not complete my assignments in a timely manner, but he wrote in my evaluation report that I completed all assignments better than planning and budgeting staff personnel. Joe Sauser was a planner and Tom Fredericks was the only budget person. Both of these white employees were promoted to administrative positions.

Why would all of the above supposedly intelligent men and leaders perjury themselves and/or give contradicting testimony in Judge Ward's court room just as Florence Creque said they would? Had they been told by the judge that he was going to dismiss all of my charges regardless of how they testified in his courtroom?

The following signed affidavits refuted the planned lies of the above City leaders, but the affidavits and my witnesses were considered insignificant by Judge Ward:

Rev. James L. Hunt, director of assessment for CEP, wrote: John P. Bond, as the deputy director of ESR, hired his white friend, George Walsh out of Italy as personnel director of ESR and prepared correspondence in an effort to have Mrs. Louise Wilson, director of ESR terminated on the grounds of incompetence. As director of CEP, Bond terminated Mr. Curtis Dixon from his administrative position using cutback in federal funds as his reason. As CAMPS secretary and assistant city manager with the City, Bond as the overseer of all federal programs, recommended that I, James L. Hunt, be terminated from my administrative position with the manpower program and he blackballed me from any future employment for six months. Bond as assistant city manager terminated Clarence Falls from his position as CEP director. Under Bond's administration, Mr. Thomas Smith resigned his administrative position with the City rather than be downgraded to a lesser non-administrative position. The above mentioned black persons were the only black administrators with the local/federal operations throughout the City excluding Mr. Wilson, Model City director and Mrs. Creque, Model City deputy director who did not come under Bond's auspices at the time. Mr. Bond often told me when he was the director of CEP that he did not consider himself 'black'; that he did not associate with 'blacks' either professionally or socially because all of his professional and social friends and associates were 'white'.

Marjorie Gregory, the Human Services director of operations, wrote: His first year with the Model City Program, Dixon designed the first PPBS system that was used within the Model City Department and he instructed the entire staff on *how to complete and analyze information. During his second year, he attended many important meetings and workshops at the regional level as a sit-in for the Model City Director. During the preplanning process for the Planned Variations Program, Mrs. Creque was Deputy Director responsible for all program activity and Mr. Dixon was acting Deputy Director responsible for all budgets and evaluation activities. From 1974-76, Mrs. Florence Creque as Human Services Director called upon Curtis Dixon at my request for his expertise in manpower in order to undo the mismanagement of the previous manpower planning director, Mr. Alexander Beaty. Without any questions, Mr. Dixon completely restructured the department, completing budgets of all activities, developing the department's first information system, developing the department's first organizational structure and office layout.*

Isaac Howard, convention center program coordinator, wrote: Curtis Dixon was an impressive and effective worker and administrator who got the job done accurately and timely. Whenever I needed any assistance or direction on pulling together any of my assignments, I went to Mr. Dixon who provided me with the necessary assistance and /or direction to get the job completed accurately. I never knew Mr. Dixon to deny assistance to anyone who asked him for it and it appeared that everyone on the Model City staff including the director and the deputy director/programs sought him out at one time or another. Shortly after the above, Mr. Howard went from being the most experienced and competent convention center coordinator to being forced out of the City as City Manager Stuart continued to govern the City with his Bible by his side and the elected officials made themselves his disciples by doing absolutely nothing to correct the dishonor that plagued the City.

Mary Freas, human services program coordinator, wrote: During early 1975 through the summer of 1976, upon the recommendation of Mrs. Creque, Mr. Curtis Dixon provided invaluable assistance to me. It was apparent from the outset of my employment that Mr. Dixon was highly regarded by Mrs. Creque and by the senior staff in the Human Services Department. His skills and expertise were sought and used by most of the staff. In the absence of any visible recognition or reward for his support and contribution to the department, Mr. Dixon maintained a positive attitude in working with the human services staff. In 1976, Mrs. Creque became seriously ill and was replaced by Mr. Alexander Beaty. Within weeks after his assignment as acting human services director by the city manager, I became concerned that Mr. Beaty was actively trying to destroy the department. His directives were in conflict with the federal regulations under which we were required to operate and, for the first time, an uncomfortable aura of racism hung over the department. At first, I attributed the changes to Mr. Beaty's inexperience and lack of knowledge about social programs. As time passed, however, his actions became very clear. He was generally cooperative and accommodative towards me and other white employees but rude, sarcastic and antagonistic toward the black employees. In that many of the black employees were senior professional staff and had key roles to play in the success or failure of the manpower programs and were being hindered from doing their jobs satisfactorily, I and several members of the staff filed a grievance against Beaty with City Manager Orville Powell. During the grievance process, Mr. Powell met with me personally and reminded me that I did not want to do anything that would hurt my career with the City. He then asked me to tell him if Curtis Dixon was the organizer and leader of the staff's grievance against Mr. Beaty. Mr. Dixon was not a member of the Human Services Department and to my knowledge he had no involvement with the grievance and I so informed Mr. Powell. Mr. Beaty, on at least one occasion, made a point of negatively criticizing one of Mr. Dixon's CETA Evaluation Reports during a departmental staff meeting. The grievance process which involved City Manager Powell, Deputy City Manager Bond, and Acting Human Services Director Beaty indicated to me and the staff that City management was not *concerned if the manpower program failed or if disallowable costs were incurred. No immediate action was taken to correct the situation or curtail Mr. Beaty's actions. At his own convenience and with no regard for what the staff was going through, the city manager removed Mr. Beaty as acting human services director in April 1977 and publicly commended him for his outstanding performance as acting human services director. By October 1977, Powell promoted Beaty to personnel director and by May 1978 to assistant city manager. The above actions on the part of City Manager Powell confirmed my suspicions that Beaty was acting against the human services staff with Powell's approval and that the entire situation was racially, as well as personally, motivated since over eighty percent of the human services staff was made up of black employees.*

Police Chief Thomas Surratt wrote: When I was Police Chief, Mr. Curtis Dixon assisted my staff setup and monitor the Neighborhood Team Police Districts within the city. The city was chosen one out of six cities in the United States to participate in this concept. Mr. Dixon was sent to California and Colorado to visit two Neighborhood Team Police Cities so that we could get a better feel for what was expected of us. After his trip, Mr. Dixon prepared a detailed report of his visit which really helped the City and the Police Department a great deal. I respected Mr. Dixon because of his competence, his support and his willingness to work cooperatively with me and my staff. I enjoyed my working relationship with Mr. Dixon because he was always very positive and supportive of the Police Department's efforts. It appeared that the policemen that he worked with and around respected him highly. In my estimation he had outstanding management potential.

Fire Chief Lester Ervin wrote: When I was deputy fire chief, Curtis Dixon invited and escorted me and A. B. Bullard, the fire chief at the time, to the City of Greensboro so that we could see the Emergency Medical Services Unit which was a part of the Fire Department. Mr. Dixon completed a comprehensive study of the EMS program within the Fire Department which really addressed and gave alternatives for resolving many of our concerns with the program. Mr. Dixon also briefed me and the fire chief on several fire truck replacement criteria studies that he had completed for the Budget Office. During the time that Mr. Dixon worked on special studies for or within the Fire Department, I was very pleased with his performance, his accomplishments and him as an employee with the City.

Joe Sauser, senior program evaluation analyst/ assistant director of planning for the Community Development Department, wrote: In 1976, at the time Mrs. Florence Creque resigned her position as the City's Human Services director, I was employed as a senior program evaluation analyst in the City's Evaluation Office. In the period following Mrs. Creque's resignation it was my belief that Mr. Curtis Dixon, with whom I worked in the Evaluation Office, was the most qualified candidate within the City for the human services director position, and I so informed him. My opinion was based primarily on the significant management and operational improvements Mr. Dixon has suggested for the Human Services Department that were subsequently implemented. In 1977, Mr. Brown assumed the role of community development director and his former position as evaluation director was vacated. Mr. Allen Joines was appointed, first, acting evaluation director by then Orville Powell. The position was filled without the benefit of an internal promotion announcement. It was my opinion at the time that Mr. Dixon was clearly more qualified, on any number of factors, for the evaluation director role than Mr. Joines. Mr. Brown apparently agreed, for he explicitly stated this to me in Mr. Dixon's presence.

Gay Pollak, president of the Executive Committee and Board of Directors for the newly formed Planned Parenthood for Winston-Salem, wrote: During the first year that the Planned Parenthood Board was established and working hard toward hiring adequate staff, selecting the proper site and

140

raising funds, Mr. Dixon played a significant role on almost all committees. He worked very closely with the fund raising committee and attended special fund raising with businesses at the request of the Chairperson. He was assigned to work with the site/building committee and as president, I sought his comments and recommendations on the selection of a site for the agency. He was appointed to the Personnel Committee and made chairman of the Finance Committee. In essence, Mr. Dixon was highly respected by the Planned Parenthood Board of Directors, its Executive Committee and the newly hired staff because of his ability, his congeniality, his willingness and cooperativeness toward making the agency a success in Winston-Salem. I personally respected Mr. Dixon because he was talented, resourceful and compassionate. He was always positive and very pleasant to work around and with. He was a thinker and he shared his talents freely.

William Clayton, manager of Bluebird Taxicab Company, wrote: I was manager of the Bluebird Taxicab Company, the only taxicab company in the City at large when Mr. Dixon was assigned from the City Manager's Office to help resolve a taxicab rate increase request misunderstanding. Mr. Dixon was truly an effective and efficient mediator in resolving all differences between me and the City of Winston-Salem. It was evident to me that he was a true leader and facilitator who enjoyed harmonious, productive relationships. I remembered commenting to him after he gave a most favorable presentation before the Mayor, the city manager, the aldermen in charge of the Public Safety Committee and myself that he must surely have had expert military training and that he was evidently now being groomed to be an assistant city manager. For Mr. Dixon's efforts, I wrote a letter of commendation on him to his superior, Mr. Bryce A. Stuart. I personally respected Mr. Dixon to the highest because he knew how to work effectively with people and he had the ability to resolve problems satisfactorily and quickly. Even my staff and taxicab drivers who met him respected him. The young man was an asset to the City of Winston-Salem.

James H. Svara, an associate professor and doctor of philosophy in the Political Science Department and director of Public Affairs Graduate Program at the University of North Carolina –Greensboro, wrote: I first met Curtis Dixon in discussions about the evaluation activities of the City of Winston-Salem in the spring of 1978. Originally, I was scheduled to talk with the Director of Evaluation (Allen Joines), but he recommended that I talk with Mr. Dixon about the City's evaluation activities. I was impressed with Mr. Dixon's knowledge of evaluation procedures and practices and further impressed with Mr. Dixon as a professional. I inquired about his educational background and discovered from him that he was attending UNC-Greensboro as a doctoral candidate in education/business administration. I convinced him that my program, masters in public affairs, would be much more beneficial to him in the City work. Mr. Dixon applied and was accepted into the program. He completed the MPA program in three semesters. I had indicated it would be difficult for him to carry a full-time course load while working full-time because of the magnitude of reading and written assignments required. To my surprise considering the circumstances, Mr. Dixon's performance was excellent. Mr. Dixon was instrumental in helping the Public Affairs Masters Program establish extension graduate classes in Winston-Salem, by recruiting seventeen students to participate in the first graduate extension class in Winston-Salem. In 1979, the Director of Budget and Evaluation, Tom Fredericks, met with the Chairman of the Political Science Department, one other professor and myself to discuss the possibility of our department completing a citizens need survey for the City of Winston-Salem. Mr. Dixon was in attendance at that meeting with a prepared agreement which completely outlined the City's requirements and the university's role. His agreement met with our approval and Mr. Fredericks verbally concurred that the agreement would be formalized between the City and the university with Mr. Dixon working closely with our staff in completing the survey. I was pleased with the arrangements and considered Mr. Dixon to be highly qualified to fill the liaison role. Mr. Dixon was transferred from the Budget and Evaluation Office, and no further arrangements were made between the City and the university to conduct the survey. Mr. Dixon was instrumental in assisting the Graduate Program of UNC-Greensboro place its first intern with the City at the Benton Convention Center in 1980. On another occasion, I inquired about the university participating in the City's Economic Development Program activities. I met with Mr. Allen Joines who brought Mr. Dixon along as we discussed the possibilities of the university playing some role in this function. After the meeting which was very positive, all my follow-up discussions were with Mr. Dixon who I assumed was given that responsibility. I was pleased with the helpful assistance Mr. Dixon provided in this endeavor. During the two years that I knew Mr. Dixon as a student and employee with the City of Winston-Salem, I saw him as a positive and dedicated individual who was an asset to the University of North Carolina-Greensboro and the City of Winston-Salem in many ways. He was an excellent student who showed leadership and made contributions that went far beyond those of most students in the program. With respect to the City of Winston-Salem, he was always a positive representative and skillful facilitator of action and intent on promoting the interests of the City. Furthermore, Mr. Dixon's performance and standing as a member of the Piedmont Triad Chapter of the American Society for Public Administration (ASPA) has been outstanding, since it was chartered in 1979. The chapter members consisting of City and county managers, governmental department heads, government professional employees and university professors showed their high estimation of Mr. Dixon by electing him vice president in 1980 and president in 1981.

Evelyn Terry, chairperson for the ABC Board, wrote: After the ABC administrator was transferred to another position, I asked the city manager to permit Mr. Curtis Dixon to act as

ABC administrator until a permanent person could be hired especially since Mr. Dixon held the credentials to perform the ABC administrator's duties and he did not appear to have a meaningful role in City government at the time. The city manager (Bryce A. Stuart) immediately appointed Lewis Cutright as acting ABC administrator because Mr. Cutright would not be a contender for the permanent position. The position was upgraded and given to Mr. Cutright with Mr. Stuart's approval.

Shizuko I. Hom wrote: I went to Mr. Bond who knew Curtis very well and he told me that he knew personally that Curtis Dixon, my husband at the time, had been unfaithful to me. Mr. Bond talked to me about many things that related to Curtis and other women.

When it came time for closing remarks from both attorneys, Judge Hiram Ward quickly suggested that the attorneys prepare a written brief defending their client(s) and he would make his decision after he received the briefs. After Court, my mom said, "Did you take note of who the judge looked at when he made his last few remarks? He looked at me and then at you. He was not about to give his decision with me, an 80 year old mother, sitting there looking him straight in his eyes. I hate to feel this way, but it doesn't matter what your attorneys write, this judge has already made up his mind." Alderman Larry Little came up to me and said, "To spite your evidence and witnesses, Judge Ward will rule against you on every one of your charges. Judge Ward has not ruled in favor of any black person since the 1974 MacLean case. He is a racist. It will take God and some more to make an honorable man out of Judge Ward when it comes to a black over a white." My attorneys, both white, were very optimistic about this approach, because they felt that everything presented in court was in my favor.

My attorneys submitted the following Plaintiff's Closing Legal Defense:

An employer's departure from normal procedures was found by courts to constitute an indication of bias, *Modammed v. Calloway*, 30 FEP 1315 1320 (10th Cir. 1983); *Williams v. Kekalb County* 577 F.2d 24, 255 (5th Cir. 1978).

An employer's failure to post vacancies, particularly when the selecting officials are white, has been repeatedly criticized as a hindrance to equal employment opportunities and as indicative of discrimination. *EEOC v. American National Bank*, 652 F.2d 1176, 1198 (4th Cir. 1981); *Baxter v. Savannah Sugar Refining Co.*, 495 f.2d 437, 411 (5th Cir.1974).

Plaintiff Dixon's prima facie case was established under *McDonnell-Douglas v. Green*, 411 U.S. 792 (1973) and *Texas Department of Community Affairs v. Burdine*, 450 U.S. 248 (1981). Since the defendants (City) did not allow plaintiff an opportunity to even apply for positions, plaintiff need not show that he actually applied for the vacancies which he never knew existed, but need only show that he would have applied if he had been aware of the position vacancies. *Teamsters v. United States*, 431, U.S. 324, 363-67 (1977).

Under *Burdine*, once plaintiff establishes a prima facie case, defendants must then articulate a legitimate, non-discriminatory reason for why they failed to select the plaintiff for the position. If the defendants do not respond to the prima facie case, plaintiff is entitled to prevail as a matter of law. According to the Supreme Court in *Burdine*, establishment of the prima facie case in effect creates a presumption that the employer unlawfully discriminated against the employee. If the trier of fact believes the plaintiff's evidence, and if the employer is silent in the face of the presumption, the court must enter judgment for the plaintiff because no issue of fact remains in the case. *Burdine*, 450 U.S. at 254 (emphasis added). The court went on to characterize the presumption as a "legally mandatory, rebuttable presumption." See *Burdine*, 450 U.S. at 255 n.7.

In Dixon's case, the defendants did not articulate a reason to why they did not follow their own policies with regard to vacancies that Dixon was qualified to fill, or why they did not comply with their affirmative action mandate. Moreover, defendants did not articulate a "reason" for plaintiff's nonselection.

Under Burdine, "the defendants must clearly set forth, through the introduction of admissible evidence, the reasons for the plaintiff's rejection."

Contrary to the policy of the City, positions were not posted or announced in advance to allow plaintiff the opportunity to apply for them, especially those which the plaintiff was most qualified to fill. This method of selecting officials supports the existence of a pattern of exclusion of blacks from upper-level administration. Payne v. Traveno Labs, 28 FEP 1212, 1235 (5th Cir. 1982).

Burdine states that the plaintiff may prevail either directly "by persuading the Court that a discriminatory reason more than likely motivated the employer or indirectly by showing that the employer's proffered explanation is unworthy of credence." That is, plaintiff has demonstrated "that the proffered reason was not the true reason for the employment decision." Burdine, 450 U.S. at 256. Accordingly, plaintiff is entitled to prevail as a matter of law.

"Preselection" has been frequently criticized by courts as depriving minorities of equal opportunity. See William v. Kelalb County, 577 f.2d at 255.

The Supreme Court has described the Burdine formulas as an "inferential" method of proving discrimination from circumstantial evidence. A plaintiff need not submit direct evidence of discriminatory intent. U.S. Postal Service Board of Governors v. Aikens, U.S. , 74 L.Ed 2d 403, 409n. 3 (1983). In Furnco Construction Corp. v. Waters, 438 U.S. 557, 579-

80 (1978), for example, the Supreme Court stated: A prima facie case under McDonnell Douglas raises an inference of discrimination only because we presume these acts, if otherwise unexplained, are more likely than not based on the consideration of impermissible factors. 438 U.S. at 577. Under Furnco and Burdine, Plaintiff is entitled to prevail in the following two circumstances: 1.) if the employer offers no reason for the plaintiff's rejection; or 2.) if the employer offers a reason, and the plaintiff proves that the proffered reason was not the true reason for the adverse decision. If the defendants offer a reason, "the plaintiff must have an adequate opportunity to demonstrate that the proffered reason was not the true reason for the employment decision, but rather a pretext. Aikens, 75 L. Ed 2d at 410 (emphasis added)(quoting Burdine at 450 U.S. at 256).

The U.S. Supreme Court stated, "It would be unwise to presume as a matter of law that human beings of one definable group will not discriminate against other members of their group." Casteneda v. Partida, 430 U.S. 482, 499 (1977).

An employer "can hardly defend itself on the basis of relative qualifications when it never evaluated the qualifications of the minority." EEOC v. Ford Motor Company, 645 F.2d 183 n.3, 25 FEP 774, 778n.3 (4th Cir. 1981).

In Lamphear v Prokop, 703 F.2d 1311, 1314-17 (D.C. Cir. 1983), Judge Wilkey found that the reason actually offered by the employer was pretextual and refused to consider another reason relied upon by the District Court but not offered into evidence by the defendants: Under both McDonnell Douglas and Burdine, an employer is held to the reason it articulates for rejecting an employee. If that reason proves pretextual, a Court is not to substitute an alternative justification of its own accord. The defendant cannot meet its burden (under Burdine) by means of a justification articulated for the first time in the District Court's opinion. 703 F.2d at 1315 n.27, 1317. Also, see

Payne v. McLemore's Wholesale Stores, 654F.2d 1130, 26 FEP 1500 (5ʰ Cir. 1981).

In Harris v. Birmingham Board of Education, 712 F.2d 1377 (11ʰ Cir. 1983), the eleventh circuit criticized a Board of Education's hiring procedure where jobs were not posted nor was any formal notification provided.

Alexander v. Louisiana, 405 U.S. 625, 632 (1972).Averments of good faith in individual selection cannot dispel prima facie cases of systematic discrimination.

The City's attorney submitted the following Defendants' Closing Legal Defense:

The plaintiff must show that the reasons stated by the defendant are a pretext for discrimination. Texas Department of Community Affairs v. Burdine, 450 U.S. 248, 101 S.Ct. 1189, 671.,Ed.2d 207 (1981).Lewis v. Central Piedmont Community College, 689 f.2d 1207, 1209, n 3(4ʰ Cir. 1982), cert. denied, 75 L.Ed.2d 792 (1983).

To the extent that plaintiff may have established a prima facie case with respect to any given position, he has failed to meet his ultimate burden under Burdine. With respect to each position, the employer articulated a legitimate, non-discriminatory reason for plaintiff's not receiving the position at issue. That reason, simply stated, is that the position was awarded to someone else who was better qualified to receive it. Upon this showing, the burden returns to the plaintiff to demonstrate that the reason presented by the employer is a pretext for discriminatory conduct. Burdine, McDonnell Douglas Corp. v. Greene, U.S. 792, 93 S.Ct. 1817, 36L.Ed.2d 668 (1973).

It is not sufficient merely for a plaintiff to persuade the Court that the employer misjudged his qualifications, because an employer is entitled to exercise his or her own judgment in this regard. Burdine, 450 U.S. at 259, 67 L.Ed.2d at 219.

A case which rests merely upon the speculation that discrimination or retaliation may have occurred is insufficient, as a matter of law, to entitle a plaintiff to any relief. EEOC V. Western Electric Co.,713 F.2d 1011, 1015 (4th Cir. 1983); Fink v. Western Electric Co.,703 F.2d 909, 915 (4th Cir. 1983);Lovelace v. Sherwin-Williams Co., 681 F.2d 230, 241-42 (4th Cir. 1982).

Of course, Judge Hiram Ward ruled in the City's favor by dismissing all of my fifteen charges, carefully distorting the facts in my attorney's closing defense while using virtually none of the information included in the City's attorney's closing defense. His findings of fact and conclusions were carbon copies of the false testimonies of the defendants. God himself could not have saved this man. He had pledged his life to dishonor with racism being at the top of his list.

The judge wrote for the evaluation director's position in1972, Bond desired to establish an Evaluation Office which in large part would be concerned with the City's use of federal money. Having worked with Brown as a HUD representative, Bond was familiar with Brown's qualifications and because of that familiarity, not because of race, chose him as the Evaluation Office's first director. The judge entered into the trial transcript that if Bond did not testify in his courtroom Gary Brown's testimony as to how and why he was promoted to evaluation director would be inadmissible. Bond did not testify at my trial, but Judge Ward used Gary Brown's outrageously false testimony anyway. The judge substituted his desires instead of complying with his own ruling.

The judge wrote for the evaluation director's Position in 1977, the most significant shortcoming was that at times his (Dixon's) work was not completed in a timely fashion, knowing full well that Brown had perjured himself when he made the above comment and the evaluation report that Brown had written on Dixon stated that Dixon completed all assignments in a very good to superior manner. In fact, Brown was the most unbelievable witness that the City used and the judge so stated in open court that he would not use any of his testimony unless Bond testified and Bond did not testify. Again, Judge Ward merely substituted his desires instead of using the facts (pretext). Judge Ward found that Powell's failure to comply with the City's written policies was insignificant even though the federal law was very clear that not announcing vacancies in advance supports the inference of a pattern of exclusion of blacks from upper-level administration and that Powell simply chose Joines because he was actually aware of Joines' administrative capabilities. But Powell never testified that Joines was the better candidate. The judge did not consider perjury and conflicting testimonies on the part of Powell, Brown, and Joines as shortcomings. Throughout the trial transcript, these individuals perjured themselves and the judge used their lies as his reasons for ruling in their favor and dismissing my complaints.

The judge wrote that even if Fran Clark was a CETA participant, this did not make her less qualified than Dixon, but because Brown said that she was the better qualified candidate to be the community development and evaluation coordinator. Brown did not say the above. Instead, he perjured himself by testifying that he did not consider me for any positions in his department because I did not apply for any positions within his department. The evidence showed that I had applied for the above position. Again, Judge Ward substituted his desires in order to favor the City and completely overlooked the facts (pretext).

The judge wrote that in April 1980, Stuart considered five or six applicants including plaintiff, for the permanent director position in the Human Services Department. Stuart found Farabee qualified through his background and experience and was particularly impressed with Farabee's performance as acting director. Stuart did not know that Cutright chose an acting director whom he thought would not be interested in the permanent position. The fact that Farabee became interested in the permanent position is not evidence of retaliation, because Stuart's decision was independently made based on Farabee's proven qualifications. The Court finds credible Stuart's testimony that his rejection of plaintiff was not tainted by retaliatory or discriminatory intent. The official trial transcript did not show that Stuart did not know that Cutright chose an acting director whom he thought would not be interested in the permanent position (pretext). Further, Joe Berrier, the immediate supervisor over the Human Services Department, testified that Walter Farabee was less qualified for the directorship of the department than plaintiff Dixon and that Farabee had told him that he was interested in the permanent position. Once again, Judge Ward discarded any facts that supported my complaint and substituted his own desires (pretext).

The judge took this same approach on every position that was not advertised in accordance with written City policies. This judge wrote; "Plaintiff filed his first charge with the Equal Employment Opportunity Commission on July, 1978. He contends that subsequent to that filing, the City retaliated against him in several respects. The court finds no retaliation. With respect to the June 1981 two week sick leave request, the City understandably sought documentation greater than that presented by plaintiff. Plaintiff's Exhibits Nos. 5-9 illustrate that the City merely sought reasonable compliance with its employee sick leave policy, not that plaintiff was being harassed. There is also insufficient evidence to substantiate plaintiff's claim that his frequent office and telephone changes were retaliatory. The renovation of city hall and plaintiff's own job changes resulted in these changes. In early summer of 1980, plaintiff, who was dissatisfied with his workload in the city manager's office, was assigned to work on an energy conservation project. Plaintiff was also dissatisfied with this assignment, feeling that he lacked needed technical expertise. Technical expertise came from an engineer assigned to the project. The City felt that plaintiff was qualified to contribute to the project but unduly delayed it. The claims plaintiff would label as retaliatory were no more than common disagreements and conflicts which arise in the course of employer/employee relationships. Nothing else appearing, the mere fact that they occurred after protected conduct by plaintiff does not make them unlawful. The same may be said of the plaintiff's testimony concerning a denial of two hours leave to attend a professional meeting. Leave was not possible because plaintiff's job required that he attend a budget meeting.

The facts from the trial transcript were as follows: At no time did the plaintiff testify that he was dissatisfied with his workload in the city manager's office or with his assignment on an energy project. Defendant Stuart testified that he assigned plaintiff to Joines in May 1980 because he (Stuart) did not have time to supervise the plaintiff.

Dr. Jim Svara, (white) associate professor at the University of North Carolina, Greensboro, testified that he worked with plaintiff Dixon and defendant Joines on an economic development project in 1980 and that plaintiff was an excellent facilitator for the City –"in fact he took the lead in spearheading the project to my satisfaction", said Dr. Svara.

Plaintiff wrote a memorandum explaining his lack of technical skills to complete energy duties in September 1980 and that technical assistance from an engineer came in March 1981, some six months later. Defendant Stuart testified that he transferred plaintiff under Joines' supervision in May 1980 to coordinate the City's energy program and perform whatever duties Joines assigned plaintiff. Plaintiff and Joines testified that plaintiff from May 1980 – October 1980 worked and completed urgent assignments that required his full attention and that were given to plaintiff by Joines. Such assignments included the City's taxicab problem (May –July 1980); the City's UDAG project (July1980); the EDA grant application (August 1980); and assisting the new economic development coordinator in completing the EDA annual report and in getting settled into her new office (Sep-Oct 1980). After completing all of the above assignments in a timely and satisfactory manner, plaintiff was told by Joines that he could begin on an energy assignment in October 1980 after he returned from an energy conference in Denver, Colorado. Also, the plaintiff testified that the energy conference revealed that engineering was the appropriate profession for the person who should develop and implement an energy program for the City and per his supervisor's instructions, plaintiff submitted plaintiff's exhibit no. 21 to Stuart explaining what he had learned at the conference. Joines was the supervisor. When Stuart disagreed with plaintiff and Joines no longer supported plaintiff as he had behind closed doors, plaintiff did not show any dissatisfaction. In fact, in October 1980, plaintiff drafted a memorandum for the city manager's signature to be sent to the various department directors who were to participate in the energy effort (plaintiff's exhibit no. 22). It took the city manager five days to sign another memo that all but told the department directors that they could assist plaintiff in their spare time and at their leisure.

Both defendants Stuart and Joines testified that plaintiff completed no work on the energy project from May 1980 – May 1981 and plaintiff listed exhibits nos. 23, 24, 25, 26, 27, and 28 that proved their testimonies to be willful, intentional and malicious perjury against the plaintiff. (Why didn't the judge address part or all of the above crucial facts that were brought out at the trial?) Evidence showed that the energy project was duly delayed by Joines and Stuart.

Dan Gilbert, a white engineer with the City, voluntarily testified that he was assigned to assist the plaintiff on the energy project in March 1981, which was ten months after Stuart assigned the technical/engineering assignment to the plaintiff and five months after Joines told the plaintiff to begin work on the energy project. Dan Gilbert further testified that his supervisor, Harold Bolick, a white witness for the defendants whom the defendants disowned in court after writing that Bolick was plaintiff's supervisor (a false statement), told Gilbert not to assist plaintiff with his work on the energy project. Gilbert testified that Bolick hindered the progress on the energy assignment by not providing the necessary instructions to complete an energy audit and it was plaintiff who insisted that Bolick give the instructions. Gilbert testified further that plaintiff did not stop asking Bolick for the instructions until they received them and they completed the energy audits with ease. (Why would a court completely overlook such crucial facts?)

The defendants did not submit into evidence that they sought reasonable compliance with the sick leave policy because there was no such policy written the way that the judge had presented it. The plaintiff presented exhibit no. 11, the City's Personnel Policy and it stated in regard to sick leave: "To be eligible for sick leave with pay, an employee must promptly report to the supervisor and/or department head daily about the employee's condition, and permit and agree to any medical examination which the City may consider necessary. Claiming sick leave under false pretenses shall be cause for disciplinary action." The plaintiff complied with the City's personnel policy by promptly informing his supervisor (Joines) of his illness. Joines, at Stuart's request, sought information from the plaintiff that was not stated in the policy and that was not required of other City employees who were out of work sick. Joines commenced to request unnecessary information from the plaintiff during his critical illness period. After defendant Joines received the first excuse from the plaintiff, he sought another and another until such time that the plaintiff's doctor wrote

Joines and said, "Please be advised that I have never received from any employer, including the City of Winston-Salem, such a ridiculous request as you have made from this patient. Lastly, after reviewing the content of your letter dated June 19, 1981, the question of what the true intent is, is seriously raised." Plaintiff testified that no other employee with the City was ever put through what he was put through and all employees were required to present doctor's excuses upon their return to work from an illness. The defendants did not contradict this testimony at trial. Why would the court consider such action against an employee who could be fired for false pretenses a common disagreement or conflict?

After plaintiff wrote Stuart about promotional opportunities, plaintiff was moved in and out of City Hall about a half-dozen times, while all other employees were moved once or twice at most because of renovations and his telephone number was changed over a half-dozen times while all other employees had no telephone change at all. Even after the renovation was complete for the city manager's complex, everyone who was displaced from that area received permanent offices except the plaintiff. Instead, he was relegated to a vault area about 6'x 6' that was used by several departments for storage. Defendant Stuart testified that the plaintiff might have had more than his share of moves and telephone changes, but the court's findings of fact and discussion did not address any of these crucial issues that incriminated the City.

At no time during the trial was it confirmed that the plaintiff was responsible for his own job changes, as the court wrote. The trial transcript showed the following job changes for the plaintiff and he did not initiate any of them: 1978 merger of the budget and evaluation offices, change for plaintiff was made by Powell; September 1979, transfer, request was made by Cutright; and in May 1980, Stuart requested a job change for the plaintiff after a newspaper reporter questioned Stuart about his not using plaintiff Dixon's talents fairly and effectively.

In regards to the denial of plaintiff to take two hours off of work to attend a professional meeting where he was president, the un-contradicted testimony of the plaintiff was that he was not permitted to attend the meeting because Fredericks said that plaintiff had to present his budgets first at a 9 AM meeting, but in reality the plaintiff was not called on to make his presentation until 3 PM. His professional meeting was from 9 AM to 11 AM, the time that he did nothing in an office meeting. The City's defense in its post trial memo was the plaintiff was permitted to attend the professional meeting after the budget meeting, a false statement that the court did not address anywhere. Further, how could plaintiff go to a 9 AM to 11 AM meeting at 3 PM?

At no point and time did the judge mention the testimonies of plaintiff's psychiatrist and physician who testified about the inhuman manner in which Stuart and his subordinate managers had treated plaintiff for years. Judge Ward had appointed himself the *gatekeeper for injustice and racism,* just as Alderman Little had said he would. Judge Ward completely dismissed his honor code in favor of an injustice that superseded racism. In my opinion, his actions were criminal, as were the many perjuries committed by the defendants. *But with dishonor being everywhere, who cared?*

It would have been virtually impossible for the judge to write the findings of fact and conclusions that were registered with the courts, because most if not all of the comments were not a part of the trial transcript and the briefs. Then the question becomes, who wrote those lies?

When I went to pick up the transcript from my trial, the recorder (a white man) said to me, "I can not believe the decision that was rendered in your case. The defendants in your case were some of the weakest that I have ever recorded for. You will not have to wait for your transcript because I took the liberty of printing it for you the day that I heard that Judge Ward had ruled against you. I knew that you had to appeal his decision."

My trial attorneys did not want to pursue my case any further. I was told something to this effect, "There is nothing more that our firm can do for you." Immediately, I started looking for another attorney. I went to the two young attorneys whom I had given their first summer jobs. I could see the fear on their faces as I talked to them about representing me. They made one comment that ended my conversation with them. It was "We have got to live here and money and power have over shadowed all of your rights." They did recommend one of their classmates named Steve Allen. He lived in Greensboro, North Carolina. I met with Attorney Steve Allen and hired him on the spot. After Allen read my transcript, he said, "I don't understand how any judge could rule against you. I recommend that you appeal the District Court's decision to the Appellate Court and the Supreme Court if necessary."

I appealed Judge Ward's decision to the Fourth Circuit Appellate Court, citing the City's violations of its written policies for any position that it thought that I would apply for and its constant harassment and humiliation tactics against me after I complained that I was being denied any and all chances for advancement.

At the appeal hearing which I attended, the appeal panel of three white judges did not address any of the perjured comments in the defendants' brief that my attorney made them aware of in a reply brief. The Panel did not comment on any of the clearly erroneous findings of fact that my attorney pointed out in the District Court's Judgment and Findings of Fact. However, the Chief Justice stated that it was clear to him that the plaintiff had not been considered for any promotion in violation of the City's personnel policies since 1972 and he asked my attorney what did he consider a fair settlement to the plaintiff for this treatment? Another justice showed concern that the City would *put me in a 6X6 storage/vault for eleven months, knowing that I had filed a race discrimination lawsuit against the City. The City's Attorney Brett (black) spoke for only seven of the thirty minutes allotted him and he gave no defense for any of the City's actions against me. My Attorney Allen spoke for thirty minutes (the time allotted). He pinpointed all of the erroneous and crucial facts about my case that should have rendered a favorable verdict for the plaintiff.*

One month after my hearing and after hearing my attorney tell me that the judges had not even read the briefs in his opinion, an unsigned statement with "UNPUBLISHED" stamped on it stated that the three judges ruled against me without discussing any of my ten claims of race discrimination and retaliation and without discussing any of the erroneous and false comments that were brought out in the hearing. I considered such behavior as highly irregular. Then I setout to review other opinions handed down by the Fourth Circuit Court of Appeals. I found from reviewing twenty cases that an opinion was always written that addressed each of the claims and further the opinions were signed by the Chief Justice.

In reviewing the outcome of one of the cases that was heard by the same appeal panel as mine and on the same day (The United States vs. Rhen Drum), an opinion was written that thoroughly addressed reasons for rejecting each claim presented to the appeal panel and the opinion was signed by the Chief Justice. Also, this case was not stamped "UNPUBLISHED" as my case was and the outcome was released to the newspaper. Why was I denied the same procedure as Rhen Drum and the twenty other cases that I reviewed? Again dishonor was everywhere I turned for justice, but who cared?

Immediately, Attorney Allen appealed the Appellate Court's decision to the Supreme Court. Without addressing any of my many complaints that were supported by facts from the trial transcript and the brief that my attorney had prepared so elegantly, the Supreme Court simply dismissed all of my complaints in one sentence and ruled in favor of the City of Winston-Salem. Did the nine Supreme Court Justices review my complaint? Did some Supreme Court clerical employee dismiss my complaint? Who would ever know the difference, with my complaint not being a high profile case that had had zero media coverage? In fact, the media refused to write anything about my many trials.

Based on the above actions, I felt that our legal system was saying without any reservations, *"Dishonor this man of Honor. Who cares?"*

Knowing that I had lived an honorable life, and that God had given me the strength and ability to earn two masters degrees, survive the Vietnam War as a decorated veteran, raise my daughter as a single parent, plan and implement several multimillion dollar programs, and complete 90 percent of all written evaluations for the City while being harassed and humiliated every day on the job, I had to continue my fight for my honor. My attorney supported my belief in myself and filed my federal complaint in state court. The one major thing that I wanted at my federal trial but was denied, I got in state court. That was a trial by jury. I felt that if twelve jurors ruled against me after hearing my evidence, I would accept that my type of honor was between me and God. My first complaint, which was filed in State Superior Court, was dismissed in favor of the City by a local judge. My attorney appealed this decision, and the North Carolina Appeals Court overturned the dismissal and granted me a trial by jury.

Prior to this trial, my neighbor Walter Marshall, a former NAACP president, a county commissioner and leader in the community, voluntarily came to me and told me that the City leaders had confided in him and told him that they had intentionally and willfully plotted, lied, and did everything unethical to destroy my character, life and standing in this community, knowing that I had been one of the City's most productive and cooperative employees. Further, Walter Marshall told me that the city manager planned to fire me as soon as this trial judge ruled against me. In essence, Marshall was telling me that the City leaders, the City's attorney, and the upcoming judge had already met and decided my fate. Of course, this man refused to testify on my behalf. The first day of the trial, seven minority jurors and five non-minority jurors were selected. Three of the jurors had attended high school with me. Right off, this told me this trial was rigged. That night, I received a call from my friend Bobby, who told me that he had overheard Judge Ross—who was presiding over my trial—tell Judge Sparrow over breakfast at the local Jolly House Restaurant that he was going to use his powers and order a directed verdict in the Dixon vs. City of Winston-Salem case. The second day of my trial, City Manager Stuart and Attorney Toney Brett walked into the courtroom with no files, folders, or paperwork to present their case. The City's defendants sat in the courtroom with smiles on their faces as I relived how inhumanely I had been treated for the past ten years. I cried uncontrollably for the first time. The City's attorney did not contradict anything that I said on his cross-examination. Marshall, my neighbor, was subpoenaed to testify on my behalf, but he refused to repeat any of the information that he had told me or written about me. Marshall said nothing to support my case. He praised the city manager and his staff, and said that he looked forward to working with them in the future. This same black community leader had written a letter to the aldermen in 1986 stating the following: "Curtis represents the best of the black community. He is intelligent and is a fine role model for our youth. However, instead of being rewarded for his achievements, he is being persecuted." *When I pulled out a large picture of my body that was completely covered with sores as a result of the inhumane treatment that I had received, my attorney angrily said, "Put that away. What are you trying to do? Destroy the defendants' careers and standing in this community completely. Put that away."* Then my attorney told the judge that he was through with Marshall and through with

160

presenting my case. Before my attorney could sit down, Judge Ross had the jury leave the courtroom. Then he went in and talked with them for about thirty minutes. When he and the jury returned, Judge Ross ordered a directed verdict in favor of the City of Winston-Salem and its defendants.

One of the jurors stayed around the courthouse so that he could talk to me. He told me that the judge had told them I was just self-centered and a complainer, even after several of the jurors told him they did not get that impression from my testimony and the cross-examination. The juror further said, "We were not about to challenge a judge who had already made up his mind about what he was going to do." My attorney also told me the day before the trial began, that he had been elected a superior court judge for the City of Greensboro, and that he would be assuming that position immediately after my trial. This meant Attorney Allen would not represent me on my appeal of Judge Ross's directed verdict. Also, immediately after my trial, my attorney told me he would be working in the same office as Judge Ross, and that he was not about to present that picture or ask Marshall questions that would possibly destroy the careers of the city manager and the other defendants. I just looked at him and said very sadly, *"Where is the honor in all of this? Does any body care about honor? Why did you take my case if you were not going to present the facts as they were so that justice could prevail? What about my career and the welfare of my loved ones who depend on me? Am I supposed to tell them that you intentionally destroyed my career to save and to join the ranks of dishonorable men?"* Before my attorney could answer, I walked away. I didn't look back as I heard him say, "You just don't understand. I will have to work with this judge. I hope that you can forgive me if I did anything wrong." Before Attorney Allen assumed his judgeship, he sent me an invitation to his inauguration ceremony. He wrote on the invitation that he would understand if I did not attend. He further wrote that he apologized if he had done anything wrong, and he wanted me to know that he planned to become a minister after his four years as a judge, so that he could do God's work honorably. I did not go to the ceremony, and I never heard from Allen again. As late as 2008, I read in the local newspaper that a Judge Ross had been appointed the executive director of the N. C. Judicial-Standards Commission.

I had to hire a fourth attorney to appeal Judge Ross's ruling. I was introduced to a local attorney, who agreed to read my transcript. If he thought it was worth submitting a brief to the State Appellate Court, he would represent me. After he had read only half of the transcript, he agreed to prepare and submit a brief to the State Appellate Court. This young white attorney was very positive, intelligent, and energetic. He felt that I had been unjustly denied all of my rights by our legal system. His complaint echoed the same sentiments, while the City's attorney simply asked for a dismissal of my complaint. That was how confident the City's attorney was that any and all judges would rule in the City's favor against me.

By this time, the bureaucratic system had beaten me down to an all-time low. I did not know day from night, heaven from hell, and I began to doubt if there was a God. I could not even remember my new attorney's name or whether the Appellate Court had reversed Judge Ross's directed verdict. I found myself just existing. My mother brought me back to life with her love and belief in God. She never left my side, and prayed with and for me day and night.

When my attorney and the City's attorney appeared before a new superior court judge, my attorney lost his ability to speak, as he gave more respect to the City's attorney than he did to the judge. Anything and everything the City's attorney suggested, my attorney accepted, to the point that my complaint went away without my understanding what had taken place. I could not believe what I was seeing. It was the truest version of a rich man/poor man scenario. As my attorney and I rode back to his office, I asked him what had just happened. All he could say was, "All my life I have wanted to work for a prestigious law firm like the one that Attorney Brent works for. Did you notice how immaculately he was dressed, and how meticulously he spoke when presenting his defense? It was not what he said, but how he said it." Having lost without presenting the defense that he had prepared was like a win for my attorney, as he praised the City's attorney and his law firm all the way back to his office. I was in shock and could not speak, because I had no one else to turn to except God. When we arrived at my attorney's office, he said he was sorry he had let me down, and that it would be useless to pursue a trial against Attorney Brent's firm, because that firm was one of the wealthiest and most influential law firms south of Washington, DC. Most judges catered to them, regardless of the merits of the cases. The attorney said he could not represent me in court against Brent's firm. Then he said repeatedly, "I am truly sorry, I am truly sorry, Dixon, but I have got to live here and survive here."

The local media never wrote or aired anything about my five trials against the City of Winston-Salem. This was completely the opposite of what the media had done with many other City employees and other individuals. After all, I was a native of this city, a highly decorated Vietnam veteran, and an academic scholar with outstanding contributions to this city. It became perfectly clear to me why the media did not say anything about me or my trials. *Were they going to report to the public that the federal district court judge ruled against me after telling the City's defendants that they should do a better job of preparing and presenting their case; that it was okay for the City's defendants to violate their personnel policies repeatedly; that it was acceptable for the City's witnesses to perjury themselves in his court room; and that it was okay for the City leaders to house Curtis Dixon in unsafe and inhumane environments when he would not accept being denied any promotions and upgrades? Was the media going to follow-up with such news as the Appellate Court and the Supreme Court confirmed the lower court's ruling that such behavior on the part of the City of Winston-Salem toward Curtis Dixon was acceptable?*

I remembered one small article published in *The Chronicle* that criticized my ability to recall the horrible treatment that I had received from so many powerful leaders over the years. The quote was, "Curtis Dixon is full of himself and knows that it is impossible for anyone to remember as much as he has written for that many years." The woman who wrote that sat in on my court session with Judge Ross in State Superior Court, and heard me tell what the City leaders had done to me with sincerity, sorrow, and truthfulness. She further saw how the judge completely overlooked my many truths, which were supported with documentation and completely had the jurors' attention. Then he ruled against me with a directed verdict, which denied me and the jurors the right guaranteed every American by the Constitution of the United States, the right to be judged by your peers. At the end of my trial, this young lady came up to me with a very sad face. As she wiped her eyes, she said, *"Please forgive me for the negative comments that I wrote about you a couple of years ago. I never dreamed that anyone could be treated the way that you have been treated here today and that so many people who have sworn to uphold the laws of this land would violate their sworn oath to help destroy you. If I did not know better, I would think that you were Jesus Christ being crucified all over again by the leaders in this city. I am resigning my job at the newspaper today and I am getting as far away from this city as I can."*

During the nineteen years that I was employed with the City, I must have voluntarily helped hundreds of City employees earn graduate degrees and get promoted; professional educators write research papers that earned them masters and PhD degrees; an alderman earn a post-graduate degree; department directors restructure and improve their departments; committees and boards improve their delivery of services to the public; family members reduce their financial problems by giving or lending them money, and assisting them in any way I could; church members bond together through singing; my fraternity receive favorable recognition throughout the city; and friends find peace and comfort through conversations and visits to my home, for relaxation, fellowship, and feasting. During my many trials, the number of people who supported me with their presence in court or a word of prayer was slim to none. However, after I had been dishonored by our judicial system, I was told that many people whom I had assisted over the years celebrated my loss. Some were my church members, as well as City employees who had encouraged me to fight for my rights.

After the above, I could not sleep day or night. A voice in my head kept telling me to proceed cautiously. I went to see Dr. Selwyn Rose, my psychiatrist, who had testified at my first trial. He also had a degree in law. Dr. Rose was very supportive and comforting, but before my session was over, he hung his head and said, "I have something to tell you that will break your heart. I checked with some of my lawyer brothers in Washington, DC, concerning your case, and the vast amount of evidence that you had against the City. Without my going into detail, they told me to tell you to drop any and all action against the City, because it was a done deal. The City leaders are willing to spend at least one million dollars to suppress your case, and the City's attorney has assured them that you will never win through the court system. Why do you think the local newspaper has never published anything about your case? Why do you think that only judges are deciding your many complaints, instead of permitting a jury to make a decision? You can not beat this bureaucratic system, and I can no longer be involved." A week after my meeting with Dr. Rose, his secretary called me and told me that Dr. Rose had been killed while flying his private plane. He had been visiting his lawyer brothers in Washington, and there were no details as to what had caused his plane to crash.

Prior to meeting with Dr. Rose, I had filed my own wrongful termination and emotional distress lawsuit in State Superior Court. After talking with Dr. Rose and hearing about his quick and sudden death, I planned to drop my lawsuit. When I appeared in the courtroom, it was as if every attorney in the city was there, and they were all looking directly at me. Stuart and Owen were hiding in a glass room directly across from where I was seated. Just before my case was called, my previous attorney came over to me and asked me why was I there. When I told him, he asked me to let him read my complaint. After he read my complaint, he advised me not to drop the complaint, but to ask for a continuance so that I could re-file it later if I wanted to. Further, this attorney said, "You will be going before the most honorable and noblest judge in this county today. He will be fair, and he cannot be bought by this system that you have gotten yourself caught up in."

When my name was called and I appeared before this silver-haired, distinguished-looking judge, it seemed that all of the attorneys in the room stopped what they were doing and stared at me. This giant of a judge, who in my eyes had to be one of God's disciples, did all of the talking. I was so mesmerized by the audience and warmness of the judge that I never got his name. Very calmly and politely, God's Judge whom I named Savior said, *"Don't be nervous and don't concern yourself with your surroundings. Just let me do all of the talking. I have read your complaint and think that it has merit, but I want you to come back to see me at a later date if you think that this is what you really want to do. Having heard and understood what I have just told you, I am granting you a continuance."* I never had to say a word. I left the courtroom realizing that God was protecting me and that everything was going to be just great for me. As I left the courthouse that day, I felt for the first time in years that honor was still alive. The honor and demeanor of that one judge, who had to be one of God's angels, had to be God's way of reassuring me that I was not alone in my struggles for honor and righteousness.

In January 1991, Walter Johnson, my first attorney, called and told me that he wanted to make things right between us. He wanted to review all harassment and discriminatory actions that had been imposed on me during and after I filed my lawsuit against the City of Winston-Salem in the late seventies. To his amazement, there were dozens. Immediately, he told me that he wanted to file a complaint in federal court against the City, citing its latest harassment acts, because Judge Hiram Ward had retired. The sitting chief justice was Sam Ervin (black). Of course, Walter wanted $3000 from me to prepare and file the complaint.

As Walter had done in the past, he did not prepare and submit the complaint by the due date. Expecting this, I had prepared my own complaint. I filed it on the due date, because I could not locate Walter. My complaint was given back to Walter at some point, but he never prepared the correct complaint, and to my knowledge no action was ever taken. At this point, I decided to call it quits and let God be my protector and benefactor. In late 1992, Walter called me again and told me that he still had time to file my complaint and win the case, but it would cost me another $3000. I said, "Thanks, but no thanks. I have decided to let God do my fighting for me. I don't have any more energy or money to put toward this losing cause. Only God can correct this injustice." I hung up. That was the last time I talked to Walter. He had lived up to every dishonorable thing that our friend and fraternity brother, Judge Henry Frye, had said about him. I knew it would only be a matter of time before Walter's downfall. In the late 1990s, I heard a news report on the radio that, *"Walter T. Johnson, Jr., Attorney at law, has been disbarred from practicing law permanently for mal-practice."* All I could think about was my mother's old saying, *"What goes around comes around?"* At that point in time, there was no closure to my legal complaints against the City of Winston-Salem.

Over a twenty-year period, the facts clearly showed that at least twenty-five ministers, four equal employment representatives, one federal district court judge, three appellate court judges, nine supreme court judges, three state superior court judges, six attorneys, two mayors and ten members of the Board of Aldermen, two city managers, and countless management personnel played dishonorable roles to support John Bond's vendetta to destroy my career and my standing in my hometown. It did not matter that I proved to them beyond the shadow of a doubt that no human being should be treated as I had been. Dishonor seemed to take precedence in each of the above individuals, the more I presented indisputable evidence and witnesses that my constitutional rights had been violated many, many times. In essence, the responses of all of these supposedly respectable people clearly echoed the following:

1. Even though I had sufficient evidence to show that my superiors willfully and intentionally set out to destroy me, my own *attorneys* refused to present many facts that they thought would incriminate the defendants, or cause them problems with their careers, even as these people were busy destroying my career, reputation and life with lies

2. Even though I was considered to be the most deserving parent in a custody dispute, the *judge* said that he always gave custody to the mother

3. Even though I did all of the leg work for new positions for my employer, *City Managers* Powell and Stuart said that I had no right to be considered for such positions

4. Even though I performed all duties that I was trained for in an outstanding manner, *City Manager Stuart* said that I had no right to an above average to superior evaluation rating, and that it was perfectly acceptable for me to be assigned duties that I was not trained to

perform and did not apply for, so that I could be evaluated as a substandard to average employee

5. Even though all employees with the City were always housed in safe and conducive working atmospheres, *City Manager Stuart and the judges* concluded that I had no right to expect the same rights as other employees, and that housing me in unsafe working environments did not violate any of my rights

6. Even though I saved the City hundreds of thousands of dollars, and I performed all assigned duties in an impeccable manner, *city managers and judges* concluded that I had no right to expect promotions, because other employees who mismanaged programs and misappropriated hundreds of thousands of dollars were promoted

7. Even though I had been a victim of unjust and inhumane treatment for years, and the *powers-above* could not refute that such treatment was in direct violation of local, state, and federal laws, they simply did not address any violations that took place against me in rendering their decisions.

What would make any young person want to be a scholar, serve admirably in the military, plan and develop programs in the work force that would benefit hundreds of underprivileged citizens if his or her outcome could be like mine was, a citizen denied any rights to the American dream? Why do these dishonorable people go to church? What God do they worship that would sanction what they have done?

John P. Bond almost caused his wife to have a nervous breakdown because he refused to stop his upstairs relationship with a man in their home. He had a liquor bar in his desk drawer at work and drank on the job. He intentionally mismanaged *over $50,000 of federal funds in order to keep his male friend close to him at all times. He rented an apartment separate from his home so that he could entertain the city manager and provide a private place for his personal consultant to live when he visited the city. He initiated this vendetta against me and other black males. And he was advised by the mayor and members of Board of Aldermen to seek employment some place else because of his overt practices.* Where was the "honor" in the City, its elected officials, its city managers and management staff, federal and state equal employment agencies, unemployment agencies, attorneys, and federal and state judges that supported the lead of John P. Bond, in order to shame, disgrace, discredit, and destroy the character, marriage, and career of one honorable employee, all because this employee would not be subservient to Bond and be a black racist? How does one explain why Deputy City Manager Bond's management style was found reprehensible, and immediately rejected in Miami and Washington, DC? Why do you suppose that the career of my friend and classmate, who became a target of Bond's racist movement in Miami, was not tarnished, but enhanced by the leaders of that city?

Where in the Constitution or the Bible does it read: Employees do not have the same rights as their managers? The wrongs of managers against the rights of employees are not admissible at the discretion of the judge? Laws are written to protect the leaders, right or wrong, and persecute the employee, right or wrong?

The mayor, the members of the Board of Aldermen, and most City employees knew me as a single parent and devoted father, the primary caretaker of my senior citizen mother, a scholar, a decorated war veteran, an outstanding contributor to the work force, an active church participant, and an honorable person all around. *Why did these leaders agree to discredit and destroy a man with such character and qualities that are so desperately needed within our society today, tomorrow and* in the future? Could such audacious actions on the part of these leaders be a contributing factor to the "Dead Beat Dad" epidemic throughout America?

According to EEOC v. American National Bank (4th Cir. 1981) and Baxter v. Savannah Sugar Refining Co. (5th Cir.1974) regarding an employer's failure to post vacancies, particularly when the selecting officials are white; according to Payne v. Traveno Labs (5th Cir. 1982) regarding the existence of a pattern of exclusion of blacks from upper-level administration by not posting vacancies; according to the EEOC v. Ford Motor Company (4th Cir. 1981) regarding an employer never having evaluated the qualifications of the minority; according to Lamphear v. Prokop (D.C. Cir. 1983) regarding Judge Wilkey's finding that the reason actually offered by the employer was pretextual and refused to consider another reason relied upon by the District Court but not offered into evidence by the defendants; according to both McDonnell Douglas (1973) and Burdine (1981), Teamsters v. United States (1977) regarding an employer being held to the reason it articulates for rejecting an employee, the reason being proven pretextual, and a Court not being able to substitute an alternative justification of its own accord, the judges at the District Court, Appellate Court, and the Supreme Court levels deviated from all of the above to dismiss my lawsuit against the City of Winston-Salem. Why would these judges violate legal precedents set in motion to deny me the same equal rights given to white citizens? Why would Judge Ward, whom God had blessed with the best of everything, sacrifice God's gifts to him for racist/perverted activities? Is there a place in God's kingdom for persons who intentionally and maliciously cause any honorable person undue harm? Or are all of these persons saying silently, who cares?

I have asked myself over and over again. How was it possible for so many leaders to display such dishonor against one individual? Why did they go to church, read the Bible, sing God's songs, and pray? God knows what is in their hearts.

Now ask yourself. Why was the complaint of a white female against the City of Winston-Salem resolved by EEOC in less than one year to her satisfaction? Why were the complaints of a black male against the City of Winston-Salem placed in EEOC's dead files for a year, not adequately resolved by EEOC after two years, held out of the court system for five years as requested by the person who intentionally violated city, state, and federal policies, and dismissed by at least five different court judges over a ten-year period, based on premeditated lies that were refuted with documented evidence? Does race supersede honor? Does dishonor promote racism? What recourse does an honorable man have when dishonor is everywhere he turns?

My answer to all of the above is: racism is alive and thriving on the dishonor of blacks and whites, who are egotistical, insecure, perverted, shallow, and not at peace with themselves and God. Is there really a legal system in place in Winston-Salem? Or is there just a buddy system? Why was the Bible used in Judge Ward's courtroom? Why would the defendants swear on the Bible, and then perjure themselves, just as Florence Creque had said that they would? Did any of the defendants truly believe in God? Or had they all pledged their lives to hell and damnation? It is written in Matthews 19:24, "It is easier for a camel to go through the eye of a needle than for a rich man to enter the kingdom of God" The riches of the above men came in the form of power, influence, and access to big bucks. And they proved God's word to be true, by using such riches to lie and attempt to destroy my honor. Have they earned the right to go to hell with their eyes wide open?

I have waited for over twenty years for at least one of the above individuals to have a conscious and free his or her soul of the wrong that he or she has caused me. Each one of them must know that there is no place in God's kingdom for them, until they make an appropriate restitution for their cruel and sinful actions. Demons could not care less about their souls or making a wrong right. They live to destroy, and they die in pain and agony. God has blessed Mayor James Allen Joines and he should no longer fear Bryce A. Stuart. Joines once told me that he considered us friends and that he hated to do or say anything that would cause another person any harm or despair, but he did. Will he save his soul and be a man of honor by publicly apologizing to me for the ungodly things that he did to and said about me? Or will he lose his soul to protect a dishonorable man? God has also blessed Orville Powell, and he should no longer have to fear John P. Bond, who died many years ago. Will Powell attempt to save his soul, or will he join his friend and confidant, John P. Bond, wherever he might be? And we all know that there is no hiding from God.

> *"A man without honor is a man*
> *without a conscious and soul."*
>
> —*unknown*

> *"Heaven has a road, but no one travels it;*
> *Hell has a gate but men will dig to get there."*
>
> —*Chinese Proverb*

> *"An honest man's the noblest work of God."*
>
> —*Alexander Pope*

A MOTHER PLEADS IN VAIN

"Now faith is the substance of things hoped for, the evidence of things not seen. For by it the elders obtained a good report. Through faith we understand that the worlds were framed by the word of God, so that things which are seen were not made of things which do appear."

—*Hebrew 11:2-3*

My mother wrote the Mayor and members of the Board of Aldermen the following letter in 1986:

Dear Mayor and Members of the Board of Alderman:

I am seventy-eight years old and the proud mother of five sons. But I am writing you this letter about my youngest son, Curtis E. Dixon, because he is my God-sent child. He has always been there for me, his young daughter, his brothers, his entire family, his job and his co-workers. I personally watched my son Curtis give his time and talents to help Mrs. Creque, Mr. Bond, Mr. Beaty, and Mr. Powell for years. Curtis has devoted his entire life to excellence and helping other people. As I sat through his three day trial in 1984, I was deeply hurt to hear the very people that Curtis had helped lie on him, slander him, plot against him and talk about him as though he was a common criminal.

Documented evidence from the official trial transcript of the Dixon vs. City of Winston-Salem case on Orville W. Powell, Alexander R. Beaty, Bryce A. Stuart, James Allen Joines, Gary R. Brown, and attorneys Roddey Liggon and Toney Brett clearly demonstrated that these individuals willfully, intentionally, and maliciously provided false information about my son and his situation with the City that has destroyed his career needlessly and will eventually destroy him if the truth is not revealed and accepted as the will of God. My son is truly a man of God and he will never give in to corruption and lies.

Is my son a sacrificial lamb for injustice? In your eyesight, is the life and career of a dishonest administrator more valuable than that of an honest employee like my son? Is deceit and underhandedness more important to you than letting righteousness and integrity preserve you? Is power and influence more important to you than peace and tranquility? In your heart and mind, if you can answer the above questions with God as your witness, my son will be vindicated and set free of this fifteen year nightmare that was started by City administrators that many of you elected officials did not think were very honorable people.

I have lived out most of my life and my son, Curtis has lived to be forty-seven years old. But his young daughter, Cheryl, whom Curtis has raised as a single parent because of interferences in his marriage from John P. Bond who started this vendetta against my son many years ago, needs to know why her father has no rights as a City employee and as a deserving American citizen. She needs to know and understand what is possibly in store for her when she grows up, especially if you concur with the actions that have been taken against her father. The sad part of all of this is Mr. Stuart's actions. I remember reading an article in the local newspaper where Mr. Stuart was quoted as saying that he was a man of God who believed in honesty, truth, understanding and that a man should not lie and cheat, but according to his testimony he showed none of those Godly qualities in regards to my son. You know as well as I do that the tone of any organization is set by the top administrator as evidenced in my son's case. It appears that the order was to destroy my son at any cost, even slander and perjury.

I am pleading with you to do the honorable thing in regards to my son. Be truthful and just. Forget about race and do what is right in God's name.

Please advise me separately or as a body so that I can inform all of my senior citizen club members. They assured me that you would be responsible and do the honorable thing. Thanks for your cooperation. And may God bless and keep you.

Respectfully yours,

/s/ (Mrs.) Georgia M. Dixon
2138 Gerald Street
Winston-Salem, N.C. 27101

These elected officials choose to support the dishonor of Bryce A. Stuart, his renegades, and the City's attorneys who made a mockery of the third commandment, "Thou shalt not use the name of the Lord thy God in vain; for the Lord will not hold him guiltless who uses his name in vain." Each of the defendants and the defendants' witness took an oath in God's name to tell the truth and nothing but the truth before testifying in court. Then they intentionally and maliciously perjured themselves about my performance and contributions as an employee with the City of Winston-Salem.

Dr. C. Matthew McMahon, in his article, *"Taking God's Name in Vain",* wrote the following noteworthy comments: 1.)

The third commandment is primary directed against the heart and the tongue. The heart is where a man's actions come forth from. If our heart is irreverent towards God, then we will use his name in vain, or in an ignoble fashion. Remember, the heart controls the tongue. 2.) When we swear by God's name falsely, we use it in vain. 3.) Whenever we make a promise and do not keep it, we are lying as a Christian and making a mockery of God's name. 4.) When we make an oath to God and do not keep it we use his name in vain. 5.) When we set God's name next to any wicked action we use his name in vain. 6.) When we use our tongues in a way that dishonors God's name we use his name in vain.

DISHONOR PERSONIFIED (1970-1989)

"The dishonor that the City's leaders and judges bestowed upon a hometown scholar, decorated veteran, devoted single parent, and outstanding contributor to the City was calculated, indecent, and unconscionable to say the least, but acceptable because where there was no truth, there was no justice. And who cared?"

—C.E.Dixon

Curtis E. Dixon, native of Winston-Salem. Education: BS, MS, MPA. Job positions: director of operations (CEP), director of evaluation (City), acting deputy director of budgeting and planning (City), and senior program evaluation analyst (City). Annual salary range for period: $11,000 to $35,000. Contributions:

1. Designed organizational structure and record keeping system

2. Developed the first city Evaluation Plan in the South-eastern Federal Region

3. Managed budgets for about fifty-five agencies

4. Assisted with the completion of $5.3 million Planned Variation Federal Program proposal

5. Assisted with the preparation of the economic development proposal that established the City's first Economic Development Department

6. Met with federal representatives to discuss strategies for dispersing PV funds

7. Met with community special committee to explain the implications of PV (responsibility of Gary Brown, who requested that I perform his duty)

8. Completed 90 percent of all evaluation studies completed for the City, with at least three analysts being hired in the department under Brown

9. Planned and implemented million dollar CETA manpower program for the City that generated hundreds of jobs for Forsyth County residents (responsibility of Assistant Planning Director of Manpower Hearn, Evaluation Director Brown, previous Manpower Director Beaty, Consultant Tom Riley, and Assistant City Manager Bond, who were all promoted after I completed the above task)

10. Completed housing study that enabled the City to establish its Community Development Department with federal funds (responsibility of Joe Sauser, who was eminently qualified to complete this task, but refused to because of some strange relationship with Brown. Both Brown and Sauser were promoted after I completed this study)

11. Represented the City all over the United States as a management, planning, and evaluation expert

12. Completed fire study that saved the City several hundred thousand dollars

13. Completed special police study that helped improve the city's neighborhood police precincts (Allen Joines was promoted to public safety director after I completed the above two studies)

14. Assisted with the completion of the City's annual budget

15. Developed the City's first Energy Conservation Plan and DRIVEC Program

16. Completed the City's economic development grant application and budget (responsibility of Joines, who was promoted to economic development director immediately after my application and budget were approved)

17. Completed a local taxicab study that defused a problem between the taxicab manager and the City's Public Safety Committee, and received a letter of commendation from the taxicab manager (responsibility of Allen Joines)

18. Performed the duties of an engineer, telecommunications coordinator, and clerk under adverse conditions and without any training and experience, and received two letters of recognition

19. Completed City organizational charts for City Manager Bryce A. Stuart, who criticized the charts after he found out that I prepared them, and then used them.

John P. Bond, native of the Maryland area. Education: BA, MBA. Job positions: ESR deputy director; CEP manpower director; CAMPS coordinator with the mayor; assistant city manager; deputy city manager in Winston-Salem; assistant city manager in Miami, FL; assistant city manager in Washington, DC; county manager in Durham, NC; city manager in Petersburg, Virginia. Annual salary range for period: $13,000 to $90,000+. Contributions:

1. Tried to get ESR Director (black female) fired by saying that she was incompetent

2. Fired the CEP planning director (considered the man too competent)

3. Fired his black friend, whom he had appointed CEP director (said that he was incompetent)

4. Demoted me because I would not agree to help him terminate black male Model City employees

5. Established a new form of racism, where the black man controlled the minds of white men

6. Mismanaged the planned variations $5.3 million federal program to keep one white man happy, and resigned before he was fired

7. Was asked to resign his position after one year in Miami, Florida (claimed that black urban league director was incompetent)

8. Was asked to resign his position after one year in Washington, DC (claimed that the black female city manager was incompetent)

9. Was asked to resign his position in Durham, NC

10. Resigned his position in Petersburg, Virginia.

Orville W. Powell, non-native of Winston-Salem. Education: BA, MPA. Job positions: assistant city manager and city manager (Winston-Salem, NC), city manager and aviation director of Gainesville, FL, city manager of Durham, NC. Annual salary range for period: $14,000 to $90,000+. Contributions:

1. Terminated a black Model City employee (college graduate) on or about 1972 for a minor incident, but recommended a white Model City employee (high school graduate) for a county manager's position, even after this employee missed about fifty days from work in one year without any valid excuses. The white employee got the job

2. Told federal representatives that the City planned to buy guns with a large portion of the planned variations grant

3. Permitted John Bond to mismanage the federal grant that employed predominantly black City employees

4. Intentionally violated City policies in order to promote white administrative assistants under his supervision over black employees with more experience

5. Created major problems with the police and fire departments

6. Hired an employees' reclassification consultant firm that acted unethically in reclassifying only my position

7. Promoted a white employee to public safety director immediately after this employee sold beer illegally, and resigned his city manager position before he was fired

8. Resigned from his position as city manager of Gainesville, FL, and accepted a lesser position as aviation director

9. Hired as city manager of Durham, NC (Powell's reason for applying for the position, as quoted in the local newspaper, was so that he would have the opportunity to get enough years of service in North Carolina to retire).

Gary Brown, non-native of Winston-Salem. Education: BA, MBA. Job positions: enlisted Army personnel, HUD trainee and area representative, evaluation director and community development director for the City, assistant city manager in Lakewood, CO. Annual salary for period: less than $10,000 to $70,000+. Contributions:

1. Visited the City about twice after the Model City staff had completed all of the work to qualify the City for the $5.3 million PV grant

2. Kept Bond happy day and night as I managed all evaluation activities, as I had done before Brown was hired

3. Used my city-wide housing study to prepare and finalize a housing proposal that established the City's Community Development Department

4. Mismanaged the newly formed Community Development Department, but was highly recommended for a promotion in Colorado.

James Allen Joines, non-native of Winston-Salem. Education: BA, MPA. Job positions: graduate student, administrative assistant, assistant to the mayor, assistant to the city manager, evaluation director, public safety director, assistant to city manager, economic development director with the City. Annual salary range for the period: none (student) to $60,000+. Contributions:

1. Assisted with the City's annual budget and odds and ends for Powell

2. Promoted to evaluation director only for pay increase and management title. I was told to continue managing the office as I had done under Brown's supervision

3. Presented on television my fire department study as his own, and Powell rewarded him with the promotion to public safety director the week after Joines was caught selling beer illegally (one of many reasons for Powell's resignation from the City)

4. Presented my completed tasks as his accomplishments at staff meetings, per the request of Stuart

5. Promoted to economic development director by Stuart, after the economic development application and budget I completed was approved)

6. Harassed, degraded, and gave false reports on me to support Stuart's vendetta to destroy my career with the City.

Alexander Beaty, native of Winston-Salem. Education: BA. Job positions: elementary school teacher in or near Tarboro, N.C., personnel specialist and personnel director with ESR, manpower director, personnel supervisor, acting human services director, personnel director, assistant city manager for the City (all promotions were made by Bond and approved by Powell). Annual salary range for the period: less than $8,000 to $70,000+. Contributions:

1. Spied on black City employees and reported negative findings to Bond

2. Mismanaged the manpower program that employed and provided services predominantly to black people

3. Attempted to destroyed the newly formed Human Services Department, which was managed predominantly by black employees, with the approval of Bond and Powell

4. Awarded his last two promotions after the human services staff filed a grievance against him; after an applicant reported him for inappropriate sexual acts; after he made sexual advances to me on an elevator; after he grabbed a fellow employee's penis in the hallway; and after he was seen peeping in the window of a co-worker, whom he had choked in her kitchen.

Thomas Fredericks, non-native of Winston-Salem. Education: BA, MPA. Job positions: graduate student, administrative assistant, budget director, budget and evaluation director with the City. Annual salary range for the period: none (student) to $60,000+. Contributions:

1. Assisted with City's annual budget

2. Responsible for the City's annual budget

3. Harassed and caused his first black budget analyst, who had an MPA from UNC-Chapel Hill, to resign her position with the budget office

4. Received a promotion to budget and evaluation director shortly after he sold beer illegally and got caught

5. Showed unnecessary biases toward black City employees assigned to the Budget and Evaluation Office.

Bryce A. Stuart, non-native of Winston-Salem. Education: BA. Job positions: assistant city manager of Charlotte and city manager of Winston-Salem. Salary: unknown to 90,000+. Contributions:

1. Harassed and degraded me in the presence of his department heads and various City employees for years

2. Relocated my office in a construction area, a vault, and a damp basement, until my health began to fail

3. Assigned me duties outside my training and experience, and made sure that my supervisors gave me low performance ratings

4. Denied me a transfer from a work environment that was seriously affecting my health

5. Terminated my employment with the City for being a man of honor. The truly sad and evil part was, Stuart used God's name to do the devil's work, which within itself is the act of a pervert (someone who obtains pleasure from inflicting pain, and who turns way from what is right and good).

There was absolutely no honor displayed by the leadership of the City of Winston-Salem during the period 1972-1989 in my regard? My resilience and brilliance literally overwhelmed them. To them, they had no other recourse but to unite together dishonorably against me. Dishonor was the order of the day for the leaders of the City of Winston-Salem. I was severely punished for my successes, while others were rewarded for their failures. But who cared, with dishonor being everywhere?

The leaders of the City of Winston-Salem told City employees for over ten years that I was a troublemaker, but they only felt secure in terminating my employment after five judges supported their lies about me. Even at my many trials, the City leaders never mentioned that I was a troublemaker. They simply lied about my performance and accomplishments with the City. I refuted their testimonies with documented evidence, but the judges still sided with the City defendants. Many of these liars went to church most Sundays, knowing that they were living a lie. Why were they going to church? There have got to be some honorable citizens in Winston-Salem, in the state of North Carolina, or in the United States, who would like to know the truth, the whole truth, and nothing but the truth about a city that would spend millions of taxpayers dollars to cover up a wrong, when it was within the power of the City leaders to do the honorable thing. The justice system proved that they did not operate using honor codes and principles. The judges overlooked all of the facts in my case, and accepted lies as their basis for dismissing all of my complaints. *What did John Bond do to the City's white male leaders that made them follow him to hell and back? Why did all of the leaders in the City fear me so much? Why did the leaders in the City use my talents and skills to get the City millions of dollars and to save the City hundreds of thousands of dollars at the same time that I was supposed to be a troublemaker?* Bond completely mismanaged millions of federal dollars that were given to the City, but still the elected officials and the city managers protected his career and destroyed mine with lies. What outstanding contributions did Bond make to the City that made him so valuable? *Were his racist and perverted practices more important to the city manager and the elected officials than the outstanding contributions that I made to the City?* Evidently they were, because only my career was destroyed with lies and deceptions, while Bond's was protected and enhanced by the elected officials. Why would the City leaders prefer to lie about me, instead of promoting me to a management position that I had earned? Why would the black aldermen initially support me, and then suddenly support the lies of Stuart and the other City leaders? Why did judges deviate from the facts to render a decision that would surely destroy my American dream?

What is seriously wrong with the above information about the City's leaders? Could such attributes of these men be a contributing factor as to why Winston-Salem has not been as progressive as Charlotte, Raleigh, Greensboro, and Durham? Which of the above North Carolina cities spent years trying to destroy its most loyal employee, to satisfy and protect a select few of its perverted and non-contributing administrators, as it appears Winston-Salem did? For over fifteen years, where did the City's leaders place their priorities? What valid justifications can any of the elected officials, City leaders, and other prominent leaders of Winston-Salem give to support such archaic behavior at tax-payers' expense? How many thousands and possibly millions of dollars do you think that the City of Winston-Salem mismanaged in order to destroy one employee's honor? How is it possible for the City of Winston-Salem to grow and prosper with the above mentality? How favorably do you think God looked upon Winston-Salem, when it bowed down to lies in support of dishonor? Who can refute that Winston-Salem's lack of progress is not directly linked to its leaders' dishonorable behavior? Dishonor was everywhere, and who cared? Certain dishonorable individuals received titles, monetary rewards, and buildings named after them, but what has the City as a whole gained?

THE LIGHT AT THE END
OF THE TUNNEL

"Do not let kindness and truth leave you; bind them around your neck. Write them on the tablet of your heart. So you will find favor and good repute in the sight of God and man. Trust in the Lord with all your heart and do not lean on your own understanding."

—*Proverbs 3*

The saddest days of my life were when my father told me repeatedly that I was going to be a failure in life, after I had accomplished tasks above and beyond the expected; when my high school principal was determined that I should fail, after I had excelled over everyone in my class; when my first wife disappeared with our daughter for two weeks, and I did not have any idea where they were; when my idol, City Manager Orville Powell, ended up being a wimp and a footstool for Deputy City Manager John Bond; when my relative Alexander Beaty, whom I had welcomed into my home and invited to my fraternity formal engagement, devoted most of his career trying to degrade and destroy everything honorable that I represented; when a black pervert and racist tried to destroy my career in my hometown without any serious concern from black and white leaders; when City Manager Stuart told local newspaper reporters that he was a Christian, and he never demonstrated any such qualities to me; when City employees all around me were promoted for their failures, and I was demoted and humiliated for my successes; when I was betrayed and insulted by the people that I respected and supported the most; when my mother's life was taken from her needlessly during her first visit to the emergency room; when I reached out to help so many people, only to be betrayed and humiliated by most of them without any just cause; when my first attorney, who was my fraternity brother, flimflammed me out of thousands of dollars and then abandoned me; when my best friend at work for over ten years told a state employment representative that he only had a casual acquaintance with me, and that he knew very little about me; when my fraternity brothers did not think enough of me to offer me a word of prayer or encouragement when I was being dishonored by City leaders; when not one elected official within the city was brave and honorable enough to be a warrior for God and proclaim the truth about my situation to the entire community, after asking me to help them write and publish a book about their accomplishments, and after using me to acquire a post-graduate degree; when City Manager Stuart, with support from his managers, set out to denigrate my outstanding performance and contributions to the City with lies; when City Managers Stuart and Powell and their managers lied ridiculously in court about everything that I stood for as a man of honor; when my own attorneys refused to use all of my evidence, which would have shown how corrupt and dishonorable the city managers and their witnesses were; when the City's attorney felt so confident that the City's many wrongs would prevail over my many rights, that he did not contradict any of my evidence and witnesses; when judges across this great nation ruled that the intentional and willful discrimination, retaliations, humiliations, perjury, and violations of local, state, and federal polices and laws were acceptable practices for the City of Winston-Salem. The saddest of the saddest day was when so many people made a mockery of

God's words. *"These six things doth the Lord hate, Yea, seven are an abomination unto him; A proud look, a lying tongue, and hands that shed innocent blood. A heart that deviseth wicked imagination, feet that be swift in running to mischief, a false witness that speaketh lies and he that soweth discord among brethren." Proverbs 6:16-19*

Two weeks after I was wrongfully terminated from my position with the City, one of my honorable friends, Principal Ben Henderson, offered me a job teaching mathematics to middle school students, only four miles from my home. I was not sure that I wanted to teach. Therefore, I told Ben that I would just substitute for a while. As I was substitute teaching that year, I had a chance to really think about a lot of things. I remembered my ninth grade mathematics teacher, Mr. C. I. Sawyer. He was my mentor before I went to college, and he said to me, "Curtis, I went to North Carolina A & T College to become an industrial engineer, but I ended up teaching mathematics. I know that you have talked about majoring in some form of engineering. I strongly recommend that you become certified to teach, just in case things don't work out as an engineer."

I never forgot what Mr. Sawyer told me, and when I graduated from Mr. Sawyer's alma mater, my major was mathematics, and I was certified to teach. With my mind running wild, it suddenly dawned on me that John Bond was Mr. Sawyer's son-in-law. Bond's wife and I had taken Latin together in high school, and Mr. Sawyer's son, Clarence, had been like a little brother to me when he went to NC A & T University. The love/ hate triangle of all of those connections was a bit much for me to digest. To me, only God could have mapped out such a path.

When my brother Lorenza, who was the superintendent of the public schools for Indianapolis, came to visit me in 1990, he asked me if I would come and work for him. I agreed. He promised to send me a contract as soon as he returned to Indiana, but he never did. In fact, when Lorenza came back to Winston-Salem, he refused to visit me. While waiting to hear from Lorenza, I applied for the economic development coordinator's position with Forsyth Technical Community College. This position came under the supervision of Lorenza's brother-in-law, James Rousseau, who was also my fraternity brother. Immediately, I was a primary contender for the position. The three people whom I asked to write character references for me sent me copies of the outstanding comments they had written to ensure that I got the position. Three months later, one of those people asked me how I was enjoying my new position at Forsyth Technical Community College. When I told him that I had not gotten the job, and in fact, I hadn't even had an interview, he said, "That can't be, because my character reference sheet clearly indicated that the job was yours if your references were in order. What is going on? Weren't you communicating with Rousseau? Doesn't he eat dinner almost every Sunday with you at your mother's home?" Of course, James Rousseau and his wife never came back to my mother's home for dinner after the above. My mother's comment was, *"Son, I hate to feel this way, but I do believe that your brother Lorenza had something to do with your not getting that position at the community college."*

During the summer, I decided to give teaching a try, since I had been blackballed from any and all management positions across the state, and even by some of my family members. When I went back to the middle school where I had substituted, I discovered that my friend, Ben, had been transferred. The new principal, Dr. Mike Schrader, welcomed me aboard as a full-time teacher without even interviewing me. His comment was, "Curtis, all of my teachers love you, the parents love you, and Ben gave you raving reviews. Welcome aboard." When I went to the central office for the school system to confirm my employment, the personnel director welcomed me with open arms, and told me that I did not have to go through orientation or take the drug test. Everyone knew I was one of the good guys, who had been persecuted enough.

When Lorenza finally decided to come visit me to see how low I had sunk, he discovered from our mother that I was teaching mathematics at a middle school. Both Lorenza and his wife said in a panic, "That can't be true. You must mean that Curtis is a substitute teacher. No one is going to give him a job." Our mother said, "You will have to talk with Curtis. All I know is what he told me, and that he goes to work every day."

Both Lorenza and his wife were afraid to confront me, so I went to them. I told them that I was a teacher under contract with the school system. I never brought up the promise that Lorenza had made with me. The looks on their faces told me that Lorenza had blocked my getting the economic development coordinator's position, and that he wanted me to fail. I could not understand why. Starting when I was twelve years old, I watched Lorenza's children every week at no charge, until I went off to college. When I started working during the summer months when college was not in session, I bought school clothes for Lorenza's son. When Lorenza went off to graduate school, I sent him spending money every time he requested it, and he never paid me back. When Lorenza finished his doctoral program and moved to Indianapolis, I was the only brother of four to visit him and his family every year. When Lorenza turned fifty, I rounded up my other brothers, my mother, and daughter, and surprised Lorenza by attending his birthday party, five hundred miles from Winston-Salem. Lorenza reciprocated by not inviting me to his party when he was promoted to superintendent, by not inviting me to his induction into the same fraternity that I had joined some twenty years earlier. He did invite his brother-in-law, James Rousseau, who asked him where was I. Lorenza even refused to bring his Indianapolis friends to my home during their first visit to the south, because my house was larger than his. Lorenza insulted my intelligence many, many times, but I kept coming back at my mother's request. Her comment to me was, "Curtis, you are my special child. Please love your brothers and always do the right thing by them. I know that it looks like most of your days are dark, but God will see you through and bless you in the end. Be patient and wait on the Lord." I heard and obeyed my mother, but I did not really understand why I always received negative results for all of my positive inputs and deeds.

The principal at Walkertown Middle School and I were the only people on staff with three or more degrees. During my first year teaching, Dr. Schrader chose me to represent the staff at central office personnel meetings. He appointed me as mediation coordinator working directly with the students, as chairman of the school's disciplinary committee, and as lead teacher for the R.J. Reynolds tutorial program. The white teachers all around me tried to encourage me to apply for a principal's position, so that they could work for me. I had learned, however, that my being aggressive and pursuing any advancement brought out the worst in administrators around me. At this point in my life, I was satisfied with surviving, making peace, maintaining good health, and taking care of my family.

The school system was considering eliminating the curriculum coordinator's position, and requested a representative from each school to defend the position. The curriculum coordinator, Elaine Pegram (white), at Walkertown Middle School requested that I represent our school, and I did. The position was not eliminated, and Ms. Pegram and I became great allies. She was an excellent mathematics teacher and resource person. When she asked to team-teach with me, I welcomed her into my classroom and we had a ball. As with everyone that I touched, Ms. Pegram was promoted to an assistant principal position two years later. The same was true with her predecessor, Ms. Madlock (white). After she stood outside my door for weeks observing me teach, she finally came into my classroom and asked if she could team-teach with me. The next year she was promoted to assistant principal. Debbie Blanton (white), who once taught mathematics at Walkertown Middle School, showed up at my classroom one day and said that she had heard I was doing great things as a mathematics teacher. She added that she wanted to be involved in my classroom activities in some form. I told her to join right in, and she did. The next year, I read she was promoted to principal of another middle school. Doss Poteat (black) was a chemistry teacher at East Forsyth High School, whom I had worked with for several years in the Upward Bound Program at Winston-Salem State University. He was hired as an NSF coordinator with the school system's National Science Foundation Program. In that capacity, Mr. Poteat spent at least two days a month for three years in my classroom, and we even partnered doing a problem-based learning case at a regional NSF conference. Shortly after that, Mr. Poteat was promoted to assistant principal, and later to principal. All of the above individuals were possibly elementary school students when I was a captain in the Air Force, serving our country in Vietnam.

During my second year at Walkertown Middle School, I planned, implemented, and managed a disciplinary/incentive program that eliminated over 90 percent of all discipline problems at the school. The program was so successful, the local Subway Store owner and manager donated one thousand dollars to the school, with the understanding that the money would be used exclusively for the disciplinary program.

At the end of my second year teaching, the entire student body met in the gymnasium to honor the teacher of the year. Instead of the principal asking the teacher of the year to come forward, Dr. Schrader asked the student body, "Who is your Teacher of the Year?" The majority of the student body stood and shouted, "Mr. Dixon, Mr. Dixon." Dr. Schrader could not get them to stop for about five minutes.

The Teacher of the Year was, in fact, Ms. Gwendolyn Johnson, a brilliant young black woman, and a member of the Delta Sigma Theta sorority, the sister sorority to my fraternity, Omega Psi Phi. We became very close friends and colleagues on the job. We shared many educational experiences with each other. She was the only black female teacher who supported me openly. After many stormy and rocky days and nights, her career in education finally soared, and she was eventually promoted to an administrative position at the central office for the school system.

Most of the white female teachers at Walkertown came to me several times to encourage me to complete my master's degree in administration and become a principal. Even the Dean of the Graduate School at North Carolina A & T University called me and told me to complete six semester credits—two classes—and he would award me my master's degree in education administration. But all I could think about was the misery, insults, and hate that came with my excelling. To test the waters, I called the dean of the graduate school at the University of North Carolina in Greensboro, where I had earned a master's degree in public administration and completed thirty-six semester hours toward a doctorate degree in education administration. This dean, who had presented herself to me as my friend and supporter when I was the president of the Triad ASPA Chapter, refused to talk directly to me. She had her secretary call me and tell me that there was nothing she could do for me, other than recommend I retake the classes in order to receive the six year degree or administration certification. The dean's secretary was very apologetic and said, "Mr. Dixon, we process requests identical to yours every day. I do not understand why my boss is denying you your request. She always spoke so favorably about you when you were the president of the Triad ASPA Chapter. Call Dr. Spruill at NC A & T University. He will work with you." I never called Dr. Spruill, because I was convinced by this dean's action that I would be rejected by the school system's administrators, just as I had been rejected by the City's administrators, and especially after Bonnie Welsh became principal at the middle school.

I approached teaching with the same zeal and fervor that I displayed as an employee with the City. I was so consumed with helping and doing the best job possible to benefit others that my first two years I worked from 7 AM to 5 PM every day, without knowing that school was over at 3 PM. After everyone had vacated the building one Friday, except for the housekeeping staff, I was told that quitting time was 3 PM Monday through Thursday, and 2:30 PM on Fridays. Even after I got home at 5:15 each afternoon, I tutored as many as twelve students per week in my home, because I could not say no to the parents of the students. When other teachers and tutorial agencies charged top dollar, I only charged half the going rate. At the end of my second year teaching, my co-workers unanimously elected me Teacher of the Year, even though I was not eligible to be considered until after I had three years of teaching experience. The three-year requirement was waived in my favor. At this point in my life, I had begun to think that there was some peace and happiness on this earth for me at last.

I was working so hard and diligently to make most of my students successful, that I missed out on my principal's indiscretion, which caused him to be transferred from the school. My third year at Walkertown Middle School was the beginning of a life of deceit, betrayal, and insults, such as I had experienced in the City. Dr. Bonnie Welsh replaced Dr. Schrader as principal. She was one of a kind. She was about fifty years old, but she wanted to be younger. She wore young girl clothes, but the wrinkles and cellulite on her arms, knees, and legs gave her away. From the beginning of her reign, she let it be known that she liked the young women teachers, and that she could take or leave the male teachers. I was like a father figure to the young women teachers. Whenever they had a problem, they confided in me. One of their biggest problems was that the principal wanted to hang out with them on weekends and spend nights at their apartments. They did not know how to handle the situation without offending the principal. Most of them ended up transferring to other schools as soon as they could.

Little did I expect that my team teacher, Jim Bott, whom I had worked the closest with, socialized with after work on Fridays, and shared many military experiences with, would betrayed me in the same manner as Bond and Beaty had done. Within two months of Dr. Welsh's arrival at the school, she relieved me of all of my non-teacher duties by labeling all of my programs as unproductive. The staff was shocked, because I was their Teacher of the Year, and I supported and assisted everyone. Even the secretaries and housekeeping staff could be found in my classroom seeking my advice. This principal went so far as to tell two white parents that if they could get five other white parents to complain about me, she would be able to get me fired. Of course, the five parents who were called informed me of the principal's plan. They assured me that they would be witnesses on my behalf, because I had been the best and most effective teacher their children had ever had. When I confronted the principal in front of my team teachers (all white), she became so disoriented that she ran into the boys' bathroom. As my team teachers laughed, I went into the bathroom to inform her that the boys wanted to use it. For at least a year, Dr. Welsh did not show her face on my hall. But she continued her vendetta against me, even after her curriculum coordinator tried to convince her that I was a positive and supportive team player. I took the insults and abuses from Dr. Welsh in stride for about seven years, still maintaining a civil relationship with Bott, whom Dr. Welsh had kicked to the curb after she had been at the school a year.

To set Dr. Welsh straight and put a little fear in her for the many evil things she had done to her devoted staff, I gave her the following letter the afternoon before Thanksgiving Day in 1999, so that she could get indigestion over the holiday. *SUBJECT: Questionable Practices. According to my documentation, you have attempted to discredit my professional standing in too many ways since your arrival at this middle school. As late as August 1998, you had me come to school a day early in an effort to show your assistant principals how you could put me down, knowing full-well that it had not been three months since my mother had passed away. At the meeting, you accused me of many unfavorable practices and you all but promised me that my performance evaluations would definitely change in the future for the worse. You even suggested that I should consider transferring to a high school. When you discovered that your accusations were totally unfounded, your comment to me in the presence of the two assistant principals was: "Let's just say that this meeting never took place and if anyone finds out about it, it will have to come from you, Curtis, because we administrators will never say anything."*

All during the past school year, I was constantly compared with a first year math teacher whom I provided direction and support (what to teach and what not to teach). I was insulted with such things as I should observe and learn from her how she taught her students to use areas of study that I had shared with her. I endured the nonsense, but enough is enough.

When I requested time away from the students so that the new math teacher and I could prepare workable pacing guides for our classes last year, you invited the guidance counselor, who had not taught math in 10 years, to oversee us perform this mediocre task. You further insulted my intelligence by stating that the counselor was an expert in math and would be in charge of the entire session. In an all day session, nothing productive was accomplished and no pacing guides were developed. You challenged anything that I attempted to contribute at the meeting. So I kept my mouth shut and let you four ladies run the show. After the meeting and without my asking, the counselor spent two days apologizing to me and telling me that she only did what you told her to do.

Even though my math students who were the low-level 8th graders showed significant growth on the 1999 Math End-Of-Grade Test, you have yet to say to me, thanks for a job well-done. Instead, you doubted the growth computation when it was prepared and presented by my team teachers in my absence. Also, at no time have you shown me any appreciation for my tutoring my students for 3 quarters without any pay when funds were available and paid to the other math teacher. I did the above out of dedication and genuine concern for the success of my students.

You had the courtesy to meet with a new teacher the day before an irate parent was to meet with us so that she could be prepared. But you told me in a note at 11:00 AM the day of the meeting that I had a 1:00 PM meeting with this same parent. At the meeting, you gave us no support. In fact, you said to my team teacher that she could be sued for what she was doing in the presence of the parent. Things like the above have convinced me that this situation is out of control and should be rectified. We, the two older teachers, found out later from the Director of Special Education that we were doing everything correct for the students, which you still have not acknowledged to us.

I have waited patiently for the past six years for you to be objective and fair with me. For some reason, such action toward me is not in your nature. And of course, you must know that the more damaging things that I have permitted you to inflict on me are not written in this memorandum. Right now, I am very angry with myself for letting you get away with the types of things that you have done to me. In my heart, I just wanted us to work in harmony, not in the fear that so many of the staff personnel voice to me.......I have done everything humanly possible to show you that I am a team player and I am here for the students. I truly feel that there is nothing that I can do to make you accept me as a true professional who does not believe in gossip and who does not participate in it.......I would really like to know what I have done to make you feel so insecure with and threatened by me. I cannot continue to work in this type of unprofessional atmosphere and I see no reason why I should have to transfer to another school for being a dedicated, caring teacher.

I wrote at the bottom of this memorandum that I was sending a copy to Dr. Welsh's boss, the assistant superintendent of middle schools, but I did not send it to him. After receiving my letter, Dr. Welsh did not return to work until a week after Thanksgiving, and she never visited on my hallway for the rest of the school year.

It seemed that everything I did for the students that involved Bott ended up a mess, just as things did with Bond. And the strange thing was that these men looked and acted as if they could have been twins, even though one was black and the other was white. I came up with a plan to raise money, so that each of my team teachers could have a television and VCR in his or her classroom. The school could not afford to buy these types of items. Before I could finish discussing my plan, Bott said that he felt that Carol Beard, a white team teacher, should be responsible for the money we earned. I said that that was just great with me, because that person would have to put up the first $400 to get the project started. When Beard said she did not have the funds, I asked Bott if he wanted to put up the funds for her, since it was his suggestion that she be responsible for all earnings. To finally get the project off the ground, Carol Beard said, "Curtis, you should manage all earnings, if you are willing to put up the $400." I agreed. Then Bott said that the first television should go to Carol. I agreed.

I put up the money for the project, purchased all of the supplies that were sold to the students during my tutoring sessions, and bought the first television at a 40 percent discount. As my team had agreed, the first television was given to Carol Beard. The next day, Beard informed me that Bott had begged her for the television, and she had given it to him. That same day, Bott told me that he did not want to be a part of the project anymore. Then he tried to convince Dr. Welsh that the project should be discontinued, because it was too disruptive. Beard was in shock. She could not believe that Bott could be so selfish, childish, and self-serving. Unknown to Bott and Beard, I had earned enough money to buy two more televisions and two VCRs. Bott was surprised and angry when he saw me hauling the new televisions and VCRs into the school for Carol and me. I said to Bott, "You can't keep a good man down." Dr. Welsh cancelled the project, hoping that I would be disappointed. When she told me, I thanked her by saying, "You must have read my mind. I have wanted to quit this project for the longest time, because it has been running me to death." Disappointed and confused, Dr. Welsh said, "You are not angry that I cancelled the project? What am I missing here? Jim Bott said …" Then I said, "My mother always said that the Lord knows best. And she was right in this situation. Thanks, Dr. Welsh and have a good day." Dr. Welsh left my classroom, shaking her head as if she was most confused.

While I was teaching at Walkertown Middle School, Jim Bott convinced me to become a part of the Center of Excellence for Research, Training and Learning Group (CERTL) with him, because, as he put it, he enjoyed working with me. However, when Bott and I were presenting a problem to a group of teacher trainees, Bott did everything in his power to make me look incompetent. When his tactic backfired because of the students participating in the exercise, the trainees criticized his lack of professionalism when they completed the daily evaluation sheet. Ann Lambros, the director of CERTL, came up to me after the session and said, "Curtis, you are truly a gentleman and scholar. Please come and work for me when you retire from teaching." Dr. Stan Hill, the school system's National Science Foundation (NSF) administrator, also came to me and said that he wanted me on his NSF team while I was still employed with the school system. When I applied at Hill's request, *Jim Bott also applied because I applied.* Bott told me that he really enjoyed working with me, even though he did not think he had a chance at getting one of the four positions. *Jim*

Bott was hired and I was not. My two co-workers in the CERTL office were devastated. I never asked Dr. Hill anything about his betraying me, and his attempts to insult my intelligence in the eyes of the CERTL staff. According to them, he had told them that he wanted me on his team, and they were the people who had encouraged me to apply for one of the positions. I was not upset, because this had been the story of my life. If any person, good or bad, interacted with me for any length of time, that person ended up getting promoted.

Before Jim Bott transferred to another middle school, I told him that I knew he had poisoned Dr. Welsh's impression of me by degrading everything I had done for the school and the students. All Bott could do was put his head down as he stroked his beard. He did say, "I am truly sorry, Curtis. I did tell Dr. Welsh many things about you, but I never thought that she would set out to try to destroy you. I must admit that you were the only teacher who stood toe to toe with her and defended yourself in staff meetings and team meetings, whenever she tried to put you or your team teachers down. I really think she was afraid of you. She did not realize you could have been her greatest ally and resource person, as you had been to Dr. Schrader and this entire staff. I guess that I was just a little jealous of all the attention you seemed to be getting from teachers, parents, and the students, not realizing how hard you worked. It took T. Sledge, the most effective and efficient science teacher in the school system, to point out to me that you had some activity going on with your students every afternoon, when the entire staff was busy getting out of the building."

My team teachers often told me that insecure people had a love/ hate relationship with me, because I was so talented and so willing to share my talents with anyone in need. Examples: When Dr. Welsh could not get any staff member to start a yearbook for the school, she had Assistant Principal Juanita Tatum ask me to do it. I took the job, and I recruited special students and certain staff personnel, who worked cooperatively with me to produce an outstanding yearbook. Of course, Dr. Welsh gave all of the credit to my selected staff and students for an outstanding job, without ever mentioning my name. Joann Vie, one of the teachers who had worked on the yearbook, called me at my home and asked me what was going on. When she had tried to tell Dr. Welsh that I was in charge of the yearbook project, Dr. Welsh completely ignored her comment. Dr. Welsh loved to use my talents, but she hated to give me any credit afterward.

After I put in for a transfer to a high school, Dr. Welsh talked briefly with me and said, "I had no idea that you kept up with everything that I had done over the years." Every day until I left the middle school, teachers would come up to me and tell me that Dr. Welsh really wanted me to stay at her school. They said she was even willing to give me the academically gifted and talented students if I would stay at her middle school. She had suddenly realized that my students' test scores were consistently higher than those in any of the other math classes. When I still refused to stay, she attempted to block my transfer. She called the principal that had hired me and gave him negative information about me. Dan Piggott, the principal of Carver High School, and I had been friends for over twenty years. He told me exactly what Dr. Welsh had said about me. He told her he was going to hire me anyway, because he had known me long before I came to Walkertown Middle School.

Dr. Welsh (white) was so fearful and intimidated by me, she did not give me the traditional exit interview, and she did not insist that I process out of her school in accordance with policy. She did not want to sit down with me one on one and have an adult conversation. After I had left the school, her secretary called me over the summer to inquire about my keys, classroom materials, and such. I told her that everything was in my classroom. Since no one had taken the initiative to communicate with me my last few days at the school, I had just left everything there. The secretary laughed and said, "You just don't have any idea of the fear Dr. Welsh has had of you since she got that letter you wrote her last November."

I continued my teaching career at Carver High School, where I permitted the principal to betray and insult me only one time. When I first arrived at Carver High School, the principal asked me to be a part of his tutorial program, because he was aware of my years of success tutoring in the middle school program. He further told me that he wanted me to be in charge of the program whenever the present lead teacher resigned. The lead teacher resigned the next school year, and Dan Piggott (black) told me that I was the lead teacher in charge of the after-school tutorial program. At the same time, the departing teacher Smith (white) told my assistant (white) that she was making her the lead teacher, and she gave my assistant all of the administrative materials for the program. When I told Mr. Piggott what had happened, he said, "I am the principal of this school, and I am the only person who can assign staff to positions. Curtis, I have given you the assignment as the lead position of the school's tutorial program. I will take care of everything and have the materials that were given to your assistant turned over to you." Mr. Piggott never talked to my assistant, and she assumed the role as lead teacher for the after-school tutorial program. The program died after one year. Other than that incident, I thoroughly enjoyed my teaching experiences in high school.

During my career as a teacher, I also volunteered my services to the Carver Road Church of Christ. My dear friend Marjorie Gregory, who passed away in 2009, and I played major roles in the planning, implementation, recruitment, evaluation, and management of one of the first charter schools in Winston-Salem for this church. We prepared and submitted a grant proposal to the Winston-Salem Foundation for financial assistance, because many of the students recruited for this charter school lived below the poverty level and needed transportation assistance. The foundation awarded the church $10,000. We also assisted with the development of operating and management instructions for the school. We did all of the above at no cost to the church. I evaluated every aspect of the school, which included the administrators, teachers, parents, and students, for the first four years of its operation. The school started with kindergarten and first grade, and added another grade each year. For my outstanding contributions, my services were soon eliminated. The first teacher hired, who subsequently became principal, told the headmaster that she did not think my services were needed anymore. In less than one year, she was removed from that position. By 2009, this charter school had become one of the most successful and progressive charter schools in the state of North Carolina, providing a quality education to students in grades pre-kindergarten to twelve.

I retired from teaching after sixteen years and was hired by Dr. Ann Lambros, Director of CERTL, as a program coordinator with Wake Forest University/Medical Educational Services Center. It was as if I had died and gone to heaven. As a senior citizen, I was now working part-time in a stress-free environment, still doing what I loved most, being productive and helping people: children, educators, and the elderly. To me, Dr. Lambros was the queen of all bosses. She exemplified the highest order of professionalism, honor, and style. Working for such a magnificent person after the riffraff I had been exposed to for years in the City and at Walkertown Middle School made going to work each day such joy. I was only supposed to work twenty hours per week, but I found myself working as many as thirty-six hours many weeks, because I enjoyed everything about my job. After one year, ole dishonor began to infiltrate this paradise.

During the seventeen years that I was being persecuted by City leaders, most of my salary and retirement earnings, which were substantially less than $40,000 per year, went toward legal fees, settlements with my two wives, taking care of my mother and daughter, and maintaining my home, so that my loved ones could continue to feel secure. My joy in life was making sure that my loved ones were prosperous and happy. So when the City leaders, along with the judges and other bureaucratic personnel, set out to destroy me, they were really attempting to destroy my loved ones and everything that God stood for. But by the grace of God, I withstood all of the persecutions and cruelties. I kept myself and my loved ones safe and secure, as I watched my dishonorable oppressors continue to receive yearly salaries that approached and then exceeded $100,000. If any of them contributed anything noteworthy for such exorbitant salaries, other than to aid in my destruction with lies and deceptions, such accomplishments have been well obscured from public view.

The happiest days of my life before, during, and after my many trials and tribulations, were when God made sure that I maintained impeccable physical, mental, and emotional health—most of the time—so that I could stay on the battle field; that I loved and cared for my father unconditionally when he became terminally ill, and I held no malice for the many cruel things he had done to me when I was a child; that I was able to further my education and receive outstanding recognition from several institutions of higher learning, despite the many roadblocks placed in my pathway; that I was able to find suitable employment at all times, and use my leadership skills to keep many of my co-workers and friends employed; that I was able to provide services to many people in need, even though some of my immediate supervisors were working vigorously to discredit me; that I never ceased performing above and beyond the call of duty on any job; that many of my students thanked me in writing after they graduated from college, for being a positive force and role model in their lives; that I was fortunate enough to go before one honorable judge and one honorable magistrate, who were dedicated to justice, equal rights, and fair representation; that I maintained the calm spirit that enabled me to tutor many students after school, ensuring their success in years to come; that my life was enriched with an extremely close bond with my mother, daughter, granddaughters, grandparents, mother-in-law, godmother, godson, brothers, other family members, and friends; that I was recognized as an outstanding father of the century in my hometown by the Alpha Kappa Alpha sorority, for devoting my life and sacrificing my career goals to raise my daughter as a single parent; that I was able to travel all over the country with my loved ones, sharing the beauties of the land and different cultures with them; that I was able to work with many intelligent, talented, and compassionate people; and that I maintained a pleasant sense of humor most days of my life with my friends, associates, and foes. Such grace from God topped all of the dishonors that so many supposedly honorable people put on my shoulders for too many years of my life.

THE C. E. DIXON THEORY

"There is no freedom on earth or in any star for those who deny freedom to others."

—*Elbert Hubbard*

"The way of peace they know not, and there is no judgment in their goings: they have made them crooked paths: whosoever goeth therein shall not know peace."

—*Isaiah 59:8*

To me, Winston-Salem was a city to love and fear at the same time, if you were a man of honor. Having grown up in this city, I remembered it as being very clannish. There were two distinct lines of racial discrimination. The expected one was whites against blacks; the worse one was blacks against blacks. I learned to cope with white racism, because most intelligent white people respected intelligent and talented black people, and would reward such blacks as long as black clan members, who practiced black on black racism, did not object. In 1970, my brother was appointed principal of Cook Elementary School. When members of the black clan reported negative comments to Superintendent Ward (white) about my brother, the superintendent rescinded the promotion without investigating the validity of the comments. My brother left Winston-Salem and became the superintendent of the Indianapolis Public School System.

My unique qualities as a native of Winston-Salem and an employee of the City and the school system were:

1. Everyone that I met, both black and white, considered me to be very intelligent, resourceful, and respectful of other people's rights, except Bryce Stuart, Sam Owen, and Bonnie Welsh

2. Everyone knew that I was devoted and dedicated to my daughter and mother

3. White people on and off the job welcomed me into their world as a friend and professional with class, brilliance, and charisma, except Stuart, Owen, and Welsh

4. Elected officials and City employees at all levels trusted me and confided in me about all aspects of the city

5. Being the first and only evaluation analyst for the City for over seventeen years, made me more knowledgeable about personnel and operations than any City employee, including the city managers and any of their subordinate managers. They all voluntarily shared many of their weaknesses and secrets with me when I talked with them one on one, even Powell, Bond, Joines, Fredericks, Brown, and Beaty. The more Powell, Bond, Beaty, and Stuart told their managers, supervisors, and other employees that I was a troublemaker, the more aldermen, managers, supervisors, and employees apprised me of what was being said about me. My main source of information was Gary Brown, after Bond favored Tom Riley over him

6. I never considered race and power when I was providing a service to the needy, when I was working on a project or job, and when someone needed my assistance. My main objectives were productivity, cohesiveness of an organization, teamwork, and outcomes that benefited the overall mission and its recipients. For some strange reason, white women were my greatest allies and supporters on and off the job, excluding Bonnie Welsh. Most white women that I knew told me that most white men would readily accept me, because they would consider me to be intelligent and resourceful. Black men, on the other hand, would be jealous and envious of my abilities and my self-confidence, and black women did not know how to appreciate my generosity and attentiveness to their expectations and desires. They wanted to own me as one owns a puppy.

I had to be special, as my mother had told me so many times, but I evidently was born at the wrong time. My aunt's white boss, Wilson Dalton, a retired Army colonel and a top executive with R. J. Reynolds Tobacco Company, told me in 1957, when I was seventeen years old, that he had never talked with any black person as intelligent and confident as I was. Then he gave me a job pass that enabled me and anyone I took with me to get a job with R.J. Reynolds Tobacco Company. Of course, I gathered up all of my neighborhood buddies and my brothers, and we all got jobs.

When I was in the Air Force, my first boss (white) told me that I was like the son he'd never had, and he paraded me all over Japan to meet all of his white officer buddies. Before he left Japan, he told me that I would have a promising career in the Air Force or in the civilian world, if I could sidetrack racism. At the first and only formal military banquet I attended, the one Air Force general (white) at the banquet spent most of the evening talking to me. When two white Air Force academy cadets were sent to Japan for a month, my colonel (white) chose me to be their sponsor. Cadet Ron Bracey was from Little Rock, Arkansas, and we became best friends. My picture was posted at all Air Force bases and AFROTC institutions with the caption, Promising Young Officer on the Rise in the United States Air Force (1962-64).

When I was discharged from the Air Force in late 1968, I drove across the United States with my Japanese wife and experienced no problem getting a motel each night. When we finally arrived in Winston-Salem, I could not believe how nice and respectful so many white people had been to my wife and me so shortly after the civil rights movement.

In 1969, I built my dream home in an all-white neighborhood outside the city limits. I was welcomed with open arms. In fact, when I had an open-house celebration for my new home, my old black neighbors and my new white neighbors came bearing gifts. It was a moment to commemorate. For two years after I moved into my new house, my white neighbor, A. E. White, cut my grass every week at no charge, because I had not purchased a lawnmower. Also, whenever I had to be away on business, Mr. White would have his teenage daughter spend the night with my wife until I returned.

In 1970, I was hired as evaluation director by Gus Ulrich, the white Model City deputy director, with the concurrence of the black Model City Director, Jim Wilson. During 1971, City Manager John Gold (white) initiated the racist movement against the black Model City employees, by telling Jim Wilson to terminate his black employees. When Wilson refused, Gold hired John P. Bond (black) as the assistant city manager, because Bond agreed to do what Jim Wilson would not do. John Gold died **unexpectedly** days after he retired in late 1971 or early 1972.

I met John Bond in 1970 when I was hired as director of operations and training for CEP. Immediately, he chose me to be his friend on and off the job. He once told me that he trusted me because we had so much in common. He said that we both were ex-military officers, and that I preferred Asian and white women, and he preferred and trusted white men. Then he said, "Why do you think I brought George (white) here from Italy and always have him by my side day and night?" When I looked at him in shock, he laughed and said, "Let's go to lunch."

When I first moved into the city manager's wing of City Hall in 1972, Bond and I were the only black professionals in that area. The secretaries brought me snacks every day, and spent at least an hour of their day talking with me about my daughter and my experiences in Japan. Even though Bond had hired young white men to supervise the black employees, all of these young white men always insisted that I come along whenever they had to explain anything about the City's federal programs to members of the community. Even Powell talked with me, until Bond turned him against me with his vicious lies about me. When the City was having a problem with its private housing specialist John East (white) in 1972, I was asked to meet with him and resolve the problem. At the end of our meeting, the problem was resolved, and he told my boss that he only wanted to work with me regarding housing matters. In 1977, when the police department was having problems with its neighborhood precinct project, the public safety director (white) insisted that I represent them in California and Colorado to find solutions to their problems. I did so, to everyone's satisfaction.

When I was in graduate school at the University of North Carolina-Greensboro, one of the upper classmen (black) told me that blacks only made Bs in their classes at this predominantly white university, regardless of how hard they worked. Then one of my white professors stated in class that he could be bought for an A grade by any student who would meet him after class at Hamm's Bar and Grill. Out of six black students, I was the only one who showed up at this all-white grill, and we continued our political science conversation over beer and burgers. I earned

213

my A in that class, and all of my other classes except one. Later, the director of the Political Science Graduate Program gave a party for my class, and the professors had a bet that I would be the only black to show up. I was. When I graduated from that university, I had made the best friends and scholars that I had ever known in my life. My closest friend, whom I commuted to class with at least four evening a week, was Lois Moses, a white housewife from Saint Paul, Minnesota. I was never treated like a black man the years I attended UNC-G (1977-79). Everyone treated me like I was an intelligent and honorable man that they enjoyed being around.

The two most memorable occasions in my life were my four years at North Carolina A&T University with my black Omega Psi Phi fraternity brothers, and my years at the University of North Carolina-Greensboro, with my black and white classmates and the young and intellectually stimulating white professors. I often asked myself, "How could there be such great honor among the professional people in Greensboro, and too much dishonor among the professionals in Winston-Salem?

When I was told by Tom Fredericks that it would take six months to complete the annual budgets for certain white department directors in 1978, because they were considered to be difficult to work with, I completed all of my budgets without any problems with any of the directors in less than three months. And of course, Fredericks gave me the most difficult department directors to work with. The rumor throughout City Hall from 1972 until Bryce Stuart showed up was, work with Curtis Dixon or get him to complete one of his magnificent studies for you, and you will surely be promoted. And it came true for every white City employee who came to me for assistance (Gary Brown, Joe Sauser, Allen Joines, Tom Fredericks, George Sweat, Pete Harles). In 1980 the chairperson of the Public Safety Committee of the Board of Aldermen and City Manager Stuart were having problems with the local taxicab company, and they did not know how to resolve the problem amicably. I was told to do what they could not do. After I resolved the problem, the taxicab manager (white) sent a letter of commendation about me to the mayor, the public safety chairperson, and Stuart. When Stuart ordered me to plan and implement a DRIVEC Energy Program in 1981 that required the assistance of Kemp Cummings, the claims and safety officer for the City, the program was extremely successful, even though Kemp (white) did not show up to assist me as promised. The fifteen young white police recruits were very understanding, and helped me do two people's jobs the first day of the training. In 1989 when Dan Gilbert (white) resigned, leaving his engineering duties, the telecommunications coordinator's duties, and my assigned clerical duties for me to complete, I performed these duties so magnificently, two white supervisors wrote letters of recognition to Sam Owen about my services to their offices.

When I walked into the office of Dr. Schrader (white) to apply for a mathematics teacher's position at his school in July 1990, he told me that I was hired without an interview. He simply stated, "All of my teachers gave me raving character references about you. The parents of the students said that you would be an asset to the school. And Mr. Henderson, the past principal, praised you to the highest." Dr. Schrader was so impressed with my abilities during my first year as a teacher, he had me chair at least five major functions at the school. When I went to the central office for the school system, the personnel director (white) greeted me and welcomed me as if we were lifelong friends.

Therefore, my work record clearly demonstrated that I had an excellent and effective working rapport with most white professionals during my entire career. Bryce A. Stuart, Orville Powell, and their subordinate managers were the exceptions, because of lies from John Bond, their demagogue. Even after Bond's racist influence on Orville Powell, Powell still secretly told me that I was one of his best and most productive employees, and that he was going to make things right. Further, I had an outstanding relationship with every white educator I had the pleasure of working with, except Bonnie Welsh. She was cut from the same cloth as John Bond. Her favorite companions on and off the job were the young white female teachers. In the City of Winston-Salem, the unwritten philosophy appeared to be *"if the black administrators and/or the black elected officials did not support a black employee, white administrators would follow the lead of the black administrators and/or black elected officials with no regard for right or wrong, because John Gold had set the pace for racism within City government in 1971. And John Gold was Orville Powell's mentor."* Based on my personal experience, too many black administrators and black elected officials abused their powers and influences in order to be favored by white leaders. For years, both of these parties told me one thing to my face and did the opposite behind my back.

Working with my black people over the years was worse than my worst nightmare. When I was a first lieutenant in the Air Force, the black enlisted men in my unit thought they did not have to salute me because I was black and I looked the same age as they were. When I was hired as an administrator of a predominantly black program, the only problems I had on the job came from the black male employees. When I was hired as an administrator in Winston-Salem, all of my problems originated from the insecurity of black men. Most of them thought that I was favored over them. Many of them thought top management gave me preferential treatment because to them, I was too aggressive, too smart, and resourceful. My relationships with all of my black superiors and co-managers were outstanding on and off the job, but they showed their jealousies and insecurities by giving top white leaders false reports on me. Too many black men at all levels in the workplace spent too much of their time drinking liquor, doing drugs, or being promiscuous, and not enough time being proficient in their jobs. Every black male employee who was hired through the Model City Program for the City between 1970 and 1972 was no longer employed with the City after 1989. If they were not dead, they had been terminated because of some negative input from another black man. John Gold's mission in 1971 was to terminate most, if not all, black Model City employees. John Bond, with support from Alexander Beaty, worked extremely hard to eliminate the black male employees. The above took place because of black on black racism. I learned the hard way from Alexander Beaty, who told me he spied on blacks for Bond, and he would prostitute his own mother if the price was right. His repulsive actions, which contributed nothing to the welfare of the city and its residents, earned him the rank of assistant city manager under Powell's administration.

In the 1970s, the so-called important citizens of Winston-Salem were busy inflicting their racist and clannish practices on its poor local citizens, and outsiders slowly took over the city. Bond was not a native of Winston-Salem, but he had married into an educated family that was highly accepted by the black clan. To me, Bond never exemplified any intelligence or savvy that benefited City government or the residents of Winston-Salem. His specialties were black racism against blacks, and convincing weak, insecure white men that he had what they needed to keep them happy and to keep blacks in line.

After Bond's appointment to assistant city manager in 1972, he immediately put his racist plan in motion. He hired inexperienced white college graduates as supervisors over at least three well-educated black Model City employees. He then hired a white man as evaluation director to replace his previous white companion, who had left town. Bond relieved me of my management positions, because I had refused to supply him with incriminating evidence on the black Model City employees. He hired my distant relative, Alexander Beaty, as manpower director for the City, because Beaty agreed to destroy the career of any black City employee that Bond wanted destroyed. To prove his worth to Bond, Beaty made a fool out of himself at our family church, by trying to make the congregation doubt my credentials when he introduced me. As he tried to make jokes and laugh in the pulpit, he said, "Curtis alleges that he has BS, MS, and MPA degrees. Curtis alleges that he was a captain in the USAF. And Curtis alleges that he received the bronze star for his outstanding service in Vietnam." When I spoke, I changed my speech and talked about insecure, devious, and destructive people like Beaty, and the unnecessary hardships that such people cause to God's children. The congregation gave me a standing ovation. At the end of the service, Beaty left the church in a hurry. Many of the church members said to me, "What was Beaty trying to do? You certainly put him in his place in a godly way. You should have seen him. I thought that he was going to fall out of his seat when you were talking." Before meeting Bond, Beaty was an elementary school teacher, with a BA degree in elementary education. Beaty and Bond had two distinct qualities in common. They both drank excessively, and they both displayed perverted and racist practices.

After the above, Bond told all of the black male Model City employees who were not fortunate enough to be placed under the supervision of young white managers that they had a month to find other employment, and then they would be fired. Bond fired his black friend, my cousin, Clarence Falls, who was the Concentrated Employment Program (CEP) director. Even though Falls committed suicide as a result of Bond's actions, the city's black clan looked the other way, as Toms were trained to do. However, there was a big uproar by many local blacks against Bond. A newsletter was published and circulated calling Bond an Oreo, whose only mission in Winston-Salem was to destroy the careers of black men. According to Florence Creque, who showed me a copy of the newsletter, Bond knew he had turned Clarence and the black publishers of the newsletter against me, but he told her he was going to implicate me as the originator of this disturbance. Bond pacified the black clan by hiring Walter Farabee (black), the nephew of the chancellor of Winston-Salem State University, as economic development director. Farabee was a high school chemistry teacher with absolutely no economic development training or experience. The only reason the City had this new economic development department was because Marjorie Gregory and I had written the proposal for the Model City employee who had been in charge of economic development for two years. He had had to find employment with the Convention Center, and he was forced out of that job under Stuart's administration. Other black male employees found employment with the sanitation division, and several left the City.

John Bond could not hide that he loved the devotion and attention of his white male companion, but he also knew that he needed some protection from members of the Board of Aldermen to maintain such a relationship. He illegally assisted with the campaign of two black aldermen, and they were reelected. Being eternally grateful to Bond, it appeared that these two aldermen supported him through all of his perverted adventures. After Bond's ordeal before the Board of Aldermen, concerning his paying his companion thousands of City dollars, the two black aldermen who supported him were not reelected during the next voting term.

It seemed that black racism and perversion were taking over the City, and everyone seemed to be bowing down to Bond and his personal consultant/companion, Tom Riley, except for City Manager Orville Powell. Powell was not a native of Winston-Salem, but he was well liked by most City employees because of his mild, non-threatening demeanor.

After spending an entire evening talking with Powell at an office picnic in 1972, I convinced myself that he was his own man, intelligent, a man of integrity and fortitude. For several weeks after the picnic, Powell made it his business to talk to me every day, assuring me that I had a promising career with the City. The man became my idol and knight in shining armor. Gary Brown, my new white supervisor, told me later that Bond finally had Orville under his complete control.

At this point, I remembered when Powell was being considered for the city manager's position, and his secretary told me that she was going to resign so that he could get the job. It had been reported to the Board of Aldermen that she was having an affair with Powell. She quit, and Powell was hired as the city manager. When Bond was the CEP Director, his secretary was as beautiful and sexy as Orville's secretary had been, and we became very close friends. Then Bond did something only a pervert would do. He told my wife that I was sexually involved with his secretary, destroying my marriage. To me, a pervert was a man who desired the companionship of another man, even if the arrangement caused problems with their wives; a man who made trouble between another man and his wife, which caused the man to chose his wife over him and leave town; and a man who misused funds from his job in order to keep the companionship of another man; or a man who would continue this relationship with another man after he had been warned about the inappropriateness of such behavior. And John P. Bond was guilty of all of the above.

When Orville Powell gave in to John Bond's nonsense, I knew all hell would break loose throughout the City, and it did. Powell had no idea what he was doing. God only knew what Bond did to Powell to make him become completely subservient to him. From 1972 until 1976, Bond had gotten away with his racist management style, hiring and firing employees in complete violation of City policies. In 1977, Powell decided to follow Bond's lead, promoting his white assistants in the same manner that Bond had done in 1972. Powell's actions clearly indicated to me that Bond was the master and Powell was the follower. Perhaps Powell thought that if Bond did it and got away with it, he could too. At this point, Powell stopped talking to me, dropping his support of me to conform to Bond's hatred of me. When Bond told Powell that I was a troublemaker and didn't deserve any promotions, Powell did not question him. When Powell was invited to a special social function that many City department heads attended, he did not go because Bond was not invited. *What would make a man give up his values and reputation for another man?* Whatever Bond was selling, Powell bought it and loved it. What would make a confident man become subservient to a pervert? Was it racism?

Prior to the above, Bond had convinced several of his white followers that he was not black. He repeatedly told his newly hired Evaluation Director Gary Brown that he was 75 percent white and 25 percent other races, and that he did not like black people. Was Bond a racist? In my opinion, he was. Not only did he say he hated blacks, he went out of his way to destroy the careers and lives of black men, so that all the citizens of Winston-Salem could see and know what he stood for. Bond hired Gary to be his companion, and Brown spent all of his time on and off the job with Bond, just as Bond's previous companion had done. And I took care of evaluation duties, as I had done before Brown's arrival.

Was Bond a pervert? In my opinion, he was, because he crossed the line with his relationships with his white friends. Bond's first companion, George, told me that Bond insisted he live with him, and when they arrived at Bond's home most evenings, Bond would follow him upstairs to his bedroom and stay with him until after midnight. Even after George's wife and children arrived, Bond still wanted to monopolize all of his free time. The situation became so unbearable that George's daughter told him she hated Bond. Even George's wife told him that she could not take the John Bond arrangement anymore. To save his marriage, George left town without a job. Then Bond hired Gary Brown to replace George. This arrangement did not last very long, because Bond hired Tom Riley as his personal consultant, and he no longer needed Brown. Of course, this did not set very well with Brown. There is nothing worse than a scorned woman, except for a scorned man. I don't think Bond ever suspected that Brown was now his enemy.

Brown sometimes came to the evaluation office and told Joe Sauser and me about Bond and Riley. Brown told us that Bond drove Tom to his motel every night that Tom was in town, and stayed with him until as late as 5 most mornings. Then Brown told us that Bond was misappropriating thousands of dollars from City funds, giving most of the money to Tom Riley. The last time that Brown talked to Joe and me, he was very angry. He said, "Bond has used me for the last time. Last night in Tom's motel room, Bond had me explain to Tom everything that was needed for a special program, so that Tom could present my work. I am going to expose him." Joe and I just listened. When Brown left, Joe said, "Curt, what goes around eventually comes around. Gary should know how you feel now. I know what Gary plans to do. He is going to give information to our friend Mark, who works for the local newspaper."

Less than a week later, a newspaper reporter came to visit Joe and told him in my presence that he had received all the necessary information to expose Bond and Riley. After this reporter's article was published, Bond had no defense for any of his actions. When he was questioned by the Board of Aldermen, he said something to this effect: "You all cannot begin to understand how invaluable Mr. Riley has been to me. I cannot put into words the services that he has provided me any time of the day and night. This man is worth twice what I paid him." For a good minute, there was not a sound in the board chambers from anyone, because we all had our mouths hanging wide open. Then one of the aldermen said, *"Get this man out of here and never bring him before this board again."* Of course, I was glad I was there personally to see this evil man fall as a result of his racist and perverted actions. But Tom Riley was not there, and has not been seen in Winston-Salem since that day. If Tom Riley were a man of honor, he would have come forward and defended Bond. If he was truly dishonorable, he would have run and hid, just as did.

Even after Bond had to resign, he continued to trust Brown and hate me. Bond had to be an awful ignorant man if he could not figure out who had access to the personal things that he did privately with and for Tom Riley. At that time, only three white men had access to everything Bond did, and I was definitely not one of them. Of course, I was told that Bond convinced Powell that I gave the local newspaper the information about him and Tom. I was the innocent bystander who was always accused of everything that went wrong under Powell's and Bond's administration, and local leaders apparently believed the nonsense.

Bond also had to resign his management positions in Miami, Washington, DC, Durham County, NC, and Petersburg, VA. I was told that his management style was rejected immediately by the leaders in the first two cities. One should ask, "What did this one black man hold over the heads of the white leaders employed with the City of Winston-Salem and the black clan of Winston-Salem that would make them accept his illicit actions for almost a decade? Why did the leaders of these other cities and counties reject Bond's management style before he could contaminate their system and send him packing?"

If an honorable judge was presented with all of the facts contained in this book, he or she would have used the proven laws to the fullest. The U.S. Supreme Court stated, "It would be unwise to presume as a matter of law that human beings of one definable group will not discriminate against other members of their group." *Casteneda v. Partida*, 430 U.S. 482, 499 (1977). But Judge Ward completely deviated from accepted case laws that supported my complaints. He knew from the evidence presented in his courtroom and from Bond's absence during the trial, that John Bond was the originator and instigator of the racist acts against me. Despite the evidence, Judge Ward followed John Bond's lead, even though Bond did not testify in his courtroom.

Long before 1980, the mayor and the Board of Aldermen knew that Powell and Bond had set the tone for destruction and confusion throughout the City, and I was one of their victims. Did these elected officials exercise their powers to correct this wrong and do the right thing by me? The answer is no. When many people outside of Winston-Salem asked me why, I gave the following answers: For some ungodly reason, they chose to maintain the dishonor of Powell and Bond, because those two individuals were their chosen top managers. I was just an honorable employee and native of Winston-Salem, who simply wanted the best for Winston-Salem and its citizens. Therefore, the mayor and the Board of Aldermen were not about to rock the boat in an attempt to change the racist and black clan philosophy of Winston-Salem to save my career.

The following uncontested quote from my book, *Evil for Good in Winston-Salem*, summed up what was happening in my hometown, with the cover-up of too many supposedly honorable people.

September 1979, as I was walking downtown, a young man walked up to me and said, "You haven't figured out yet why you haven't been promoted or treated fairly by your superiors in the City?" I didn't say anything. Then he said, "Do you participate in orgies? Do you like groupies? Do you go in for big time liquor drinking? Do you like games of all types?" I shook my head to all of his questions, without speaking or slowing down my pace. Then he said, "Curtis, you have given yourself the answers to your problem with the City's top managers. You are not a team player. Your bosses are more corrupt than you could ever imagine. I wish you luck." Then the following questions came into my mind: "Why did John P. Bond put his career on the line for a man whom I introduced to him in 1972? Why did Orville W. Powell put his career on the line for a young man that he had hired in 1971?"

When I returned to my office in City Hall, one of the secretaries in the City attorney's office (Sarah Puryear, whose career soared after the following) cornered me and said, *"Do you know that the City Attorneys, Ron Seeber and Roddey Ligon, are going to hold your case out of court for five years? I heard Orville Powell ask them not to try or settle your lawsuit until five years from now. Curtis, they know that they have done you wrong. I wish that you could have heard them talking about you – all nice things."* I thanked the young lady and walked away with tears in my eyes.

That alone should have told me that I never stood a chance for any form of justice through the courts in Winston-Salem, especially when the five-year deal came true. It appeared as though Judge Ward was working with the City and not for justice. Otherwise, how would the City leaders know in advance things that only the judge would have known?

Knowing all of the above, and that Winston-Salem had been labeled clannish by many outsiders, the mayor and the Board of Aldermen—which consisted of four white aldermen and four black aldermen—hired Bryce A. Stuart in 1980 as the city manager. At least three of the aldermen complained to me that he was the least qualified of the six finalists, but they never publicly challenged any of his evil practices against me. The cruelest difference between Stuart and Powell was that Stuart stated publicly that he would govern the City with the Bible by his side, and he quoted scripture about honesty, truthfulness, fairness, and doing the right thing. Then he openly surpassed any act that Powell and Bond ever attempted against me, so that the mayor, the Board of Aldermen, and all City employees could witness. The mayor and the Board could have permitted Acting City Manager Lewis Cutright to promote me before Stuart was hired, and the local black clan would have supported me because they knew the truth. Instead, both of these groups stood quietly by and let Stuart harass, humiliate, and almost destroy my career and health. I can truthfully say, "If I had not seen Bryce Stuart face to face, I would have sworn that he was a black racist hired to finish what John Bond started, destroying my career with lies. He could not be a white man like Cutright or Powell, because Acting City Manager Lewis Cutright and former City Manager Orville Powell never lied about my talents, performance, and contributions to the City, as Stuart did. Powell used my talents and accomplishments to promote his white cronies. Stuart used the same white cronies to lie about my performance. Hell will not be hot enough for this evil man."

Then it was as if I never existed in Winston-Salem. The local newspaper did not write anything about my case. The local television stations did not air anything. Of the dozens of citizens that I had helped get jobs and promotions with the City, not one of them called me and said anything. My two loyal black friends, Jerry Clark and Marjorie Gregory, and many white friends stood by me until the end. Only white professors and leaders who lived outside of Winston-Salem called me and said, "What is going on in Winston-Salem? Are the people over there living in the Dark Ages? Why would they cover up such a simple wrong instead of correcting it? Do they think that they can keep the world from knowing how backward that city is by keeping the real story out of the media? Are they determined to preserve the city's clannish philosophy at any and all cost?"

Dishonor just might be everywhere, but my hometown, Winston-Salem, topped any and every city that I visited in the United States, in my opinion. Who would ever believe that one man, who was an outsider, could destroy an honorable man's career without any resistance from citizens of the entire city, and especially black citizens? Who would ever believe that the honor of one black man, who was a proven scholar and outstanding contributor to the success of Winston-Salem, could bring out the worst in so many of society's most influential and powerful white and black leaders? I was the only boy in my high school class who was inducted into the national honor society, ranked in the top one percent of my class, and voted the male student most likely to succeed, but I was denied access to my American dream in Winston-Salem. Every one of the girls who was inducted into the national honor society with me achieved her American dream in cities other than Winston-Salem. Even the black males who were ranked academically within the top ten percent of my graduating class, achieved their American dream in cities outside of Winston-Salem. I was the only one of my college classmates to pursue a career in Winston-Salem. Everyone else became hospital administrators, principals, engineers, and social service directors in other cities and states. How can this city ever grow to be a successful metropolitan city with a clannish philosophy that promotes such dishonor? What future would the next generations of blacks and whites have in this city if dishonor remains the order of each day, as it was from 1970 through 1989?

Since 1989, Winston-Salem has continued to move away from being as progressive as other cities in North Carolina. It has gone from being the second largest city in North Carolina to the fifth, with no airport or train station. If I could plan, implement, and evaluate many city programs, that resulted in the City both receiving millions of dollars and saving hundreds of thousands of dollars, and created hundreds of jobs for its residents, and if I could maintain the respect and confidence of city managers, county managers, college professors, and other professionals as the vice president and president of the Piedmont Triad Chapter of the American Society for Public Administration for two full years, while I was under constant duress in the 1970s and 1980s, just imagine what contributions God would have enabled me to made toward the growth and prosperity of Winston-Salem, if the City leaders had set aside their dishonor. We will never know, because dishonor was everywhere and nobody cared.

In 1990, I was invited to talk to a class of high school seniors about my experiences with the City. Most of the students were white. The more that I talked about the contents of my book, *"Evil for Good in Winston-Salem"*, which many of them had read as a project for their class, the angrier the students became. Their solution to my problems with the leaders of the City was to off them while they were sleeping, or when they were having one of their group gathering. When I said that was not the right way to resolve a dispute, several of them said, "You tried going through the courts. What did that get you?" I did not know what to say after that comment. I was saved by the bell ringing, ending the class.

I sincerely believe that there is no city in the United States like Winston-Salem. If God does not step in and demand some honor, Winston-Salem will probably be regarded as a town off the beaten path of success by 2020.

THE PRICE PEOPLE PAY FOR SUCCESS

"It is best to live with honor for just a day than with dishonor for many decades; better a short lived celestial swan than a century lived crow."

—Sri Sathya Sai Baba

"No weapon that is formed against thee shall prosper and every tongue that shall rise against thee in judgment thou shall condemn. This is the heritage of the servants of the LORD, and their righteousness is of me, saith the LORD."

—Isaiah 54:17

After living the honorable life that I did, I firmly believed that God used me to show the world how unethical and self-serving many people are, even after they have been blessed with many worldly advantages. Most of these people were churchgoers who tithed, and even sat on boards and committees that supported justice for all. An old saying that our parents have told us and we have told our children, and I even told my students for sixteen years to always remember is: *What goes around comes around many times two-fold.* Therefore, anyone who thinks that he or she can escape the wrath of God is sadly mistaken.

Each and every one of us will have a day with destiny two-fold, for everything that each one of us has imposed selfishly on an innocent person. Fancy words and trickery might work with man, but not with God. He is the master of this universe. Are you prepared for the consequences of your actions?

My high school principal, who denied me every opportunity and advantage to succeed after high school, *committed suicide one year* after I graduated. It was rumored that he was caught embezzling school funds.

My high school math teacher, who was also the assistant principal, really disappointed me. When I requested that he give me a character reference for a job, he wrote that I was one of his average math students. He knew I admired his mathematical abilities, and that I excelled over every student he taught during my four years in high school. My mathematical giant showed me that he did not wish me well. I was told that he spent many years alone in his basement drinking liquor until he died.

My cousin Clarence Falls, who decided to forsake me and unite with Bond, *committed suicide* after Bond caused him to be terminated from his position as CEP director. He was less than forty years old.

My best friend on my first job as a civilian worker, Winfred Turner, whom I grew up with, gave false and damaging reports to Bond about me, to keep me from advancing in the City. When Winfred developed heart disease, he came to me and apologized for the cruel and false reports that he had given on me. However, he continued his vendetta against me behind my back. As fate would have it, *he died unexpectedly while babysitting his two young sons.* He was less than forty years old.

Florence Creque, who had a fear of Bond and had both an envy and appreciation of my talents, was *a contributor* to my demise. She did show some heart and courage when she testified favorably at my trial, and she alerted me that Stuart and the City's attorneys had coached their witnesses and defendants to lie about my performance. Florence died a horrible and embarrassing death from cancer, with the rumor flowing throughout the city that *she also had AIDS*. She was less than fifty years old.

John Bond, who was *the originator, creator, instigator, and number one perpetuator* of the destruction of my career, was diagnosed with terminal cancer shortly after Judge Ward ruled against me. It was reported to me that Bond *suffered miserably for years before dying a very sad and pathetic death*. None of his cronies whom he had provided jobs made any comments about their great giant in the local media after he died.

Judge Hiram Ward, who gave me the impression that he hated me the first day he saw me, ruled that City administrators, who had perjured themselves, intentionally violated written personnel policies, and humiliated and demoralized me, had used acceptable practices in his courtroom. After he came out of retirement some ten years later to dismiss a complaint that was submitted on my behalf, he died *unexpectedly*. In my opinion, this person went to hell screaming and crying with his eyes wide open, for the intentional wrongs that he imposed on innocent people; or he went to heaven peacefully with a smile on his face for the many honorable deeds that he contributed to the innocent.

The CEO of one of the largest industries in this city refused to stop the dishonor that was being brought against my closest friend and one of his faithful church members, when she came to him for his assistance. He acknowledged to her that she had done absolutely nothing wrong to deserve the cruel treatment she was receiving, but he did not want to rock the good ole boy boat in support of her. Shortly after he turned his back on this person, he went on a camping trip in the mountains, miles from civilization. There he had *a massive heart attack and died* before he could be brought back to civilization. He was less than fifty years old.

William Hill, personnel director for the City, told Sam Owen to document me and fire me. He proudly delivered Stuart's termination letter to my home as a good Tom always does. Before he could retire and rejoice for his betrayal of a black man he did not even know, he died of cancer.

Tom Fredericks received a substantial increase in pay because I was assigned to his office. He showed his gratitude to top management by trying to humiliate and degrade me at every opportunity. I was told that Fredericks had a heart attack shortly after he retired from the City.

The irony of all of my experiences came under the administration of City Manager Bryce Stuart, whom I considered to be completely amoral. Stuart was the only dishonorable person who came to the city boasting that *he was a man of God,* even as he openly surpassed any evil and corrupt thing that Bond had ever thought of doing to me. I can remember the scene as if it was yesterday. One alderman refused to run for his position on the board again, saying, "Enough is enough of this nonsense. I no longer want to be a part of this circus." Mayor Martha Wood and all but two of the remaining aldermen met and talked with me. Each of them told me that they knew I had not done anything wrong, and they knew many unethical practices had taken place throughout the City. They further assured me that I would soon be vindicated. However, these elected officials never made any attempt to end the trial proceedings. They had to know the trial was rigged against me. If they were truly honorable people, they would have put an end to the charade. Following my last trial in state court against the City, Stuart terminated my employment with the City, citing false allegations that did not nearly match the mismanagement practices of the previous city manager, deputy city manager, and the community development director, that had cost the City thousands of dollars. The Board of Aldermen made special provisions for them to acquire comparable employment with other cities, by giving each of them outstanding references. At no time did the Board of Aldermen consider terminating these dishonorable men for violating City policies. Further, Stuart was given the maximum salary increases each year until he retired. For his sinful contributions, which evidently met with the approval of the mayor and Board of Aldermen, a city building was named after him. In my mind and soul, the desires of the mayor and the Board of Aldermen had to have been to make me, Curtis Dixon, disappear from being an employee with the City. God must have a very special homecoming for Stuart and his supporters. Shortly after he was hired as the city manager, he had surgery on his hemorrhoids, and the police chief at the time stated that Stuart was now a perfect asshole, which he was toward me for nine years. Around the time he retired, I was told that he had heart surgery. Is this man following in John Bond's footsteps right up until the end? *"....In judgment thou shall condemn."*

Many dishonorable men and women seem to escape the wrath for their unrighteousness for a little while, but only they know that it's just a matter of time. Dishonor among a few powerful men has caused pain and hardships to thousands upon thousands of children, mothers and fathers, and innocent people in general. I know that God, who has shielded me from all harm and destruction, will never accept an intentional wrong as right, or bless the guilty for punishing the innocent, or sanction a money receiver over a cheerful giver. Such dishonorable people will meet with destiny sooner than they expect. And I am quite sure that they are not looking forward to going where dishonor is written on the gate entrance. My mother had a favorite saying for many sinners who went to church regularly. It was, *"A sinner (dishonorable person) does not have to go to church or tithe at all in order to go to hell, because there is no charge and no pretending necessary. The gates to hell are always open."*

SUCCESS FOR A LITTLE WHILE

"The battle is not always won by the swift, but by those who can endureth forever. It could be God's test of man's belief, strength, endurance, and righteousness. How many people have walked in an honorable man's shoes or better still how many young students, entry level professionals, and young leaders in the work force will take the high road to please God for eternity or the low road to please a dishonorable man in order to be successful for a little while."

—*C .E .Dixon*

After about thirty years in the workforce with no appreciable advancements commensurate with my education and accomplishments, I held steadfast to my beliefs in integrity, a sense of humor that could lighten up any room, a desire to stay physically and mentally fit, an insatiable concern for eating the right foods, a willingness to help young folks develop workable goals and careers, and my belief that God was the center of my universe, directing my every path. I knew that I was protected by God and that my life's course had to be directed by God, using me to prove that the beliefs and practices of too many men are in direct contradiction with the Bible. How many of my oppressors will be able to stand before God when the time comes and say, *"God, I am worthy of your praise. I have atoned for my many sins. I have personally asked everyone that I have falsely caused undue harm to forgive me."* Of the many people who caused me undue harm, only ten people personally asked me to forgive them for any wrong they visited on me.

The first person was my father. When he was told he had just a few months to live, he wanted only me to take care of him. That meant I had to prepare all of my father's meals, bathe him, read the Bible to him, and take care of any of his needs and desires. I did these things at seventeen years old without ever complaining, because I knew this was my father's way of asking me to forgive him for how he had treated me. Two days after my father passed away, our next door neighbor, a seventy-five-year-old lady, sat me down and told me that my father had truly loved me, but he always felt he was too old to tolerate me when I was growing up. She went on to say, "Just before your father died, I caught him trying to put on your shoes. And when I asked him what was he doing, he said with a glow all around him that if he could just get your shoes on his feet, he would be forgiven for the way that he treated you for so many years and that God would welcome him into his kingdom." All I could do was cry, because I genuinely loved my father, even though I had never understood until that day why he had always treated me so differently from my other brothers.

The second person was the minister who stole my truck, but returned it to me with a sincere apology and several hundred dollars of back pay that he owed me one month before he died.

The third person was Allen Joines, who privately asked me to forgive him for being a weak person and not supporting me when I was being wrongfully treated by so many people, especially City Manager Stuart. Joines told me that he knew that his career would be over if he said or did anything to support me. Joines stated further that he feared City Manager

Stuart more than anyone he had ever worked for, because Stuart had shown everyone that he got great pleasure out of abusing his power and hurting anyone who did not agree with his management style. Joines continued by saying that he knew he could never repay me for the invaluable services I had provided him and many other City employees. He said he was grateful that I had advised him to turn down a promotion to an assistant city manager's position in Oakland, California, where they would have expected him to do the caliber of work that I had done for him. Joines told me often that he wished he had my religious convictions and strength, to stand boldly for integrity and for what was right. And he apologized over and over to me for being a weak person who really wanted to do the right thing by everyone. Joines valued my opinion and remained with Stuart, where he was promoted to assistant city manager before he retired. After he retired, J. Allen Joines was elected mayor of Winston-Salem. Further, Joines's secretary spoke favorably about me on one occasion in City Hall, and she was immediately relocated out of the city manager's wing to the basement area of City Hall, as the secretary to the Information Office.

The fourth person was George Alston, who was a program coordinator with the City's Model City Department in 1971. During George's employment, he participated with the other black Model City employees to work against me. He thought management favored me over them, and I did not socialize with them. Some fifteen years later, George showed up at my home unannounced. When I asked him where his old Model City buddies were, he said that he did not know. Then he said, "Curtis, I know that you put your career on the line to save my job with the City, and I treated you like the enemy. Man, you will never know how many years I have wanted to come to you and thank you, and to ask you to forgive me for being such a jackass. I was much older than those young fellows that I followed. You just don't know how much you are respected and hated by so many people in this city. They don't understand you,

236

because you are your own person. If you can't help a person, you will not do anything to hurt that person. You stay away from any specific group, but you help anyone who requests or needs your assistance. I really saw you for what you are as you struggled under Bond's administration." I stopped George and said, "Where are you going with this confession?" Then George said, "Curt, I am dying, and I need for you to forgive me." I told George, "I forgave you when I told Bond that I would not destroy your career, and I forgive you now." George and I spent the rest of the afternoon together talking about pleasant things that happened in our lives. After about five hours, George left my home and I never saw him again.

The fifth person was my first wife Akie. Before she took her last trip to Japan, she came to visit me. The visit was one of the best times that she and I spent together. When she returned from Japan, she came to visit me again. Only this time, she brought some of everything that I loved about Japan. She must have bought me ten gifts. As she was leaving, she hugged me and said, "Thanks for being my best friend. Thanks for being there for me, even when I did everything possible to hurt you. I hope that you enjoy the goodies that I brought you from Japan." One month after Akie's return from Japan, she had a stroke, went into a coma, and never regained consciousness. At Akie's funeral, I realized that she was asking me to forgive her the Japanese way, when she brought me so many gifts from Japan. I can only hope that she knew I forgave her by the way I continued to be there for her years after we separated and divorced.

The sixth person was my brother Lorenza. Two weeks before he died, he simply asked his three brothers together to forgive him if he had ever done anything to cause any of us any harm. At this time, Lorenza wanted me to read a special passage from the Bible to him over and over. However, during this private time I spent with Lorenza, he never tried to make amends for the many cruel things he had said about and done to me over the years. In fact, I held Lorenza's hand a few days before he passed away, in the same fashion as I had done with my brother William two years earlier, and my mother seven years earlier. I received a firm hand grip of love and assurance from each of them. Lorenza, though, refused to grip my hand at all. After Lorenza died, I continued to brag about his successes whenever the opportunity arose, knowing that he had done everything within his power to belittle and destroy my reputation and character when he was alive.

The seventh person was the young lady who wrote the one and only article about me and my situation with the City. It was published in *The Chronicle*, a private local newspaper. She all but accused me of lying about everything that had happened to me over the years, and of attempting to destroy innocent, decent people. She recanted everything that she had written after attending one of my trial hearings. After witnessing the covert agenda of the presiding judge to deny me due process, after I presented my evidence of abuse, humiliation, retaliation, and violations of many City policies without any contradictions from the City's attorney, she apologized to me for having written those negative comments about me. She asked for my forgiveness in the presence of my family. I accepted her apology. With tears in her eyes, she stated further, "I am resigning my job with the newspaper today, and I am leaving this godforsaken city forever. I never dreamed that people could be so cruel and evil. Why?"

The eighth person was a reporter from the *Washington Post* who interviewed me concerning the qualifications of Assistant City Manager John Bond, who had just been recommended for the assistant city manager position in Washington, DC. I gave the reporter my honest opinion about Bond's qualifications, but the reporter considered my comments to be negative and of an envious nature. The reporter told me she would not be using any of the information I had provided. She further said that she was very disappointed in me, because she had been told I was a man of great honor and integrity, who was the most knowledgeable person in Winston-Salem about the City and about Bond. The interview ended with me telling the reporter that the truth would show itself in one year. One year to the date, I received a call from the reporter, who said, "I don't know if you remember me interviewing you a year ago in your home, but I am the reporter from the *Washington Post*. Have you read the latest article that was published on John Bond, which quotes verbatim everything that you told me a year ago that he would do on this job in Washington?" I said, "Yes, I have the article in front of me. What more do you want from me? I told you that this would happen, and you told me that I needed to get over my envy of Bond." In a soft voice, the reporter said, "Maybe I should not have called, but I owe you an apology for what I said to you a year ago. Everything that you said came true, just as you said it would. This man created nothing but chaos the entire year that he was on the job, and he was terminated exactly one year from the time that he was hired, just as you said he would be. How did you know this? What is happening in your life? Please accept my sincere apology, and may God continue to be with you in years to come."

The ninth person was Willie Smith, the manager of Russell's Business School, the first black secretarial/business school in the area. When I was the acting deputy director of planning and budgeting for the Model City Department, he constantly made negative comments about me to anyone who would listen to him. When Smith became terminally ill, he called me and asked me to come to his home. When I arrived, he greeted me at the door as if we were the best of friends. Immediately, he started apologizing to me for all of the degrading things he had said about me. "Dixon," he said, "I just want you know that I truly did not mean any of those mean things that I said about you. I just followed the crowd. Everyone felt so threatened by your abilities, your confidence on the job, and more so when you continued to work cooperatively with everyone, even after we were disrespectful toward you and did conniving things to you. I am saying all of the above to say, you never did anything wrong. You did everything right. It was if you were God sent, and that frightened the hell out of most people, including me. I even found out years later that my program lasted two extra years because of you, and you never said anything to me. I just want you to know that I called Assistant City Manager Beaty and told him that this vendetta against you has got to stop." As Smith began to get weak, his wife said that it was time for him to take a nap. I stood up to leave, but Smith stopped me and told his wife to get out the family sterling silver. "I want you," he said to me, "to take whatever you want from that twelve-place setting of sterling silverware that has been in my family for forever." Before I could say anything, he added, "Dixon, make a dying man happy, and become an honorary member of my family by at least taking a place setting." I chose one place setting, and Smith and his wife wrapped the set up for me. Before I left the house, Smith said again, "I am truly sorry that I ever played a part in that jealousy trip against you. Just from this one visit to my home, I want you to know that you are one of the most honorable people that I have ever had the opportunity to know. You are you, true blue, and everything is going to work out just fine for you. I hope we will meet up again on the other side." As I was driving home, I looked into the bag. There were two place settings and a note that read; "You are the greatest, and may God continue to bless and take care of you." Willie Smith's wife saw me in the grocery store three weeks later, and she told me that Smith died with a smile on his face the night after my visit.

The tenth person was Attorney Walter T. Johnson, my first attorney in my fight for justice against the City of Winston-Salem. He took it upon himself, without my permission, to file a wrongful discharge and harassment complaint in Federal District Court on my behalf. But Judge Hiram Ward came out of retirement to block Walter's forgiveness tribute to me by dismissing the complaint. Determined to make at least one of his many wrongs right with me, Walter appealed Judge Ward's dismissal to the Appellate Court, where the complaint was also dismissed in 1995. At this time, Judge Ward, who had been labeled the gatekeeper for racism by many minority leaders, also had been given special privileges at the Federal Appeals Court level. I have not seen or heard from Walter Johnson since early 1992, but I have prayed that God will forgive him for the many wrongs he might have caused many people, and show him some favor for the two rights that he attempted on my behalf.

When I was sixty-nine, an educational institution asked me to help increase the performance of several high school students, who had ranked the lowest in their county the previous year. Despite resistance from several students and parents, I persevered, using my normal honor tactics and strategies. With my help, as many as 85 percent more students passed the performance requirements, than any of the full-time teachers achieved. One of my students, who passed the performance requirements with flying colors, told me that this was the first time he had passed a state-mandated test in his eleven years of schooling. This was like a message from God to me saying, "Be patient, my son. I am not through with you yet." To me, this meant that I could possibly have a long, healthy, and prosperous life beyond the comprehension of man, so that I could continue to do God's work.

As a seventy-year-old retired senior citizen, I continued to work about twenty hours per week educating high school students; twenty hours per week working with teachers, so that their jobs could be easier and more rewarding to the students; countless hours per week helping my daughter raise her two daughters; and at least one hour per week tutoring my cousin in mathematics. Further, I assumed the full responsibility for the care and education of my godson, from high school through college. Otherwise, my godson would never have had the opportunity to go to college. I can truly say that my beliefs and drive for excellence were not altered by the years of insults and betrayals from so many people. In fact, the greater the backlashes, the more determined I was to excel and serve mankind in the manner that God would have me. Consequently, I was able to provide a valuable service to the young and the old, and to the supporters of children and the elderly.

If God had not directed my path, a number of heinous crimes could have been committed as a result of the injustices inflicted on me. Many people throughout this land, who were treated much less dishonorably than I, have been featured in the media for killing many people, because they felt treated unjustly by one person. Many of those killed were judges, lawyers, principals, administrators and managers, elected officials, college students, and innocent children and adults. Still, dishonor is alive and thriving more and more. However, during the 2008 general election for president of this great nation, as well as other key public positions, the philosophies of many of the candidates as they related to honor involved the health, educational, and employment welfare for the entire population, not just the welfare of the elite. As a result of those concerns, the politicians whose philosophies were more honorable and supportive of the little person and the country as a whole, versus the wealthy and top managers, were voted into office across this country.

During my forty-year struggle for success and happiness, for some favorable opportunities, and for justice through the courts, I was denied any semblance of the honor and support that Barack Obama found, when he received overwhelming support from more people than any other president in the history of the United States. I only asked that twelve jurors decide the merits of my case. But an elite group, judges and attorneys, made sure that my complaints and concerns were never reviewed and decided by those twelve jurors, who might have been honorable men and women. Consequently, I was denied my full measure of happiness.

"We remain a young nation, but in the words of Scripture, the time has come to set aside childish things. The time has come to reaffirm our enduring spirit; to choose our better history; to carry forward that precious gift, that noble idea, passed on from generation to generation: the God-given promise that all are equal, all are free, and all deserve a chance to pursue their full measure of happiness."

Quote from Barack Hussein Obama,
President of the United States, Inaugural Address,
January 20, 2009

From the President of United States to the lowest citizen, I, Curtis Eugene Dixon, would like to know: *Where did I go wrong? What should I have done differently? If an honorable man can not get justice through our legal system, what recourse does he have?* Such information might prove invaluable to our grandchildren and their children, and make them aware of such pitfalls that have the potential of destroying their careers and livelihood.

REWARDS MORE GRATIFYING THAN MONEY/ POSITION

"By God's grace, I am what I am."

—*1 Corinthians 15:10*

When I was eight years old, I was knocked from a swing that was over fifty feet off the ground. My brother Artemas told me that I sailed through the air like a kite and bounced on the ground like a rubber ball. After being unconscious for over an hour, when everyone thought that I was dead, my brother and friends carried me to our church. I woke up in the arms of my mother with no injuries.

When I was seventeen and had to pick my brother up from work at 1 AM, I fell asleep at the wheel of my father's car and drove safely through five curves in the road, before crashing into a telephone pole a few feet from a gas station. The policemen who arrived on the scene said to me, "God was with you this morning, young man. Not only did you escape death by hitting this pole, you only have one small scratch on your hand."

When I was twenty one and cruising with my friends, the young lady who was driving the car lost control of the car.

Everyone in the car panicked except me. I climbed into the front seat and turned the car just in time to keep it from crashing into the sharpest point on the rail of a bridge.

When I was twenty-five years old and a captain in Vietnam, I bought a motorcycle and rode it with a friend most nights until midnight. Many nights, I passed or rode with Vietnamese men riding with women on the backs of their cycles. The last night that I rode my motorcycle, two GIs were shot and killed while on their motorcycles by a Vietnamese woman riding on the back of a motorcycle. When her picture was circulated on the base after she was killed, I saw she was the same woman who had passed me and my friend many times when we were riding my motorcycle.

While in Vietnam, I worked from 6 AM until 6 PM six days a week. On one particular day, my boss gave me an assignment that was due the next morning. I planned to work until 8 PM so that I could finish the assignment, but then decided to call it quits for the day at 6:30 PM, before finishing the assignment. The next morning when I arrived at my worksite, it had been mortared completely to the ground, and six soldiers in nearby sites had been killed. I was told that the attack took place at about 7:00 PM which meant that I would have been killed had I stayed at work until 8 PM, as I had planned.

When I was forty-five, a deadly tornado severely damaged my neighborhood, and the largest tree in my yard was blown down. The concussion from the tree hitting the ground shook my entire house. After the tornado subsided, I went outside to assess the damage to my property and the neighborhood. I discovered that the tree, which was about five feet in diameter and about a hundred feet tall, landed parallel to my house, perfectly straight on my driveway. However, when my neighbors looked at the breaking point on the lower part of the tree, they told me that the tree should have hit my house. Anyone in any of the rooms on that side of my house would have been killed instantly. Something had turned the tree away from my house after it started to fall. My mother and I were in the danger zone of my home when the tree fell.

When my mother became critically ill, I was not thinking coherently. Just before I was about to crash head-on into another car, the sky lighted up. The driver of the other car saw me and was able to avoid me.

When my cousin Wendell Clarence Falls was fired, he grieved for about six months before committing suicide. However, each time that I was terminated from a job, I persevered, stronger than ever, on the next job, and the next job, and the next job. I knew that I was on solid ground with God, who had ordained me with an honor that no dishonorable man could destroy. Every job that I held, people who had contact with me, from chief executive officers to city managers to the lowest-paid workers, sought me out at one time or another for my expertise or advice. I was a man of few words, but the charisma and reverence that I projected captured everyone's attention. I never had to volunteer for any assignment, because I was always singled out. Without my being aware of everything that was happening around me and to me, the honor that only God could have bestowed on me was readily seen by everyone. Yes, they used me, abused me, betrayed me, insulted me, and did everything humanly possible to destroy me, but I just kept on coming back to save the children, the elderly, and future generations.

All of the above could have been death situations for me, but by the grace of God, I was protected.

Once, I did notice something that I thought was awful strange. One morning, the owner of a car repair shop, a minister, two businessmen, and I were standing in a parking lot talking, when a homeless man walked up to us. He walked straight over to me and asked if I would give him a dollar so that he could get a cup of coffee. I gave him the dollar, and the man thanked me and walked away. The other men asked me if I was the savior. They wondered why the homeless man approached me, when the other four men all looked more successful. And of course, the minister and the two businessmen said that they would not have given the homeless man anything, because he was only going to use the money to buy alcohol or drugs.

I felt that I was one of the few people born during my era who was truly blessed, and who lived a fulfilled life, completely different from most people. I learned to know and accept that the path of my life had been directed and protected by God. Without God and honor in my life, I could easily have been a mass murderer, a suicide victim, a bum, a thief, or any dishonorable person, out of self-pity and disgust from a lifetime of disappointments. Instead, I held steadfast to my belief in God and the honor that God had bestowed upon me. Whenever I would think of anything destructive, my mother's face would appear before me and her voice would say, *"Would what you are thinking be pleasing to God and beneficial to you and your loved ones?"* And the pain would always go away, and I would have new energy to travel on with positive thoughts and actions. Whenever I wanted to drink and smoke because most of my friends and associates were drinking and smoking, my doctor's voice would always intervene and say, *"Remember that I told you that drinking any form of alcohol and smoking of any kind would mean an early death for you, because of the makeup of your internal organs".* Consequently, I never smoked or drank, and I never suffered the illnesses that my father and brothers experienced at relatively young ages.

As a City employee, I loved the challenges of the various tasks and responsibilities so much, I was never absent from work during my first ten years. Everyone seemed to depend on me, and I enjoyed being useful. I never concerned myself with what other people were doing on the job. If any employee came to me for assistance, I would assist him or her if I could.

When I was director of development, operations and training for the Concentrated Employment Program, I vividly remember one of the employees of a new department with the City of Winston-Salem requesting my assistance, to help her deliver fuel and food to community residents who were in dire need. None of my staff with the federal manpower program was willing to volunteer, but I did. For what I considered a positive gesture, John Bond and many employees viewed my actions as being "holier than thou". All I did was help out for a worthy cause. Two months later, Bond deleted my position and I was without a job.

Florence Creque was known for telling her friends and fellow employees that I did not work for money. I was just a dedicated, enthusiastic worker, who enjoyed helping people and completing difficult tasks. When I told her that I had the same responsibilities as she and everyone else, and that I needed the same advantages on the job as the next person in order to pay my bills, she said that I was too sensitive. But she continued to tell top managers that I was not ready for a management position, in order to keep me from advancing.

Being your own person and not the person someone else wants you to be may mean a road of many heartaches, headaches, pains, and disappointments, but through the grace of God, your life can still be as fulfilling and rewarding as my life was. My dream was to get a quality education, marry and father four children, be successful at my job, build a beautiful home, have adequate transportation for me and my family at all times, take care of my mother, and be in a position to help other people. Even though I did not realize my "American Dream," God gave me the wherewithal and strength to help anyone who crossed my path and genuinely needed my assistance, even though my funds were limited and my leadership roles were diminished. I built my dream home and was able to keep it through many storms. I married twice, fathered two children, and raised three children. I maintained excellent credit, which enabled me to take advantage of interest-free credit cards to help my family, friends, and work associates. I used my leadership and managerial skills throughout my work career to help others get promoted, to secure other people jobs, and to assist many insecure leaders by being their unpaid consultant. These were the joys of my life. I loved helping people and being productive. People like Creque, Bond, Powell, and Stuart praised me for my accomplishments, but they refused to acknowledge them publicly. For some strange reason, I found it difficult not to help dishonorable leaders, if my services would benefit others in need.

What were the odds that I, Curtis Dixon, an ordinary citizen, would spend my entire life interacting or communicating personally about my *"honor"* with President Lyndon Johnson; Secretary of Defense Harold Brown; military personnel ranging from generals to enlisted men; Japanese generals; school principals and teachers; mayors and other elected officials; city managers and regular City employees; domestic, civil, and criminal attorneys; federal and state judges; the CEOs of major industries; medical doctors and doctors of philosophy; and even the homeless, without some input from God? And I showed each of them my positive side, and only the Winston-Salem group responded to me "most *dishonorably"*. Ask yourself, "Why? Why would anyone love to use, but hate to reward?" Who can say without a doubt that what happened to me my entire life was not the work of God? When I was a young man, my life was shielded in several death situations. During my work career, over 50 percent of the individuals who set out to cause me undue hardship, left this earth for a better or worse place before they reached three score and ten years of age (70). The loved ones of many of those deceased told me that their mates died peacefully after meeting and talking with me. Was this a sign that God forgave them, and they made it into heaven?

One assistant city manager apologized to me many times for being too weak and fearful as a person to speak the truth about what was happening to me, because he feared repercussions from the city manager. He was the only assistant city manager out of five who became a popular and polished public official. Was this the work of God? In the midst of the cruelest tactics imaginable, I served as coordinator, vice president, and president of the Piedmont Triad Chapter of the American Society for Public Administration for four major cities. I was chosen for these positions by city managers, county managers, professors, and other professional personnel, before Stuart appeared on the scene. How do you suppose I got the strength to undertake such responsibilities? Judges from all levels of the judicial system ruled against me, and City Manager Stuart terminated me from my job. Soon after that, I was told that more black City employees were being promoted to higher level positions than ever before. Secretaries became professional level employees or supervisors, professional level employees became division or department heads, and department heads became administrators. Did God use the dishonorable intent of so many people to make something positive and great happen for many deserving citizens?

Having held steadfast to the great honor that God embedded in my soul, I never missed a beat. When I walked into the office of the personnel director for the Winston-Salem/Forsyth County School System, I was welcomed with open arms. In less than three years with the school system, I was named Teacher of the Year.

Even though I was wronged for most of my life, I always felt that God made sure I was healthy, educated, happy, employed, and able to spread his honor everywhere I went. What are the chances that influential and rich leaders who act dishonorably will receive any favor from God? Only God has the answers to all of the above questions, but every man should be mindful that God has also given us wisdom and strength to make honorable choices.

I thanked God every day of my life for giving me a kind and forgiving spirit, and the strength and wisdom to live a positive and generous life in the midst of harm and despair. My only regret was that I might leave this earth for a better place before I could secure a stable lifestyle for my daughter, my two young granddaughters, and my godson. Even then, I held my head high and said, *"To God be the glory. Only his will shall be done."*

To my heart and soul, a wise man spoke the following words just as I was about to give up on mankind ever replacing dishonor with honor:

"America. In the face of our common dangers, in the winter of our hardship, let us remember these timeless words. With hope and virtue, let us brave once more the icy currents, and endure what storms may come. Let it be said by our children's children that when we were tested we refused to let this journey end, that we did not turn back nor did we falter; and with eyes fixed on the horizon and God's grace upon us, we carried forth that great gift of freedom and delivered it safely to future generations."

President Barack Hussein Obama
Quote from Inaugural Speech on January 20, 2008

EPILOGUE

"Trust in the Lord with all your heart. And lean not on your own understanding. In all your ways acknowledge him. And he shall direct your paths. Better is the poor who walks in his integrity than one perverse in his ways, though he be rich."

Proverbs 3:5-6, 28:6

In my opinion, dishonor has enabled many people to acquire high-ranking job positions, exorbitant salaries, leadership roles and social status in a community, beautiful homes, extravagant vehicles, control over innocent people's careers, and, for many, death before three scores and ten years. Further, dishonor has the capability to destroy the hopes and dreams of thousands of people. Dishonor can also destroy families, communities, businesses, schools, churches, and governments. In my case, the dishonor shown toward me has amplified my honor. The more dishonorable people concentrated desperately to destroy my honor, the more I held my head high so that God could see my light shine. After over thirty years of insults, betrayals, and lies, I was still standing tall. This told me that I had to possess some godly qualities that my oppressors feared and longed to have.

After the birth of my two granddaughters in 2005 and 2006, I realized that my life's course had not changed *since I built my dream home and earned two master's degrees in the 1970s.* I transported my granddaughters to their day care school most mornings in 2009, as I had transported their mother thirty-five years ago. Also, I gave the same love, care, and devotion to my granddaughters that I had given to my mother until she passed away; to learning and excelling for over forty years; to my two wives for twenty years; to my daughter and my godson every day of their lives; to my stepson for ten years; to my brothers and family members for as long as I can remember; to my godmother until she passed away; to my jobs, to friends, neighbors, and associates at all times; and to everything good and positive in my life forever. At seventy years old, I still had my dream home that God enabled me to build for my family when I was only twenty-nine; a professional job status that had remained stagnant for forty years, thanks to the dishonor of many powerful people; and good health that enabled me to be mistaken as a fifty-year-old by my co-workers, as I continued to contribute to the lives of the young and the elderly. Only God could have brought me through such a storm and left me happy with how I lived my life, healthy enough to enjoy my granddaughters, and most grateful for protecting me and using me to show the world what true honor really is.

Despite minor bouts with subtle racism from a select few white leaders, my military career soared. Was it because there were no black officers assigned to any of my units? When I was only twenty-three years old, I supervised as many as seventy-five troops. I earned two outstanding unit awards and the Bronze Star before I was twenty-seven. I interacted with and was respected by different ethnic groups worldwide without any difficulties. Then I returned to my hometown, Winston-Salem, and started working with mostly black people for the first time. It was worse than a nightmare, worse than Vietnam. I contributed much more to society as a civilian leader in Winston-Salem than I did in the military, but my black brothers and sisters concentrated all of their energies and efforts on discrediting me, envying me, lying about me, and doing everything possible to make me fail. Their envy and destructive attitudes were unreal and unforgivable. During all of this black on black racism, most white leaders marveled at my abilities and accomplishments, and used my talents to enhance their careers.

Based on the facts presented throughout this book, my career with the City was destroyed by John Bond, my initial co-manager and black friend, with support from Orville Powell, Bryce Stuart, Gary Brown, Alexander Beaty, Allen Joines, Tom Fredericks, Sam Owen, the mayor and the Board of Aldermen, and members of our judicial system from 1972 through 1989. Also, the facts clearly indicate that the following dishonorable practices could have played a significant role in the decisions of the above individuals against me: (1) cover up perverted activities,(2) envy within the same race, (3) Uncle Toms who were willing to do anything for a few pieces of silver, (4) racism that seemed to be an acceptable practice by many blacks and whites in powerful positions, (5) an evil way of life for many people, (6) a clan that strongly felt it had the God-given right to decide who succeeded and who failed, (7) judges who supported illicit activities and set aside the code of honor for their own personal gratification.

If the above individuals did not discriminate and harass me for years, why was their entire defense against me based on false information that I refuted in court? If the lower judge was truly seeking justice, why did he use the false testimonies of the defendants as his primary reason to dismiss my many complaints, after telling the defendants in open court that they needed to do a better job of preparing their defense? If the higher judges were truly seeking justice, why did they refuse to challenge the false reports of the lower court, after the facts were presented to them without any contradiction from the City's attorney? Hate and envy are despicable qualities in any man or woman, but even worse is condoning and supporting such destructive traits. What mother or father would welcome their son or daughter being victimized by such underhanded and dishonorable tactics? Would Judge Ward have gladly and proudly removed my name from his judgment and replaced it with his son's or daughter's name? Would Bryce A. Stuart, Orville Powell, Allen Joines, Gary Brown, and Sam Owen have lied on their son or daughter to support the wrongs of another individual? Why did these people find it necessary to lie about Curtis Dixon's performance and qualities after benefiting from them for years? Why did so many judges support the defendants' malicious lies? What sin could be more unforgivable in God's eyes? What mother or father could be more distraught and disillusioned? What son or daughter could be more confused and hurt by such corruption and dishonesty? But who cared? Did the elected officials who talked with Dixon and made false promises to him, concern themselves with honesty? Did the local ministers who avoided him after hearing how repulsively he was being treated daily on his job, act as disciples of God? Did his attorneys, whose greatest concerns were the welfare of his oppressors, truly care about honor? There was no honor, and all of these individuals knew that no one really cared.

As I struggled to survive and be treated equally as others around me, I began to understand why my mother said that I was her special child, why I was always used and later abused, and why so many powerful people felt compelled to destroy what I represented. I was my own person, a self-starter, a pioneer who loved being productive, useful, resourceful, and honorable at any cost. As early as 1969, I was the only person at my job who built his own home, completely furnished it, and bought two new cars after being employed for only six months. I was the only employee pursuing a master's degree, after trying to get other co-workers to attend graduate school with me. I was the only employee who was always selected to prepare budgets, to plan and implement new programs, and to meet with state and federal representatives regarding the status of various federally-funded programs and projects. Even when the city manager attended federal meetings, I was invited to come along. Whenever there were any legal discussions about the programs, I was always asked to be present. I did all of the above, because that was how God made me, an individual who wanted the best for himself, his loved ones, and his fellow man. I really considered myself an asset to the City.

I never dreamed that black people would hate me, and that white people would decide my success or failure based on what another black person said about me. Florence Creque did tell me that I had crossed the line by building such a home at a younger age than the black doctors, lawyers, and renowned society folks did. Florence Creque and John Bond, both who pretended to be my friends, felt threatened by my honor and accomplishments. Their greatest fear was that I might expose their incompetence as managers, even though I had always made them shine by performing many of their duties for them. These people destroyed the great dreams that I had for my family, friends, and mankind.

As years went by, I also knew I would never have survived as an administrator with the City, if it meant conforming to the standards of Florence Creque, John Bond, Gary Brown, Alexander Beaty, Orville Powell, Bryce Stuart, Allen Joines, and Sam Owen. These people were incapable of appreciating the advantages that God had given them, because they had no honor. Their professional record with me clearly showed that they spent too much of their time doing what other people expected of them, or reacting to what others had told them about me, instead of sharing their talents with the city and its residents as I did. They never got a chance to like themselves or me, because they doubted their own abilities as competent and efficient administrators. They evidently never experienced true honor, because after learning that I was not their enemy, but was in fact their strongest ally and greatest asset on the job, they still wanted to destroy everything that I stood for. Their track records clearly indicate that they thrived and survived on the dishonor around them. If any of them had had one tenth of the honor that I shared with them, there is no telling what great things God would have permitted them to accomplish. Further, if I had to work directly for the elected officials that rewarded city managers and others for their failures, my life would have been miserable, and I would have left this earth long before three score and ten years. If more people in general would accept honor over dishonor, the world would definitely be a better place.

In cities like Winston-Salem, managers are considered better citizens than non-managers, and whites are considered superior to blacks. And the really sad part is, too many blacks feel and act as if whites are superior. (John Bond and Alexander Beaty were living examples.) When a manager violates a policy or loses favor with his superior, he is rarely if ever fired, and his "punishment" is to move him to a higher paying position or help him secure comparable employment elsewhere. If a black non-manager violates policy or challenges his leaders, he is instantly fired or harassed, humiliated, and then fired, with support from black community leaders and the legal system. If a white non-manager challenges management, corrective action is taken immediately to ensure that everyone involved is happy. It appears that managers are only prosecuted when the federal government brings charges against them, and most non-managers are deemed guilty by both the state and federal judicial systems before they go to court. Where is the honor in such dishonorable practices? Does the above also mean that managers' families are better, or deserve better opportunities than non-managers' families? Where are such practices written in the Constitution or the Bible? If any of the above is true, crimes will continue to escalate, many careers and lives will continue to be destroyed needlessly, and our younger generations will have to search for a better way to live all by themselves. Does Winston-Salem fit the above profile? After sixteen years of teaching, I can truthfully say that dishonorable practices were still being embedded into the minds of students by the actions of the older generation. And as late as 2009, too many of my students clearly demonstrated dishonorable practices with one another and with adults every day. What a shame! But who cares? Do you?

What did I represent that made so many people in the Winston-Salem area want to cause me harm? Why haven't any of them crowed to the world their victory over me? Were they afraid that their dishonor might not be received favorably outside of Winston-Salem, as it was in Winston-Salem? Orville Powell left the state of North Carolina shortly after he retired, moving to Indiana. Why would he leave a state that made it possible for him to help or destroy anyone that he pleased? As of 2006, Powell was living the life of an honorable man in Indiana, where he wrote at least two books. He was appointed the first executive director of the Indiana Municipal Management Association (IMMA), and he was a clinical associate professor in the School of Public and Environmental Affairs at Indiana University. I wonder if he has been honorable enough to share with his colleagues and students his experience with Curtis E. Dixon, a young black City employee who idolized him, but whom he chose to destroy. Or did Powell just tell the world about his success stories?

Throughout my entire life, I have strove for perfection, and I have been competitive, but I have never been envious or jealous of anyone. I have always been a servant to mankind, and I have never caused another human being any harm. I am a man of honor. My body and soul are completely free of the hatred and dishonor that others inflicted on me over several decades. And still I say to each one of them, "Enjoy your worldly accolades while you can, because the day of reckoning will come when you least expect it. May God have mercy on your soul."

I have prayed every day that no one on this earth will have to endure the agony and heartache that I had to deal with. I know that black people do not like to hear the truth, but we are our own worst enemy. Black people are forever favoring and uplifting Toms, whom we know cause black people more harm than good. John Bond did not hide that he did not like black people, and he terminated several black men from their jobs with support from other black leaders throughout Winston-Salem. Alexander Beaty told me personally that he spied on black employees for Bond, so that they could be fired. Beaty and I grew up in the same church and were distant relatives, but he lied about me for years, in order to be favored by Bond and white superiors. For being a Tom, he received promotion after promotion, as well as praise from many black leaders of Winston-Salem. I planned and implemented a million dollar manpower program for the City, and a black high school classmate of mine told me he would not be the director of that department if they asked him. I caught him doing a black slave dance for the white leaders in City Hall, and was told that my classmate was a good ole boy who wanted to be the director of the manpower program. My classmate giggled his way to the directorship, with absolutely no experience. But to the white leaders, he was a good Tom.

After my career had been destroyed, a black woman who worked closely with me for years told me that she had been present at many meetings when Bond and Beaty discussed how they planned to destroy my career. For her silence, she was promoted to a director position. My own brother, whom I loved unconditionally and whose children I helped raise, volunteered to give me a job, but then refused to visit with or call me. My fraternity brother, who was also this same brother's brother-in-law, received character references from three of my professional friends concerning a job position with his institution, yet he never offered me an interview. My black neighbor knew that City leaders were lying about me, but he refused to do the honorable thing and support me. Instead, he pledged his alliance to a dishonorable white man. A black classmate from kindergarten through twelfth grade refused to acknowledge that he knew me, after he befriended Bond and was elected an alderman for the City of Winston-Salem. Further, this same man was the only member of a three-man property revaluation review board, who insisted that the value of my home should be increased by $50,000 when the house needed major repairs. The lead member (white) of the review board recommended that I appeal their decision to the state review board. When I did so, the $50,000 increase was reduced to $20,000. Several black ministers, after hearing how I was being treated by the City leaders, refused even to inquire about the situation, and never spoke to me again.

Black elected officials supported black administrators with the City who mismanaged millions of federal dollars (Toms), but they refused to support a black man of honor who saved the City several hundred thousand dollars. My own fraternity brothers were not compassionate enough to offer me a word of prayer and encouragement when I was fighting for my career. My black attorneys and the black attorney who represented the City were totally unethical and self-serving. My attorneys aided the City's defendants by making sure that no facts were presented that might malign their careers. The City's attorney presented false information about me, and he coached black and white leaders with the City to lie about my accomplishments and performance, according to Mrs. Creque and the facts presented throughout this book. The black EEOC representatives gave inferior service to black clients and superior service to white clients. Many black entrepreneurs gave black clients faulty service for outrageous prices. Based on my experiences, there was no race of people as divided as the black people in Winston-Salem from 1970 through 1990. From 1990 until 2009, I completely separated myself socially, mentally, and psychologically from all dishonorable people in Winston-Salem, to the best of my ability.

I sincerely hope that my life's story can be of some value to all honorable young men and women, especially young black men. Together we shall overcome our inadequacies and fears, and grow to be greater contributors to society and mankind, and better fathers to our children. Divided, we will continue to be disrespected and not treated as equals to black women, white women, and white men in the workplace.

I fought a good fight for myself and all honorable men and women, but especially honorable black men. I honestly feel that my efforts were not in vain, even though I was not able to do all of the great things for my family and mankind that I knew I was capable of. Such was not the master's plan. Who was I to question God's plan for me? I did many times, but I found myself staying the course that he wanted me to travel.

One thing for sure, I will not leave this earth an unhappy man, because I know that God knows I was an honorable man, who contributed handsomely to mankind in a dishonorable environment.

If I had not lived this horrible nightmare, I would not believe what happened to me was possible. But it did. In writing this book, I always reminded myself:

"Integrity is telling myself the truth.
And honesty is telling the truth to other people."

—Spencer Johnson

This book is my honesty.